Jesuit Student Groups, the Universidad Iberoamericana,
and Political Resistance in Mexico, 1913–1979

Jesuit Student Groups, the Universidad Iberoamericana, and Political Resistance in Mexico, 1913–1979

DAVID ESPINOSA

UNIVERSITY OF NEW MEXICO PRESS • ALBUQUERQUE

© 2014 by the University of New Mexico Press
All rights reserved. Published 2014
Printed in the United States of America

First Paperback Edition, 2022
Paperback ISBN: 978-0-8263-6385-5

Library of Congress Cataloging-in-Publication Data
Espinosa, David, 1962–
 Jesuit student groups, the Universidad Iberoamericana, and political resistance in Mexico, 1913–1979 / David Espinosa.
    pages cm
  Includes bibliographical references and index.
  ISBN 978-0-8263-5460-0 (cloth : alkaline paper) — ISBN 978-0-8263-5461-7 (electronic)
   1. Student movements—Mexico—History—20th century. 2. College students—Mexico—Societies, etc.—History—20th century. 3. Jesuits—Political activity—Mexico—History—20th century. 4. Universidad Iberoamericana (Mexico City, Mexico)—History—20th century. 5. Catholic Church—Mexico—History—20th century. 6. Church and state—Mexico—History—20th century. 7. Government, Resistance to—Mexico—History—20th century. 8. Mexico—Politics and government—20th century. 9. Mexico—Social conditions—20th century. 10. Mexico—Economic conditions—20th century.
I. Title.
 LA428.7.E73 2014
 378.1'98109720904—dc23
                         2013051117

Designed by Lisa Tremaine
Text set in Janson; display face is Univers Bold Condensed.

For Cleo, David, and Chris

CONTENTS

	Acknowledgments	*ix*
	Abbreviations	*xi*
	Introduction	*1*
ONE	Church-State Relations from the Porfiriato to the Mexican Revolution, 1876–1917	15
TWO	The Asociación Católica de la Juventud Mexicana, the Mexican Revolution, and the Cristero Rebellion, 1912–1929	35
THREE	The Unión National de Estudiantes Católicos, the University of Mexico, and the Partido Acción Nacional: Student Politics, National Politics	53
FOUR	The Revival of Catholic Higher Education in Mexico, 1943–1952: The Centro Cultural Universitario	75
FIVE	The "Mexican Economic Miracle" and Vatican II, 1952–1967: The Universidad Iberoamericana	91
SIX	Tlatelolco, the Corpus Christi Massacre, and the Transformation of the Universidad Iberoamericana, 1968–1979	113
	Conclusion	*139*
	Notes	*145*
	Bibliography	*181*
	Index	*191*

ACKNOWLEDGMENTS

I wish to acknowledge the debt that I owe to the mentors, colleagues, family, and friends that made this work possible. First and foremost, I wish to recognize the many debts that this work owes to my mentor Dr. Sarah Cline (University of California, Santa Barbara), as well as the many contributions that I received in my professional development from Dr. David Rock, Dr. Héctor Lindo-Fuentes, Dr. Fernando López-Alves, and Dr. Francis Dutra. I am deeply grateful for all their efforts over the years. I also wish to recognize the support that my scholarship has received in the past from Dr. Benjamin Fallow (Colby College) and Dr. Manuel Ceballos Ramírez (El Colegio de la Frontera Norte).

Mtra. Maria Teresa Matabuena Peláez of the Universidad Iberoamericana's Dirección de la Biblioteca Francisco Xavier Clavijero was of enormous assistance to me in my research at that institution, as was Berenise Bravo Rubio of the *Archivo Histórico del Arzobispado Primado de México*. I also wish to acknowledge my debt to Mtra. Lourdes Margarita Chehaibar Náder and her hard-working staff at the Universidad Nacional Autónoma de México's Instituto de Investigaciones sobre la Universidad y la Educación for their assistance to me over the years. Without their help and cooperation, this work would not have been possible.

I have always received nothing but the strongest encouragement from my friends and colleagues at Rhode Island College in support of my scholarship. I especially wish to acknowledge the support that I have received from Dr. Ronald Dufour, Dr. Robert Cvornyek, Dr. Joanne Schneider, and Dr. Karl Benziger. I am truly fortunate to have the opportunity to work with such wonderful friends and colleagues who have created an atmosphere at Rhode Island College where both teaching and scholarship are strongly promoted. The Rhode Island College administration has also been generous and supportive of my scholarship.

My wife Cleo has been greatly supportive of me throughout my academic career and for that and many other reasons I am enormously grateful to her and to my wonderful sons David and Christopher. My mother, Imelda, and my father, Donato, provided me, a child of Mexican immigrants, with the opportunity to go to college, an option they themselves did not enjoy, and I will always be grateful to them. My parents also instilled in me a sense of discipline and taught me never to be afraid of hard work. And finally, I wish to mention and acknowledge two men, my grandfathers, who in different ways awoke in me from an early age a passion for history: Luis Espinosa Monge and Enrique Flores Ramírez.

ABBREVIATIONS

ACJM   Asociación Católica de la Juventud Mexicana, Mexican Catholic Youth Association
AHUIA   Archivo Histórico de la Universidad Iberoamericana, Iberoamerican Historical Archive)
CCU   Centro Cultural Universitario, University Cultural Center
CEC   Centro de Estudiantes Católicos, Catholic Student Center
CGT   Confederación General de Trabajadores, General Workers' Confederation
CNE   Confederación Nacional de Estudiantes, National Student Confederation
CNECM   Confederación Nacional de Estudiantes Católicos de México, National Confederation of Catholic Students
CROM   Confederación Regional Obrera Mexicana, Mexican Regional Labor Confederation
FEU   Federación de Estudiantes Universitarios, Federation of University Students.
FICSAC   Fomento de Investigación y Cultura Superior Asociación Civil, Civil Association for the Promotion of Investigation and Advanced Cultural Studies
IPN   Instituto Politécnico Nacional, National Polytechnic Institute
LNDLR   Liga Nacional Defensora de las Libertades Religiosas, National League for the Defense of Religious Liberty

MURO	Movimiento Universitario de Renovadora Orientación, University Movement for Restored Orientation
PAN	Partido Acción Nacional, National Action Party
PCN	Partido Católico Nacional, National Catholic Party
PNR	Partido Nacional Revolucionario, National Revolutionary Party
PRD	Partido de la Revolución Democratica, Democratic Revolutionary Party
PRI	Partido Revolucionario Institucional, Institutional Revolutionary Party
SEP	Secretaría de Educación Pública, Secretariat of Public Education
UAG	Universidad Autónoma de Guadalajara, Autonomous University of Guadalajara
UNAM	Universidad Nacional Autónoma de México, National Autonomous University of Mexico
UNDC	Unión National de Damas Católicas, National Union of Catholic Ladies
UNEC	Unión National de Estudiantes Católicos, National Catholic Student Union

INTRODUCTION

Jesuit Student Groups, the Universidad Iberoamericana, and Political Resistance in Mexico, 1913–1979 analyzes the Roman Catholic Church's efforts to influence twentieth-century Mexico through Jesuit-led organizations dedicated to the education and indoctrination of the nation's middle- and upper-class youth, who the Jesuits considered to be the "living forces" of Mexican society. It focuses on the Asociación Católica de la Juventud Mexicana (ACJM, Mexican Catholic Youth Association), the The Unión National de Estudiantes Católicos (UNEC, National Catholic Student Union), and the Universidad Iberoamericana and emphasizes how each individual organization was tailored to the unique political, social, economic, and religious conditions of their day; it highlights the active role that the young people of these organizations made to many of the great historical events of twentieth-century Mexican history, including the Cristero Rebellion of 1926–1929 and the Mexican Student Movement of 1968.

These organizations did not achieve their original goal of transforming Mexican society into one based on ultramontane Catholic values that were at war with the modern Western world; rather, and much to the regret of Catholic conservatives, Mexican society became increasingly secular during the course of the twentieth century. Nevertheless, these organizations and their members left important imprints on Mexican society. Both the UNEC and the ACJM made their marks by defending the church's interests in periods of intense anti-clericalism that descended into bloodshed, thereby helping to maintain the church's position in Mexican society during extremely difficult times. And these Jesuit-led organizations trained a generation of political activists who played important roles in the creation and development of the Partido Acción Nacional (PAN, National Action Party), a key political institution in contemporary Mexican society that is the current ruling party. The Universidad Iberoamericana and the UNEC in turn contributed to the development of Mexico's private university system, whose importance to the system of Mexican higher education has grown significantly over the decades.

The ACJM was established by the French Jesuit Bernardo Bergöend in 1913 with the goal of indoctrinating elite young men in the Roman Catholic Church's social doctrine, as enunciated in Pope Leo XIII's landmark encyclical *Rerum Novarum* (1891) and fueled by a desire to "re-Christianize" Mexican society. This meant a rejection of the modus vivendi that the Roman Catholic Church had achieved during the reign of the authoritarian liberal dictator Porfirio Díaz (1876–1911) and a combative stance toward the reformist liberal revolutionaries that had overthrown him. Bergöend's ACJM took a leading role in the Roman Catholic Church's struggle against the anti-clerical Constitution of 1917 that had been drafted by the victorious revolutionaries, a conflict that culminated in the tragic Cristero Rebellion that left the ACJM in tatters and tens of thousands of people (the vast majority non-ACJM Catholic peasants) killed or displaced. The ACJM, radicalized by the brutal civil war in which many of its members had been killed, was eventually brought under stronger ecclesiastical control through the vehicle of the newly introduced institution Catholic Action in order to prevent it from undermining the *Arreglos* of 1929 that had brought the conflict to a formal end.

The UNEC emerged in 1926, on the eve of the Cristero Rebellion, as an organization of male Catholic preparatory and university students who felt persecuted by pro-government educational officials because of their religious and political beliefs. During its early existence, the UNEC was little more than a branch of the more established ACJM and, like the latter, was battered and broken due to its involvement in the Cristero Rebellion; however, in the 1930s the UNEC made its own mark as an institution through its heavy involvement in the world of student politics, combating the influence of Marxist students and helping to defeat socialist-inspired curriculum reform efforts. While the UNEC's ideology was identical to that of Bergöend's ACJM, its goals were far more modest; the UNEC did not seek to overthrow the government by breaking the Arreglos of 1929, but it did seek to preserve and expand the church's role in Mexican education. However, the UNEC was ultimately undone by the ACJM's growing antipathy to that organization, with which it competed for high-value recruits, and a growing reconciliation between Mexico's increasingly conservative one-party state and the Roman Catholic Church during the early 1940s that made the high-profile UNEC a political liability to the latter. Former UNEC members played active roles in the founding of the PAN in 1939, which grouped together both religious and secular conservatives who were in opposition to the leftist policies of President Lázaro Cárdenas (1934–1940) and occupied key leadership positions in that party in subsequent decades.

The Universidad Iberoamericana was established in 1943 by the church hierarchy by using the material and human resources of the UNEC. Known originally as the Centro Cultural Universitario (CCU, University Cultural Center), the Jesuit-led Iberoamericana allowed the church to maintain the pedagogical functions of the UNEC but in an organization more suited to this new era of improved church-state relations. A key factor behind the Iberoamericana's success was the economic patronage that the fledgling institution received from the increasingly powerful business community who provided the funds needed to build the university campus and to cover operating deficits. In return, the Iberoamericana offered an innovative curriculum satisfying Mexican industry's need for trained professionals in an era of rapid economic development (1940s–1960s). The Iberoamericana's board of trustees, which organized economic support among the business community for the institution, was comprised of former UNEC members, who were now successful businessmen and continued to be dedicated to Catholic education.

The 1960s brought profound changes to the Iberoamericana and the Roman Catholic Church as a whole. The 1962–1965 Vatican II Council and the reforms that it spawned dramatically undercut the Iberoamericana's original mission of promoting Catholic culture in Mexican society through the education of Mexico's elites. The Iberoamericana's promotion of an intransigent "Catholic culture" was out of step with the church's new emphasis on openness to the non-Catholic world and its support of the ecumenical movement. In addition, the Iberoamericana's mission of educating elites to serve as agents for the "Christianization" of Mexico was undermined by the decision of Pedro Arrupe, SJ, the Superior General of the Society of Jesus, to redirect the Order's human and material toward the needs of the poor. The Jesuit Order's historic attention to the educational needs of society's select few at the expense of the masses was denounced by the Jesuit hierarchy itself. The Conference of Latin American Bishops of Medellín (1968), which Pope Paul VI attended, endorsed the concept that the Roman Catholic Church would have what was later termed a "preferential option" for Latin America's poor.

By the late 1960s, the cumulative effect of church reform made the Iberoamericana's original raison d'être an anachronism. The Iberoamericana's *Ideario* of 1968, or "statement of ideals," was that institution's effort to make the Iberoamericana relevant to the new circumstances; it emphasized the university's commitment to the scientific investigation of Mexico's social problems and was the essential first step in attempting to resolve them. Inspired by Vatican II's call to open the Roman Catholic Church to the world, the Iberoamericana became a forum for the analysis of left-wing doctrines and theories it had once rejected. Iberoamericana faculty members enjoyed much greater academic freedom than had been the case before advent of church reform. The degree to which the Iberoamericana had been transformed was demonstrated during the Mexican Student Movement of 1968. Iberoamericana faculty members (both Jesuits and non-Jesuits) and students participated in anti-government protests characterized by conservatives as being Marxist-controlled. This activism in turn generated conflict between leftist elements at the Iberoamericana against Mexico's authoritarian one-party state government and its own conservative business class patrons as well as conservative Catholics opposed to the church reform movement. The college's leadership managed to navigate these multiple political traps that threatened not just the Iberoamericana's academic freedom but its very survival and emerged strengthened and dynamic, becoming the leading institution of Mexican higher education that it is today.

Chapter 1 analyzes the critical nature of church-state relations that emerged in Mexico in the aftermath of the Mexican Revolution. It begins at the turn of the century, in the waning days of Porfirio Díaz's dictatorship (1876–1911), when Catholics used the so-called social question to reassert themselves into Mexico's political and social discourse, after half a century of liberal hegemony. These so-called social Catholics utilized the coming of political freedom under Francisco Madero's revolutionary government to form the Partido Católico Nacional (PCN, National Catholic Party), under the auspices of the Catholic Church hierarchy. The PCN endorsed the social, political, and economic thought encapsulated in Pope Leo XIII's encyclical *Rerum Novarum* (1891) and addressed social issues neglected by Díaz's regime. Although it was benefiting politically from Madero's rule, the PCN failed to support his regime when it was assailed by anti-democratic forces in the federal army and the ruling class. Elements associated with the PCN openly supported the 1913 military coup by Victoriano Huerta that overthrew Madero's government. Revolutionaries attacked Catholic clergy and institutions as punishment for its collaboration with the military dictatorship (1913–1914). The anticlerical provisions of the 1917 Constitution were enacted by the victorious Revolutionaries for the purpose of destroying the Roman Catholic Church's influence in Mexican society. These constitutional articles defined the parameters of church-state conflict in the post-Revolutionary era.

Chapter 2 analyzes the history of the ACJM. Study circles lay at the heart of the organization, in which its members were taught ecclesiastical history, Mexican history (from a Catholic perspective), and neo-scholastic philosophy. The Catholic Youth Association served, in effect, as a substitute Jesuit university. The Catholic Youth's Jesuit spiritual director also believed these elites could be effective agents for the resolution of the social question, with its study circles emphasizing the teaching of Catholic sociology, as enunciated in the papal encyclical *Rerum Novarum* (1891). Bergöend believed that their standing in Mexican society would place them in a position to enact social legislation in accordance with Catholic doctrine in the future.

Catholic Youth members played an active role during the Cristero Rebellion, providing much of the urban organizational strength of the Liga Nacional Defensora de las Libertades Religiosas (LNDLR, National League for the Defense of Religious Liberty), the umbrella group that coordinated the 1920s Catholic rebellion. Members of Bergöend's Catholic Youth Association participated as fighters during the conflict, while a few were implicated in terrorist attacks against the life of the Mexican strongman and former president, Álvaro Obregón. The church hierarchy decreed the demobilization of Bergöend's Catholic Youth Association at end of the Cristero Rebellion. It had grown too militant and was out of step with the Catholic Church's post-Cristero strategy of seeking better relations with the Mexican state.

Bergöend's Catholic Youth Association was effectively supplanted in the 1930s by another Jesuit-led organization—the UNEC—which was led by Ramón Martínez Silva, SJ, during much of its brief existence. Its history is analyzed in chapter 3. In many respects, the UNEC's functions overlapped that of Bergöend's Catholic Youth Association: it sought to groom a cadre of elite Mexican men to serve as the agents for Mexico's Christianization. However, the archbishop of Mexico granted the UNEC exclusive rights to recruit its members from Mexico's university student population. In the name of academic freedom, the UNEC rose to prominence by opposing the implementation of the Socialist Education program at Mexican universities. Beginning with the Universidad Nacional Autónoma de México (UNAM, National Autonomous University of Mexico) in 1933, left-wing academics and students attempted to impose socialist education on the Mexican higher education system. They sought to transform the nation's universities, traditional bastions of conservatism, into agents for creating socialism in Mexico. These Marxist forces found their most determined opponents to be the UNEC.

The UNEC's significance was not limited to the realm of student politics, however. The UNEC created a generation of political activists that helped to found the PAN, a right-wing political organization that emerged in opposition to President Lázaro Cárdenas's left-wing political, social, and economic policies. Members of the UNEC went on to occupy key positions in the PAN's hierarchy and also founded its official newspaper.

The reestablishment of a modus vivendi in church-state relations in the 1940s had a dramatic but predictable impact on the UNEC. Once again, the Catholic Church hierarchy was faced with a militant lay Catholic organization at a time in which the hierarchy was seeking to establish more cordial relations with the federal government. The church leadership withdrew their support from the student organization and directed the Jesuits to a new enterprise, the establishment of a Catholic university, which became the Universidad Iberoamericana.

Chapter 4 details and analyzes the complex series of factors behind the founding of the Jesuit university, which in its infancy was known as the CCU. The Universidad Iberoamericana continued the Jesuit's long-standing work of promoting the development of Catholic culture in Mexico, tasks entrusted to the UNEC and the ACJM in previous decades. Unable to obtain government recognition for its academic titles and degrees, the Iberoamericana affiliated itself with the UNAM. This complex and often troubled relationship between the two institutions severely affected the Iberoamericana's curricula development, and for this reason these issues are analyzed in depth.

Chapter 5 examines the special contributions that the Universidad Iberoamericana made to Mexican higher education during the 1950s and the early 1960s. The Universidad Iberoamericana prospered during this period by offering business-oriented courses, some entirely new to Mexico and Latin America, which addressed Mexican industry's increasing need for trained professionals during this era of rapid economic growth. Through these courses, the Jesuit institution propagated orthodox Catholic doctrine on the issue of labor-capital relations. The Mexican business class reciprocated by providing the Iberoamericana with economic support it desperately needed to cover its operating deficits and the construction cost of its campus, which opened in 1963. The downside to such a close relationship with the Mexican business community only became apparent in the late 1960s, when under the influence of the Vatican II Council the Roman Catholic Church reasserted its emphasis on promoting social reform after downplaying it during the conservative, strongly anti-communist pontificate of Pope Pius XII (1939–1958). The Vatican II Council's promotion of dialogue with the Catholic Church's ideological enemies, including the formerly despised Marxists, was another issue that was to eventually generate conflict between the Universidad Iberoamericana and its business patrons as the Iberoamericana and its Jesuit leadership moved to embrace the message of Vatican II.

Chapter 6 examines how the Roman Catholic Church's reform movement of the 1960s affected the Universidad Iberoamericana and how the Jesuit institution responded to this change. My argument is that the reforms promoted within the Roman Catholic Church in the 1960s radically restated the Iberoamericana's role in Mexican society. In the post–Vatican II era, the Iberoamericana had to justify its continued existence now that the Roman Catholic Church hierarchy in much of Latin America was criticizing the neglect of the education of the popular classes and proclaiming a "preferential option for the poor." These new positions were fully supported by the Jesuit Order's superior general. The ecumenical movement also eliminated the goal, vigorously promoted by the Jesuits in decades past, of implanting an exclusionary, intolerant Catholic culture in Mexican society, for the Iberoamericana's founders established the university in 1943 on the premise of Catholic education.

The Jesuit leadership of the Iberoamericana responded to these changes by altering the institution's mission in Mexican society. Instead of promoting a xenophobic Catholic culture, the Iberoamericana became a forum of more open intellectual debate. In this way, the university contributed to the call of Vatican II to bring the Roman Catholic Church into greater contact with the world. The Iberoamericana addressed the Roman Catholic Church's renewed concern for issues of social inequalities in a variety of manners. One was by pledging the university—in its *Ideario* of 1968—to employ the social science investigation carried out at the institution toward the solution of Mexico's social ills. In addition, a form of social service was instituted for the Iberoamericana's student body, in which they were sent into Mexico City slums. The goal of this was not only to have them assist the poor but also to have these well-heeled students meet face to face the social injustices of Mexican society.

The participation of Iberoamericana students and faculty members in the Mexican Student Movement of 1968 heralded to the larger Mexican society the important changes that Vatican II had brought both to the Mexican Jesuit Order and the Iberoamericana. Unfortunately, it also raised the specter of the Iberoamericana, experiencing the same type of governmental repression that the UNAM and National Polytechnic Institute suffered. And it created an estrangement between the Iberoamericana's conservative business-class patrons and leftists within the college, which threatened both the Iberoamericana's academic freedom and future economic viability.

Primary Sources

The most important archival sources for the ACJM was the UNAM's Miguel Palomar y Vizcarra Collection, a rich collection of documents from Catholic organizations and personal correspondence of leading lay Catholic activists. The Universidad Iberoamericana's Acción Católica Mexicana Collection and the Historical Archive of the Arzobispado Primado de Mexico were the key archival sources for the UNEC.

Additional valuable information was provided by the UNEC student paper *PROA*.

The most important primary sources for the history of the Universidad Iberoamericana are found in the Archivo Histórico de la Universidad Iberoamericana (AHUIA, Iberoamerican Historical Archive) and the UNAM's Centro de Estudios Sobre la Universidad at the university's historical archive. The AHUIA contains the minutes of the Iberoamericana's council meetings (from 1956 on), as well as those of the University Senate, after it was constituted in 1970. The Iberoamericana's archive also contains documents and interviews collected for an early, unpublished history of the university. University catalogues and journals—the most important of which was the social science publication *Comunidad*—provided critical information for this study. The catalogues contain information on curriculum development and the role of the business community in this process. The journal *Comunidad* gives testimony to the intellectual diversity at the Iberoamericana in the 1960s: the open discussion of issues previously condemned out of hand. This journal recorded Professor Ángel Palerm's analytical, yet poignant, reflections on the Mexican Student Movement of 1968, in which many of the Iberoamericana's social science major students participated.

The Centro de Estudios Sobre la Universidad Archive of the UNAM contains important documentation on the Universidad Iberoamericana, because the UNAM exercised direct control over the Iberoamericana for thirty years. The official relationship between these two institutions is recorded in the documents contained in the UNAM's *Dirección General de Revalidación y Incorporación de Estudios* collection. These documents give testimony to the importance of explicitly articulated political factors in the UNAM's decision-making process as to whether or not to recognize new academic programs at the Iberoamericana. These documentary sources are complemented with a number of oral interviews I conducted with informants who played important roles in different phases of the Iberoamericana's development.

Articles written by Jesuit clerics in the journals *Pulgas* and *Christus* shed light on the participation of both progressive clerics and Iberoamericana students in the Mexican Student Movement of 1968. The ideas and beliefs expressed by these are far removed from those defended and expounded upon by earlier generations of Jesuits in organizations like the Universidad Iberoamericana, the UNEC, and the ACJM. They give fascinating testimony to the profound impact of church reform movement within the Order, as well as how these changes divided the Roman Catholic clergy in Mexico into progressive and conservative factions. They demonstrate how far some Jesuits moved away from the church's pre–Vatican II positions on economic, social, and political issues.

Secondary Sources

Histories of lay Catholic organizations, written by former members, form the most significant secondary sources used in this work. Uniformly apologetic in nature, these histories are nonetheless extremely useful. More important than the details of the institutional life that they provide (recorded in tedious detail) is the information that they provide on the ideological values that they promoted. They flesh out what was meant by phrases such as "Catholic culture" and "Christianization," the promotion of a militant, intolerant Catholicism at the expense of rival ideological, philosophical, and religious systems. This is clearly seen in Antonio Rius Facius's *La Juventud Católica y la Revolución Mexicana* (1963) and *Méjico Cristero: Historia de la ACJM 1925 a 1931* (1960)—the unofficial histories of Bernardo Bergöend's ACJM. Harsh judgments concerning Roman Catholicism's enemies—defined as all those who were not orthodox Roman Catholics—permeate Rius Facius's works. Prominent on this enemies list are Jews, Protestants, Marxists, socialists, and liberals. Luis Calderón Vega's *Cuba 88* (1959) is the basic work on the other great Jesuit-led Catholic student organization—the UNEC. Written in a confusing and turgid manner, it is a work that must be carefully mined in order to extract useful information. Again, as in the case of the works of Rius Facius, the most significant data in *Cuba 88* is that which pertains to the set of values promoted at the institution. Its appendix is of particular use, containing the entire program and conclusions of the 1932 Iberoamerican Convention of Iberoamerican Students, providing in detail the UNEC's analysis of a wide host of political, social, and economic issues facing Mexico and, to a lesser degree, Latin America.

Biographies of Bernardo Bergöend and Ramón Martínez Silva, spiritual directors of the ACJM and the UNEC, respectively, were used in this study. Andrés Barquín y Ruíz's *Bernardo Bergöend, S.J.* (1968) and Manuel Ulloa Ortíz et al.'s *Semblanzas de un Maestro* (1974) are sympathetic works written by former Catholic student activists. In addition to detailing

Bergöend's relationship with the ACJM, Barquín y Ruíz's work explains the Jesuit's contributions to the PCN of 1911 and to the LNDLR of the 1920s Cristero Rebellion. The study highlights the example of European Catholic organizations, especially of those of Bergöend's native France, in generating ideas for Bergöend's projects.

Historical works authored by Jesuit scholars are significant to this work, providing information on the institutional history of the Jesuit Order and church-state relations in Mexico. In addition, the historical perspective presented in these works is important in their own right, as they formed an integral part of the Catholic culture that Jesuit student organizations promoted. The works of Mariano Cuevas, SJ, and José Bravo Ugarte, SJ, are the most salient to this work, for both taught classes at the Universidad Iberoamericana and gave presentations at the UNEC during the 1930s. Both works present an intransigent Catholic vision of Mexican history, which denounces the influence of Protestantism, Liberalism, anarchism, socialism, and Marxism in Mexican society. These works present a form of Catholic nationalism based on antipathy to the United States, which sees Mexican Protestants as agents for U.S. imperialism. Cuevas and Bravo Ugarte were not reconciled to the Roman Catholic Church's political defeat in the nineteenth century, while the fire of their hatred toward the Mexican Revolution and its aftermath burned fiercely in their histories. The institutional history of the Society of Jesus in Mexico is presented by José Gutiérrez Casillas, S.J, in his *Jesuitas en México durante el Siglo XIX* (1972) and *Jesuitas en México durante el Siglo XX* (1981). Gutiérrez Casillas's work builds upon that of Gerardo Decorme, SJ, who completed his two-volume *Historia de la Compañía de Jesús en la República Mexicana durante el Siglo XIX* in 1921.

The historiography of church-state relations in the twentieth century centers on a period before 1940, comprising the events surrounding the Mexican Revolution, the Cristero Rebellion of 1926–1929, the Maximato (1929–1934), and the presidency of Lázaro Cárdenas. Jean Meyer is the foremost historian of the Cristero Rebellion, including its origins and consequences. His three-volume *La Cristiada* (1973) remains the standard work on the subject, as is his study of the 1930s Sinarquista Movement, *El Sinarquismo: ¿un fascismo mexicano?* (1979). Soledad Loaeza's *Las Clases Medias en México* (1988), though concerned specifically with the textbook controversy between the State and Mexican conservatives of the late 1950s, does examine in depth the reestablishment of the modus vivendi in the 1940s. Loaeza maintains that the consensus between Mexico's ruling political elite, the Roman Catholic Church hierarchy, and the business community created in the 1940s was founded on a common fear of Communism in Mexico.

Mexican educational issues of the 1920s and 1930s are well studied in the historiography. The most significant English-language study of Mexican higher education during this period is David J. Mabry's work on the UNAM.[1] Spanish-language histories concerning the Socialist Education controversy at the UNAM include Julio Jiménez Rueda's *Historia Jurídica de la Universidad de México* (1955) and Sebastián Mayo's right-wing work *El Asalto a la Universidad Nacional* (1964). Enrique Krauze's *Caudillos Culturales en la Revolución Mexicana* (1985) offers a sophisticated analysis of Vicente Lombardo Toledano and Manuel Gómez Morin, two of the most distinguished Mexican statesmen of the twentieth century and fierce antagonists in the Socialist Education controversy.

Finally, scholars within the Iberoamericana community itself have examined their institution. José de Jesús Ledesma's *Trayectoria Histórico-Ideológico de la Universidad Iberoamericana* (1987) is a comprehensive, but uncritical, study of the Iberoamericana. Ernesto Meneses Morales's *La Universidad Iberoamericana en el Contexto de la Educación Superior Contemporanea* (1979) analyzes the Iberoamericana's role in Mexican higher education and society after the turbulent 1960s, a decade that ushered in profound change within the Roman Catholic Church, the Jesuits, Mexican politics, and higher education in Mexico. Meneses Morales's rectorship of the Iberoamericana during this period makes this work particularly significant.

This work advances twentieth-century Mexican historiography in several fields. It analyzes the relationship between the Roman Catholic Church and the Mexican right in post-Revolutionary Mexico and, concretely, the importance of Catholic ideology to the Mexican right. The issue of church-state relations is also central to this work. It places the founding of the Universidad Iberoamericana, the first Catholic university for the education of laity in post-independent Mexico, in the context of long-term efforts by the church to promote Catholic culture through Jesuit-led lay organizations. It emphasizes the importance that the Roman Catholic Church, through the Jesuits, placed on educating young elite males, who, they expected, would be Mexico's future movers and shakers. This was a goal that the church pursued with tenacity in the face of barriers placed against it by a succession of anticlerical governments.

The Roman Catholic Church's leading role in anti-government opposition movements in post-Revolutionary Mexico, culminating in the religious-based civil war of the Cristero Rebellion (1926–1929), gives historical saliency to its educational activities. This manuscript emphasizes the Iberoamericana's strong ties to Jesuit-led, right-wing, lay-student organizations, such as the ACJM of the 1920s and the UNEC, with whom it shared a common ideology and a common goal—the promotion Catholic culture—and the historical bonds between the Iberoamericana and Mexico's conservative opposition party—National Action.

The critical role that the UNAM played in the founding of the Iberoamericana is prominently analyzed in this study. In addition, this work sheds new light on the UNAM's salient role in combating the government's Socialist Education program in the 1930s by incorporating Catholic preparatory schools whose studies the government refused to recognize. By validating the studies done at the Universidad Iberoamericana, the UNAM, in effect, allowed Catholics the opportunity to shape Mexican higher education. This came when the anticlerical State denied them other options.

This study highlights the Iberoamericana's significant contributions to Mexican higher education, pioneering new academic programs designed to satisfy the private and public sector needs for trained professionals during Mexico's post–World War II economic boom. It also details the active role that the Mexican business community played in shaping the Iberoamericana's curriculum and providing the university critically important financial support.

The Universidad Iberoamericana is a key case study for the examination of the far-reaching consequences that the 1960s church reform movement brought to the conservative, and historically militant, Catholic Church in Mexico. The reforms unleashed by the Vatican II Council, and furthered by the Conference of Latin American Bishops at Medellín, forced the Iberoamericana and the Jesuits to radically rethink their roles in Mexican society. This work shows how these reforms forced the Iberoamericana to abandon its original mission, that of imposing the hegemony of Catholic culture on Mexico, to become a forum of dialogue between Catholics and society at large. The Jesuits also abandoned their long-standing belief, promoted at the Universidad Iberoamericana, that elites could be transformed into agents for the implementation of Catholic social doctrine on the "social question." To justify its continued existence, the Iberoamericana was transformed from an institution that instilled a paternalist concern for the poor into their well-heeled students into a research center that critically examined Mexico's social problems using modern social science methods. This study of the Universidad Iberoamericana also offers a microcosm of the conflicts that the 1960s church reform movement generated within Mexico's Catholic community between progressives and traditionalists, both within the church hierarchy and among the laity.

CHAPTER ONE

Church-State Relations from the Porfiriato to the Mexican Revolution, 1876–1917

> *Persecution has unleashed all its fury. Clergy have been expelled, Catholic schools closed . . . priests have been arrested and the celebration of the mass impeded. . . . All Hell has broken out.*
>
> —Letter from Miguel Palomar Vizcarra to
> Gabriel Fernández Smollera, 1914

Introduction

The early decades of the twentieth century were characterized by dramatic twists and turns in the Roman Catholic Church's fortunes in Mexican society, an institution that had once exercised a near hegemonic influence in Mexico from the time of the Spanish Conquest until the final triumph of anticlerical liberals over their church-supported conservative rivals in 1867. Utterly discredited as a consequence of its disastrous support of the ill-fated, French-installed regime of the Austrian Archduke Maximilian, the Roman Catholic Church had recovered a measure of its lost vitality during the lengthy dictatorship of General Porfirio Díaz, a hero of the war against Maximilian's French-supported government. Unable to exercise a formal political role in Mexico during the so-called Porfiriato (1876–1911), the church instead concentrated its efforts in unglamorous but highly significant institution-building activities. New parishes were created and staffed by Mexican-born priests educated in recently established seminaries, which served both to increase the church's contacts with the general population as well as to strengthen the national identity of the clergy. However, during the last decade of the Porfiriato (the first decade of the twentieth century) the church and lay social Catholic activists began to take a decidedly more open political stance; these players were reacting both to political factors endogenous to Mexico as well as to the religious-ideological currents emanating from the Vatican and the broader Catholic world.

The church and social Catholic activists responded both to the abject failure of the Porfirian regime to constructively address the legitimate needs and demands of the Mexican laboring classes and the emphasis that the Roman Catholic Church had recently given to the "social question," most importantly in Pope Leo X's encyclical *Rerum Novarum* (1891), by holding a series of conferences that paternalistically examined the nation's severe social ills. These gatherings, held in different cities in central Mexico from 1903 to 1909, also created a cadre of militant politically active Catholics eager to shake off the subservient role that practicing Catholics and the church had occupied in the nation's political life since 1867. These efforts bore fruit in 1911 when taking advantage of the democratic opening created by Francisco Madero's successful revolution against Díaz's regime. Established in close coordination with the Catholic Church hierarchy, the Partido Católico Nacional (PCN, National Catholic Party) soon became one of the country's most influential political parties, winning offices at the federal, state, and municipal levels. Despite the fact that Mexican Catholics had been one of the principal beneficiaries of the political freedoms ushered in by Madero's revolution, the church hierarchy and its political arm failed to support the new government; indeed, these forces welcomed Madero's overthrow in February 1913 and supported General Victoriano Huerta's brutal counterrevolutionary government.

The fallout from the Catholic Church's disastrous political decisions became all too apparent as revolutionary armies, seeking to overthrow Huerta's de facto regime, took numerous opportunities to punish the church and its institutions as they victoriously advanced toward Mexico City. The revolutionaries' anticlerical ire, manifested in a more or less unorganized fashion during their struggle against Huerta (1913–1914), was codified in the Constitution of 1917; this document formed the epicenter of the church-state conflict that afflicted Mexico in the coming decades. Drafted by the often-dysfunctional revolutionary "family," the 1917 Constitution reflected the revolutionaries' determination to break the influence of the Roman Catholic Church on Mexico. The Catholic Church's refusal to recognize the Constitution of 1917 hampered the consolidation of the new political order. The revolutionary general Álvaro Obregón, who became president in 1920, sidestepped a frontal confrontation with the Catholic Church by not enforcing the Constitution's anticlerical provisions.[1] Plutarco Elías Calles's determination to enforce the law during his administration (1924–1928) was met with fierce opposition by the Roman Catholic Church and its supporters. The rigidity of the positions taken on both sides played a fundamental role in transforming strained church-state relations into a brutal civil conflict, the Cristero Rebellion (1926–1929), which is analyzed in the next chapter.

Catholic Revival during the Porfiriato: The "Social Question"

The thirty-five-year period of Mexican history dominated by Porfirio Díaz, known as the Porfiriato, was fundamental to the nation's political, economic, and social development. During the Porfiriato, the Mexican economy was reintegrated into the world economic system. Long-term political stability was attained for the first time since Mexican independence in 1821; however, there were severe limitations to the regime's accomplishments that manifested themselves with clarity during the Mexican Revolution (1910–1920), which abruptly terminated Díaz's long rule. These limitations included an unequal distribution of the benefits of economic expansion, the destruction of peasant communal landholding communities, the negation of the right of Mexico's working class to establish labor unions, and the lack of political rights and legal protection for the vast majority of the Mexican population.

Porfirio Díaz also initiated a new era in the relations between the Mexican state and the Roman Catholic Church that allowed him to conduct the pacification of the nation. For much of its post-independence history, Mexican society had been embroiled in political and social conflict that pitted reformist Mexican liberals against clerical-backed conservatives. At the heart of this discord was the issue of the Roman Catholic Church's position in Mexican society with Mexican liberals promoting the separation of Church and State and the church attempting to preserve its position in society.[2]

The Catholic Church hierarchy's rejection of the liberal Constitution of 1857, which stripped the church of its landed wealth and thus its political muscle, led to the War of Reform (1858–1861) and its corollary, the War of the French Intervention (1862–1867). In 1867 liberal president Benito Juárez executed the French-installed puppet emperor of Mexico, Archduke Maximilian of Austria, and so confirmed the total political defeat of the Roman Catholic Church and its allies.[3] In 1873 Juárez's successor, Sebastián Lerdo de Tejada (1872–1876), used the Laws of Reform of the 1857 Constitution to enforce the secularization of public schools.

Lay Catholics and the Catholic hierarchy mounted resistance to these policies; Catholic peasants waged scattered revolts over a wide region in central Mexico from 1874 to 1876 that continued until Porfirio Díaz's 1876 military uprising overthrew Lerdo de Tejada's government.[4]

In 1876 Porfirio Díaz seized control of a country that for the past sixty-six years had known little more than civil war and economic chaos. Mexico's chronic weakness had tempted foreign powers to engage in naked military aggression that had led to the loss of half of its national territory (1846–1848) and its attempted recolonization (1862–1867). Díaz, with his well-developed political acumen, understood that if he was to remain in power and create the sort of stable authoritarian regime that had eluded Mexico's notorious strongman of earlier decades Antonio López de Santa Anna, he had to stimulate economic development in order to have the resources all strong central governments require. The essential prerequisite for such economic growth was political stability; however, there would be no such political stability if Mexico's political leaders remained at war with the Roman Catholic Church, which still claimed the support of millions of ordinary Mexicans.

It was Díaz's political pragmatism that led him to ease enforcement of the anticlerical provisions of the 1857 Constitution while never formally revoking them.[5] This was in keeping with his overall policy of maintaining the charade that Mexico was a formal democracy by holding rigged elections and giving the appearance of separation of powers when in fact none existed; it was anger and outrage at Díaz's mockery of democratic values and practices that ultimately led Francisco Madero to challenge him in 1910.

The Social Question: "Rerum Novarum"

The Roman Catholic Church took full advantage of the modus vivendi during the Porfiriato to strengthen its presence in society; Mexican novices filled the newly constructed seminaries, thereby ensuring that the clergy in Mexico would be progressively national in orientation and not as reliant on foreign-born clergy.[6] The church also expanded its educational network of parochial and preparatory schools and thereby increased its ability to ideologically mold the educated elites of Mexican society. However, it was the emergence of the "social question" and the publication of Pope Leo XIII's encyclical *Rerum Novarum* in Porfirian Mexico that provided the Roman Catholic Church with a potent issue that allowed it to challenge the country's liberal political elites; the social question allowed politically active Catholics to once again openly influence the social, economic, and political discourse in Mexico.

Rerum Novarum synthesized the programs of nineteenth-century Catholic activists, men who had sought to address the "social question" posed by the European industrial revolution. These Catholic social reformers, many of whom belonged to the aristocracy whose social position was being challenged by the rising industrialist class, went beyond the Catholic Church's reactionary condemnation of liberalism and defense of the caste system of privilege of the ancien régime; they actively sought to use this hierarchical social model for the promotion of social reform. Wilhelm von Ketteler (the bishop of Mainz), Count Albert de Mun of France, and Baron Karl von Vogelsang of Austria were the most influential of these Catholic social activists. They upheld the corporatist social model derived from Aristotle's *Politics* and embraced by Thomas Aquinas in his *De Regime Principum*, in which society was likened to a human body, consisting of mutually interdependent organs (social classes) arranged hierarchically. They agreed with Aquinas's assertion that this hierarchical, mutually interdependent social order was divinely ordained and corresponded to human reason.[7] According to these Catholic thinkers, liberalism allowed humans to escape from their fundamental social obligations to one another by promoting the "cult" of individualism. They blamed liberalism for both revolution and the advent of radical working-class ideologies; by failing to recognize any divine authority in the political/legal relationships governing human beings, liberalism had prepared the stage for the exploitation of the weak by the strong, such as during the Industrial Revolution. According to the Catholic reformers, the failures of liberalism had spawned three anti-liberalist movements: utopian socialism, Marxism, and anarchy.[8]

Pope Leo XIII's encyclical *Rerum Novarum* asserted that the solution to the tensions present in an industrial society could not be found outside of the teachings of the Roman Catholic Church. The pontiff reminded the wealthy that all human beings, including the poor, possessed natural dignity, and he denounced the oppression of the poor by the powerful in the savage world of early laissez-faire productive capitalism in unequivocal terms: "to exercise pressure upon the indigent and destitute for the sale of gain and to gather one's profit out of the need of another is condemned by all laws, human and divine."[9]

In addition, *Rerum Novarum* emphasized the social obligation of the state toward the people it governed. The state had the burden of protecting the "spiritual and mental interests" of the workers and of implementing policies that "benefited every class" in society. Governments were to allow the formation of workers' organizations, as long as they did not threaten society with revolutionary violence; furthermore, the church viewed social reform as the best mechanism for staving off the labor strife and revolutionary violence that threatened the entire social and political hierarchy of Europe. Pope Leo XIII denounced radical working-class ideologies in his encyclical; he condemned the doctrine of class warfare and put in its place the concept of a hierarchically organized society in which the social classes were mutually interdependent.[10] The institution of private property was also defended as being in accordance with natural law.

In Mexico, the social question arose as a corollary of Porfirian political and economic policies. Díaz's economic policies had created a modern working class, but its members found themselves unable to express their socioeconomic concerns in the closed Porfirian political system, and Porfirian agrarian polices had favored the expansion of the large estates at the expense of Native American communities and mestizo peasants, who found no effective peaceful means to address their grievances. Díaz ruled the nation through an elaborate system of personal alliances with regional elites, a system that excluded the vast majority of Mexican civil society. Workers in the new industrial complexes created by Mexican and foreign entrepreneurs found their aspirations to promote union organization and political participation blocked by the state.[11] The state's response to this new social phenomenon was one of brutal repression and was most apparent during the 1905 Cananea copper mine strike and the 1906 Río Blanco textile strike. The importance and dynamism of the economic sectors in which these workers labored gave them a social and political significance that dictated the utilization of more refined mechanisms for addressing their needs. Similarly, Mexican peasants were subjected to state repression by the paramilitary Rurales if they dared to openly protest the alienation of their lands by the politically connected hacendados (estate owners).

Despite the grievous social problems faced by the vast majority of the population of Porfirian Mexico, political considerations delayed *Rerum Novarum*'s diffusion in Mexico. As noted by the prominent Mexican scholar Manuel Ceballos Ramírez, the proclamation of this encyclical coincided with the highpoint of the "policy of conciliation" between the Porfirian state and "liberal Catholics" within the ecclesiastical hierarchy and among prominent lay Catholics.[12] During the 1890s, the Porfirian state was at its apogee and the Roman Catholic Church hierarchy was loath to provoke a disruption of its relationship with the dictator that had been so fruitful to that institution. And so for the first decade of its promulgation, this encyclical left no real imprint on Mexican society.

The year 1903 marked the turning point in the history of *Rerum Novarum* in Mexico, when the first of four national Catholic conferences (1903–1909) of clerics and lay Catholics was held with the expressed purpose of promoting this encyclical and applying it to the realities of life in Porfirian Mexico. The reason for this about-face was the growing crisis of the Porfirian state, as more and more social groups that had negatively been affected by the economic and political policies of the Porfirian dictatorship expressed their dissent with the regime. Anarchists and traditional liberals were increasingly vocal in their criticisms of the Díaz dictatorship, while there was increasing labor unrest along with the ongoing strife in the Mexican countryside created by Porfirian land policies, which had led to the alienation of millions of hectares of land from Native American communities and other small landholders; these anticlerical dissidents were also highly critical of the regime's conciliatory policies toward the Catholic Church.[13] Overshadowing all of these growing tensions and problems was the issue of who was going to succeed the rapidly aging dictator. This reality created growing tension within the Catholic camp between those clerics and laity who still identified with the regime and the so-called social Catholics who embraced the message of *Rerum Novarum* and rejected Díaz's politically out-of-touch government.

The lay participants of these Catholic congresses were drawn from the educated, urban middle class: lawyers, doctors, journalists, intellectuals, and students; some were also large-landed estate owners, while the Catholic clerics included both bishops and lower-ranking priests.[14] The initiative for holding these conferences came from the Catholic Circle of Puebla, one of a number of lay Catholic organizations located in the main cities of central Mexico: Guadalajara, Mexico City, and Puebla.

These societies were part social club and part center for instruction in Catholic doctrine, which sought to teach its members to live and interact with one another in a Catholic manner.[15]

The Puebla Catholic Circle took advantage of the twenty-fifth anniversary celebration of Pope Leo XIII's ascension to the papacy in 1903 to call the first Catholic Congress, which it also hosted. The thirty-nine delegates of the Puebla Congress agreed that measures needed to be taken in order to combat alcoholism among the poor and promote Catholic charity.[16] The Puebla Congress commission that examined Mexico's "Indian problem" proposed that the hacendados enact a series of reforms to ameliorate the lives of the peasants who labored on their properties. It recommended that the hacendados provide their workers with schooling, medical attention, low-cost basic goods, and old age and accident insurance.[17] Notably absent from the list of proposed remedies was any mention of land redistribution as a means of addressing Mexico's grave social inequalities; this is a significant omission given the fact that land reform emerged as one of the central issues of the great conflagration that broke out less than a decade later.

The next Catholic Congress, held in Guadalajara in 1906, was overshadowed by the recent bloody strike at the Cananea Copper Mine. The impact of Cananea is clearly seen in arguments presented by delegate Nicolás Leaño, who first expounded on the concept put forward by Pope Leo XIII's encyclical *Rerum Novarum* on the matter of the wages necessary to sustain the worker and his family in "frugal comfort" and then applied his analysis to the Mexican reality of 1906. The recent Cananea strike had, according to Leaño, proved the existence of socialism in Mexico and highlighted the urgent need to "Christianize" labor-capital relations.[18] Leaño warned of the consequences if Mexico's social ills were not addressed in a Christian fashion: "The poor's moral, religious, and cultural criteria are so infinitely limited that there is no doubt that they will embrace, with fanaticism and horrible furor, any act of rebellion . . . against their masters."[19]

The 1909 Oaxaca Conference discussed the issue of the length of the workday and promoted the improvement of hygiene in the dwellings and the work places of the proletariat. It also gave rise to a new association of Catholic social activists, the Catholic-Social Study Circle of Santa María of Guadalupe, commonly known as Operarios Guadalupanos. Comprised of journalists, lawyers, engineers, priests, and landowners, they were committed to the promotion of Catholic social reform for the benefit of the working class, they defended the rights of yeoman farmers (the ranchero class), and they rejected the liberal Catholic policy of conciliation with the Porfirian regime. Their four-hundred-strong membership was concentrated overwhelmingly in the cities of central Mexico—the Catholic heartland. Two-thirds of the Operarios Guadalupanos were laypeople, and one-third were clerics.[20]

Agricultural congresses were held in this same decade to gain "the moral and material improvement of the peasantry."[21] The Archbishop of Mexico José Mora y del Río, a supporter of the social Catholic line within the church hierarchy, sponsored these assemblies. The paternalistic nature of the proposed reforms is manifested in the language utilized by archbishops who enjoined estate owners to "love their peons."[22] In return for these improvements in their lives, Archbishop Mora y del Río eagerly predicted that the peasants would demonstrate tremendous loyalty to their masters, that "they would be only separated by only death." The conferees demonstrated a special concern for the behavior of "their" peasants, whom they viewed as prisoners of the vices of drunkenness and concubinage. Conferees used a more socially critical perspective when they addressed issues of infant mortality and rural illiteracy.

One of the most significant outcomes of these Catholic congresses was the creation of a network of Catholic political activists; this was not an incidental outcome but rather an actively pursued objective. This goal of creating Catholic political activists is apparent in a letter from José Elguero, the social Catholic militant from the city of Morelia, to Miguel Palomar y Vizcarra of Guadalajara. In it, Elguero spoke of the impending crisis that would be created by Porfirio Díaz's death and the need for Catholics to gain power either through the electoral path or through revolutionary means. Elguero's views reflected a new political awareness of a younger generation of militant Catholics who rejected the political line embraced by clerics like Gillow. Reflecting upon the views of the previous generation of Catholics, Elguero wrote: "We Catholics have stated until now that we should not step into the political arena, due to the fact that our fathers emerged in so disadvantageous a position from the last political-religious war,[23] they lost their nerve . . . and now the word politics is synonymous with disgrace and loss of patrimony, etc. I believe that the present generation, sprouting from the old roots, must have more courage and enter into national politics, because the Republic is ours and not only the fatherland of the Liberals."[24] Mexican Catholics were approaching a moment of decision, wrote Elguero, and they needed to be ready for the moment when Díaz departed the scene. He believed that in order for this Catholic political revival to take place, the cooperation of the bishops and lesser clergy was essential: "It all depends on the village priests, who have over the masses absolute authority. But as the priests depend on the bishops, these latter should initiate the political work, even though they lead from the laity."[25] Elguero hoped that through the networks established by the delegates at these congresses, a "Catholic Masonic Society" would be created that would be of invaluable importance for the day "in which we need to conspire, either peacefully or in revolutionary fashion." The culmination of these efforts came in 1911 with the creation of the PCN.

Not all the members of the Catholic clergy were happy with the new directions that the church was taking toward the government. The social Catholics' frontal assault upon Porfirian social policies was attacked as ill founded by Bishop Gillow of Oaxaca, a conservative cleric known for his close, personal relationship with the dictator Porfirio Díaz and for championing the modus vivendi in church-state relations; Bishop Gillow's cautious approach to these new initiatives highlights the divisions that existed between the socially progressive Catholic reformers and those, primarily in the church hierarchy, who sought to continue with the politics of conciliation.[26]

Partido Católico Nacional

Francisco Madero's decision to challenge Díaz's hold on power in the 1910 presidential elections found an echo in many sectors of Mexican society, including disaffected regional elites as well as elements of the middle class. The scion of a wealthy northern family, Madero proposed in his electoral campaign a vision of a democratic society governed by the rule of law that he had originally set forth in his work *La Sucesión Presidencial en 1910* (1908). Madero's presidential candidacy electrified the nation but landed him in jail—imprisoned by a frightened regime. However, Madero refused to back down and escalated his conflict with Díaz by taking arms against the dictator. Madero's military challenge to the Díaz regime, enunciated in his *Plan of San Luis Potosí* (1910), was seconded by the bolder victims of Porfirian political and economic policies. These included peasants whose land had been confiscated by commercial agricultural producers and vaqueros (cowboys) displaced by the enclosure of the open ranges of northern Mexico; Madero's political revolt inadvertently became the midwife for a social revolution.

As the revolution gained steam and Díaz's regime faltered, the dictator anxiously sought the support of Catholic activists in a desperate effort to buttress the crumbling foundations of his political authority. However, Archbishop Mora y del Río, the head of the Catholic Church hierarchy in Mexico, had no desire to tie Catholic fortunes to those of a floundering, decrepit regime. In fact, Mora y del Río had something very different in mind—the creation of an independent Catholic political party.[27] Mora y del Río turned to Gabriel Fernández Smollera, the lay Catholic leader from Mexico City, as his instrument for the founding of a new Catholic party.[28] Fernández Smollera used the informal political network built up through the Catholic congresses, gathering a national assembly of Catholic activists in May 1911 comprised of Catholic circles members and Operarios Guadalupanos activists.[29] The resulting PCN was formally established on May 3, 1911, with Gabriel Fernández Smollera as its first president.[30]

Francisco Madero was at Ciudad Juárez negotiating with the Díaz government's representatives for the transfer of power to Madero when he received a memorandum from the leaders of the PCN informing him of the party's creation; a copy of the PCN's platform was enclosed with the document. Madero was sympathetic to the new undertaking, generously stating that he considered "the organizing of the Mexican Catholic Party as the first fruit of the freedom that we have conquered" and praising its political agenda, believing that "it reveals advanced ideas and the desire to collaborate in a sober fashion and within the Constitution for the advancement of the fatherland."[31] Despite these initial warm words, the long-term relationship between Madero and the PCN proved to be complex and oftentimes difficult.

The PCN endorsed Madero for the presidency in the October 1911 elections, which were held to ratify the military victory that Madero had already attained.[32] The PCN supported the Porfirian diplomat Francisco León de la Barra for the vice presidency, however, instead of Madero's candidate José María Pino Suárez. The PCN's selection of such a prominent representative of the old regime for the nation's second highest post was a telling decision. De la Barra had become interim president as a result of the Treaty of Ciudad Juárez negotiated between Madero and

Díaz. While in office, De la Barra successfully employed a stratagem of exacerbating preexisting fissures within the revolutionary supporters of Madero, sowing the seeds for an eventual overthrow of the new regime. His darkest act was initiating a ferocious counterinsurgency campaign against Emiliano Zapata's peasant movement in Morelos. Zapata had only been reluctantly persuaded by Madero to abide by the terms of the Treaty of Ciudad Juárez (May 1911) by disarming his fighters when León de la Barra moved against him. For Zapata, the author of this treachery was Madero himself, and it led the Zapatistas to declare themselves in rebellion against the Madero government in the "Plan of Ayala" (November 1911).

Relations between the PCN and the Madero administration were often difficult and contradictory. During the 1912 political campaign, the PCN brought forward accusations of electoral manipulation and violence against the Madero administration, particularly in the state of Chiapas.[33] Conversely, the PCN supported Madero in his conflict with the Zapatistas. Indeed, the PCN, reflecting the class and ethnic interests of its middle- and upper-class leadership, advocated draconian measures in order to contain the "Zapatista hordes," calling on Madero to "energetically repress all popular tumult, because nothing creates more alarm in foreign circles and is at the same time a symptom and a cause of anarchy; and . . . never support socialist parties and clubs, nor awaken alarm in private property owners, nor uncontrollable desires within Indians and workers with agrarian laws that interfere with the natural evolution and progress of . . . civilization."[34] Madero's failure to energetically deal with the Zapatistas was an important factor in the final estrangement between his government and the PCN. The PCN's true feelings toward Madero's government became tragically evident in the Decéna Trágica (Ten Tragic Days) Coup of February 1913.

The PCN tallied notable electoral successes in the 1912 campaign in spite of the alleged electoral fraud; they won four seats in the federal senate and the governorship of the state of Jalisco, adding to the Querétaro governorship they secured in the October 1911 elections.[35] The PCN also scored important victories in the state assembly of Jalisco as well as the municipalities of the state, making Jalisco the party's national stronghold.

Campaign literature demonstrated the influence of the Catholic social doctrine, as synthesized in *Rerum Novarum*. PCN flyers assured the Mexican electorate that "we Catholics are in possession of a set of doctrines which neither liberals nor socialists can accept and which are the only ones which can redeem the poor from their state of misery. . . . The Catholic Party shall fight to save the poor from the clutches of the moneylender and to make him a private property owner, in a step-by-step fashion, promoting his education and not through the art of demagoguery; we will fight to consolidate and increase small property ownership, which is the fountain of the prosperity of the nations."[36] The PCN emphasized to the electorate that it promoted public security as well as social reforms. This was a direct slap at the Madero regime, which was struggling to maintain itself in power as it was confronted with one military uprising after another; in addition, the party sought to demonstrate the viability of its program by citing the success of Catholic political organizations in Europe, which also advanced the doctrines contained in *Rerum Novarum*.

Mexican Catholics and Counterrevolution: 1913–1914

Francisco Madero's troubled presidency came to a violent and tragic end in February 1913, when he and Vice President José María Pino Suárez were overthrown and killed by General Victoriano Huerta, a senior commander in Díaz's Federal Army. Huerta then proceeded to establish a military dictatorship that sought to compensate for its lack of legitimacy and popular support by engaging in state terrorism against its opponents. Huerta's policies merely served to make his regime more odious to the bulk of the Mexican population, and soon enough new revolutionary armies arose determined to avenge Madero and overthrow the usurper's illegitimate government.

The participation of PCN members in Victoriano Huerta's government (1913–1914) was a monumental political error for which the entire Catholic community in Mexico paid dearly. The PCN offered candidates for the presidential, gubernatorial, and congressional elections held during Huerta's rule, and individuals associated with the PCN served in Huerta's fast-changing cabinets. But while Huerta courted the PCN for a period of time, he eventually turned against it, as he had with many of his erstwhile allies. In the end, Catholic political figures and the Roman Catholic Church hierarchy found their fates were too intertwined with that of Huerta to break free completely from the regime. Huerta and the Catholics became bound together by their common fear and hatred of the revolutionaries pressing down on the central government, and both were to suffer at the hands of those eager to punish the Huerta regime and its allies.[37]

Without having to contend with pro-Madero candidates, the officially tolerated PCN was able to build on its previous electoral successes, winning two more governorships in the regions of Mexico still under Huerta's control.[38] The PCN also participated in the long-delayed presidential elections originally stipulated in the *Pacto de la Ciudadela*, the pact brokered by the US Ambassador to Mexico Henry Lane Wilson that had paved the way for Huerta's ascension to power.[39] The PCN offered its presidential candidacy to the important Huertista military field commanders Joaquín Maas and José María Mier, who each declined the offer in turn; the PCN's ultimate presidential candidate was the acting Mexican foreign minister Federico Gamboa.[40]

Despite this relative success, the PCN still had to contend with the Machiavellian nature of the Huerta regime. The dysfunctional nature of Huerta's government is well illustrated by the controversy surrounding the nomination of Eduardo Tamariz, a PCN congressman, to be the head of the Ministry of Public Instruction. The granting of this ministry to a member of the PCN represented a major triumph for the cause of Catholic education.[41] However, true to his authoritarian nature, Huerta had not deemed it necessary to obtain the prior consent of the Federal Chamber of Deputies for Tamariz's appointment, and the filling of this position sparked a congressional revolt. Liberals within the legislative body opposed the "imposition" of a Catholic to such a politically sensitive post.[42]

By a vote of 108–20, Tamariz was denied permission to leave his congressional duties and assume the leadership of the Ministry of Public Instruction; this act of insubordination was joined by the Senate in October of the same year when that body voted to hold an investigation to clarify one of the more notable political crimes of the Huerta regime: the assassination of Senator Belisario Domínguez following an antigovernment speech in the senate chamber. Two days later the Chamber of Deputies was encircled by governmental security forces. Huerta ordered the chamber's dissolution and the arrest of the majority of its members for being "enemies of the state"; however, only one member of the PCN was arrested in this political crackdown.[43]

Huerta's closure of the national Congress brought to light fissures within the Catholic political camp. The Catholic Mexico City daily *El País* strongly rebuked this latest act of political repression by the de facto regime; however, the editors of *El País* were in turn criticized by high-ranking clerics of the Mexican Roman Catholic Church. Differences between the lay Catholic politicians and the church hierarchy were further widened as a consequence of the presidential election that was held on October 23, 1913. Huerta's government manipulated the election to such an extent that a humbled legislature declared the results void and determined that Huerta was to remain in office until July 1914.[44] The PCN eventually confronted the Huerta dictatorship, but only when it felt the sting of its repressive policies, accusing the government through its journal, *La Nación*, of prejudicial vote rigging against its candidates.[45] Repression was the price the PCN paid for its tardy defiance of the Huerta regime; its leader Gabriel Fernández Smollera was thrown into jail by the authorities and later forced into exile.[46]

Although Huerta had neutralized the PCN as a national political force, neither the ecclesiastical hierarchy nor Catholic political activists were prepared to identify with the armed groups threatening the central government's existence. Conservative Catholics considered the revolutionary forces to be by far the worst of the two evils, as indicated in this revealing letter penned by the PCN militant Rafael Contreras to the PCN deputy from Jalisco, Miguel Palomar y Vizcarra:

> There is still time for our fatherland to be saved, as long as the Catholic Party so wishes it. Are there not enough persons in the Party [PCN] to lead a counter revolution, along with the current government [of Victoriano Huerta]? Are the high clergy so lacking in patriotism as to not propel Catholics to take up arms in defense of the fatherland? . . . Is it not propitious for Mexican Catholics, united en masse, to exterminate the revolution? . . . If we remain indifferent before the danger we will lose all: God, Fatherland, and Liberty.[47]

To the dismay of Mexican counterrevolutionaries, nothing proved to be able to stem the revolutionary onslaught, and the Roman Catholic Church and its supporters were left to face the consequences of their political decisions.

The Constitution of 1917

By the summer of 1914, the revolutionary armies of Venustiano Carranza, Francisco Villa, and Emiliano Zapata had delivered Mexico from the Huerta dictatorship and were punishing those who had collaborated with that regime. Catholic ecclesiastical and political figures became favorite targets of revolutionary ire. The leader of the Constitutionalist revolutionary faction, Venustiano Carranza, maintained that Catholic political and ecclesiastical figures had played a leading role in the February 1913 coup d'état against Francisco Madero's government, and for that reason members of both the higher and lower Catholic clergy were targeted for retribution by his troops, with the Catholic bishops fleeing Mexico altogether.[48]

The ideological and political contradictions within the revolutionary coalition that overthrew Huerta's regime proved to be too great to surmount and opened the door to yet another round of conflict in war-torn Mexico. The conflict was decided in favor of Venustiano Carranza and the Constitutionalist faction, who in 1915 under Álvaro Obregón's skillful generalship convincingly defeated the combined forces of Francisco Villa and Emiliano Zapata. Once in power, Carranza called a constituent congress to draft a new federal constitution, which assembled in Querétaro in December 1916. From the outset, the constituent congress was divided between the moderates, who merely sought to rectify the weaknesses in the old 1857 Constitution, and the progressives, who were determined to deal with the social and political needs exposed by the Mexican Revolution. Carranza led the moderate faction at Querétaro, while the radicals received the support of Álvaro Obregón.[49]

The new constitution was strongly anticlerical; indeed it was one of the most anti-clerical documents ever drafted and set the parameters of church-state conflict in the post-revolutionary era.[50] It contained articles that barred the establishment of monastic orders, prohibited the holding of public religious ceremonies, nationalized church properties, and provided the government with the legal authority to regulate the internal activities of the Roman Catholic Church.[51] Predictably, the Roman Catholic Church bitterly contested the Constitution's anticlerical provisions, and Article 3, the key anticlerical provision of the 1917 Constitution, proved to be one of the most intractable of political issues of the post-revolutionary era. Article 3 dealt with the nature of educational instruction in government-operated schools as well as the authority of the state to regulate the instruction imparted at private institutions. In essence, Article 3 dealt with the issue of who was going to control the intellectual and ideological formation of Mexico's youth—the revolutionary state or Mexican civil society. The Roman Catholic Church was the specific target of the state's expanded role in education, as it was principal operator of private educational facilities.[52]

Carranza's proposal for educational reform, introduced at the constituent congress, was a further manifestation of the extent the president was wedded to the Mexican liberal *Reforma* tradition of the nineteenth century. Carranza's educational plan read as follows: "There shall be complete liberty of instruction, but the instruction imparted in the official educational establishments shall be secular and free at the elementary level of these same institutions."[53] The most important advance in this proposed reform over previous legislation was that primary education was to be free of cost at government schools. It reaffirmed the principle that a secular curriculum would reign at public educational institutions, without interfering with the right of religious groups to promote religious education in their own schools. Conversely, Carranza's proposal did not guarantee any official recognition of any titles or degrees granted at private schools, which left intact a long-standing impediment to the expansion of Catholic education in Mexico.

At the constitutional congress, the commission dealing with Article 3 took a far more strident line on the role of religious institutions in education. Led by Francisco Múgica, a political firebrand whose social and political views differed strongly from those of Carranza, the commission issued its own draft that went much further than Carranza in curbing the role of the Roman Catholic Church in education. The proposed article stated that education in Mexico would be secular in both the state elementary schools as well as private ones.[54] The proposed article struck directly at the Catholic Church's efforts to transmit its religious, philosophical, moral, and political values to Mexican students through education. The members of the commission made clear their rationale for opposing the Catholic Church in the arena of education: "The Roman Catholic Church is the cruelest and most tenacious enemy of our liberties; its doctrines have . . . placed the interests of the Church above those of the fatherland."[55] Private schools would be subject to official inspections by the state in order to ensure the fulfillment of this clause.

Carranza's supporters in the Congress raised objections to the Múgica committee's resolution. Delegate Félix Palavicini, who had served as

Carranza's minister of public instruction, stated that the proposed measure represented an assault upon cherished liberal precepts of freedom.[56] José Natividad Macías, delegate to the congress and rector of the UNAM, objected to the resolution, describing it as "oppressive Jacobinism" that played into the hands of the right-wing opposition. He maintained that it "justified the campaign of vilification carried out by the Roman Catholic clergy in the United States against the Revolution by throwing into the mud the most elemental rights of mankind."[57]

Obregón's political support of the constituent Congress's progressive bloc was instrumental to the final outcome of the debate over Article 3; after two days of passionate debate, the delegates voted on a clause favoring the commission's radical resolution over the one introduced by Carranza's supporters. Article 3 of the 1917 Constitution, as adopted by the congress, defended the principle of freedom of instruction; however, it also maintained that religious instruction was to be barred in both public schools as well as in the elementary schools supported by civil society. Religious corporations and ministers were barred from establishing or being directors of elementary schools, and privately operated elementary schools had to accept governmental inspection in order to operate. This provision was included to ensure that private elementary schools were indeed refraining from engaging in religious instruction; however, a loophole for the supporters of Catholic education was retained, for clerics were not barred from teaching at these private elementary schools.[58]

Carranza had been defeated in the struggle to draft the constitutional article concerning education in Mexico; however, as president of Mexico he enjoyed wide discretion in the formulation of regulations implementing the provisions of the Constitution. In his 1918 initiative for the modification of Article 3, Carranza noted the prevailing fear existing at the constituent congress of Querétaro that the Catholic clergy would take advantage of the freedom of instruction in order to "shackle the conscience" of Mexican youth, but he rejected these objections as being ill-founded.[59] Carranza stated that his decision to propose the amendment of Article 3 was because it "satisfies neither the intrinsic generosity of revolutionary principles, the [principle] of equality under the law, nor the promotion of the education of populace. On the contrary, [the article] has been counterproductive to the diffusion of culture, creating frequent political or administrative problems which no form of reasoning can be seen as useful to the collective progress [of the nation]."[60]

The Catholic bishops of Mexico responded quickly and sharply to the Constitution, issuing a manifesto on February 24, 1917, from their exile in the United States; in it they denounced the Constitution of 1917 as another of the "systematic abuses carried out by the revolutionaries against the Catholic Religion, its churches, its ministers, its educational and charitable institutions since a few months following the revolution of 1913 to the present."[61]

With reference to Article 3 of the 1917 Constitution, the bishops stated that "on the one hand it restricts freedom of instruction, as it bars religious instruction even in the private school, [and] on the other it denies priests the faculty which all men have to teach, and finally, it attacks the right of parents to educate their children according to their consciences and religious beliefs."

The manifesto concluded with the following statement: "We protest against such actions and against all the rest contained in the Constitution dictated in Querétaro on February 5 of the present year [1917], which goes against religious freedom and the rights of the Church, and we declare that we refuse to recognize any action or [public] statement from any person in our diocese, even if he be an ecclesiastic and invested with dignity, if it contradicted our declarations and protests."[62]

The Mexican ecclesiastical hierarchy's rejection of the 1917 Constitution set the stage for church-state conflict in the following decade and served to revive moribund lay Catholic organizations that had lain dormant since their recent mauling at the hands of vengeful revolutionaries. Lay Catholic organizations like the Mexican Catholic Youth Association assumed leading positions in the church's efforts to defeat the anticlerical provisions of the 1917 Constitution and found themselves engulfed in the Cristero Rebellion of the 1920s, a conflict that killed and displaced tens of thousands of people.

Conclusion

The Roman Catholic Church reaped great benefits from the policy of conciliation that the church hierarchy forged with the Porfirian dictatorship, allowing it to build the new seminaries, parishes, and churches that helped the church recover its strength after the catastrophes of the early nineteenth century. Porfirio Díaz's pragmatism on the religious issue was based on his desire to consolidate his hold on power by pacifying the nation. Díaz's neocolonial economic policies generated high rates of economic growth and provided him with the resources to establish a strong centralized dictatorship.

This policy of conciliation broke down, however, due to a complex and interrelated series of factors; one was the increasingly obvious social and political costs of Porfirio Díaz's policies, which were generating the tensions that would eventually erupt into the Mexican Revolution; another factor was the dissemination of the papal encyclical *Rerum Novarum* in the Catholic congresses of 1903–1909, which created a cadre of politically intransigent social Catholic activists eager to confront not only the decrepit Porfirian regime but also its enemies on the political left, primarily anarchists and socialists.

The political aspirations of these social Catholics were realized when, thanks to Francisco Madero's successful armed revolt against Porfirio Díaz, they were able to establish the PCN. While this political organization enjoyed a measure of success, it was ultimately undermined by its tacit acceptance of Victoriano Huerta's counterrevolutionary government, which made the PCN and the church hierarchy natural targets of revolutionaries determined to punish all those who had endorsed Huerta's murderous regime. The victorious revolutionaries went on to codify their anti-clerical sentiments in the Constitution of 1917. Although the church and its institutions had emerged from the Mexican Revolution badly mauled, its outrage over the new Constitution led to a rapid rebuilding of its organizational strength, with social Catholics leading this effort; this set the stage for the open warfare between the Catholic Church and its supporters against the revolutionary state.

This conflict will be analyzed in the next chapter, which focuses on an all-male, Catholic youth group dedicated to the formation of social Catholic activists, the Asociación Católica de la Juventud Mexicana (ACJM, Mexican Catholic Youth Association), and the French Jesuit priest who created and organized it, Bernardo Bergöend. The ACJM was created as a means of promoting Catholic culture in Mexico's young men through the vehicle of education, and of then turning these indoctrinated young men into the active agents of Mexico's so-called re-Christianization. Chapter 2 examines the fates of these young men and of their organization during the brutal Cristero Rebellion of 1926–1929 and highlights the fissures within the Catholic camp that this conflict brought to the surface.

CHAPTER TWO

The Asociación Católica de la Juventud Mexicana, the Mexican Revolution, and the Cristero Rebellion, 1912–1929

> *[Our goal] is nothing less than the coordination of the living forces of Mexican Catholic youth for the purpose of restoring Christian social order in Mexico.*
>
> —ACJM, "General Statutes"

Introduction

The Asociación Católica de la Juventud Mexicana (ACJM, Mexican Catholic Youth Association) was the creation of a French Jesuit cleric, Bernardo Bergöend, and represented a part of a greater social Catholic effort to refashion Mexican society or, in the words of Bergöend, to "re-Christianize" the nation in accordance with Catholic social doctrine. Bergöend's ACJM targeted the "living forces" of Mexican society; it educated young men drawn primarily from urban Catholic middle-class families who, thanks to the indoctrination carried out at the ACJM's study groups, would become the agents of Mexico's transformation. According to Bergöend, the ACJM also served as a surrogate Catholic university in a country where such an institution could not exist due to the political realities of the day.

Bergöend's demand that the members of his organization become active agents of Mexico's so-called re-Christianization meant that it was inevitable that these young men would be drawn into the bloody Cristero Rebellion of 1926–1929, a conflict that cost the lives of some 90,000 people, with uniformly disastrous results.[1] This conflict exposed bitter divisions within the church hierarchy between those who wanted a negotiated settlement to the war and those who rejected any agreement that allowed the hated revolutionaries to remain in power. Archbishop

Pascual Díaz, the leader of the clerics seeking a modus vivendi, used the newly introduced Catholic Action in order to rein in radicalized Catholic organizations like Bergöend's ACJM that opposed the church's truce with the government. The ACJM lost its former dynamism once it came under stricter control by the ecclesiastical hierarchy and the internal democracy that existed within the organization had been eliminated.

The history of Bergöend's ACJM is an important stepping stone in the story of the creation of the Universidad Iberoamericana. The ACJM indoctrinated young men who later on contributed to the Iberoamericana's creation and development. And, as will be seen in chapter 3, the ACJM helped develop the The Unión National de Estudiantes Católicos (UNEC, National Catholic Student Union) that in the 1930s was a major player in the world of university student politics. The UNEC went to form a generation of Catholic political activists that assumed leadership positions in the newly created Partido Acción Nacional (PAN, National Action Party), one of contemporary Mexico's major political institutions, after it was created in 1939. President Felipe Calderón (2006–2012) was, in fact, the son of the 1930s UNEC leader Luis Calderón. Chapter 4 of this work will then demonstrate how the UNEC was used by the church hierarchy to provide much of the material and human resources to create the embryonic Universidad Iberoamericana.

Origins of the Asociación Católica de la Juventud Mexicana

The ACJM owed a great deal to the Roman Catholic Church's resurgence during the late Porfiriato, emerging from the milieu created by the Catholic congresses of the early 1900s. The ACJM's history is inseparably linked to the energetic Jesuit priest Bernardo Bergöend. Born in the Alpine region of France in the year 1871, the short, bespectacled cleric entered the Jesuit Order in 1889 and served in Spain before being transferred to Mexico in the early 1900s, precisely at the moment when Catholics there were beginning to study and embrace, at least in part, the social and religious message contained in *Rerum Novarum*. Bergöend entered fully into this environment, training and educating Catholic labor leaders in Guadalajara, traditionally a conservative Catholic city, and drew up plans for a "Political-Social Union of Mexican Catholics" that sought to take advantage of the progress that Mexican Catholics had made in creating an independent political voice during the recent

Catholic congresses, a goal brought to fruition in 1911 with the creation of the Partido Católico Nacional (PCN, National Catholic Party) following Francisco Madero's successful challenge to Díaz's dictatorship.[2]

In 1912 Bergöend managed to persuade the archbishop of Mexico, José Mora y del Río, to allow him to create the organization that became his life's work—the ACJM, which he modeled on the French social Catholic reformer Count Albert de Mun's Association Catholique de la Jeunesses Français.[3] Bergöend articulated his organization's goals and importance to his lifelong friend Miguel Palomar y Vizcarra in the following terms: "In Mexico, as everywhere else, one needs well-molded men, and as you well know, only the young can be molded."[4] Bergöend wanted to mold these young men, who he described as Mexican society's "living forces" for the purpose of "restoring Christian social order in Mexico."[5] By restoring Christian social order in Mexico, Bergöend meant to regain the religious and cultural hegemony the church had enjoyed during the colonial era and which it lost to Mexican liberals in the mid-nineteenth century. Bergöend was convinced that once the archbishop fully understood the significance of the ACJM, he would agree that it should "take precedence over any other social project" that the archbishop was considering.[6]

Bergöend's embryonic organization was one of the Catholic organizations targeted by revolutionaries as they attacked Huerta's counter-revolutionary regime and it was forced to temporarily cease operations after Huerta's fall in 1914. Bergöend, like other members of the Catholic clergy, was forced to go into exile in order to escape revolutionary retribution, and the ACJM ceased operations. Surprisingly, however, the ACJM did not disappear into obscurity; rather, it vigorously reemerged in the late 1910s in order to help combat the effects of the anti-clerical 1917 Constitution. The rebuilding of ACJM was entrusted to Bergöend by the Jesuit Father Superior of Mexico as soon as the cleric returned to the country in 1917; in the next decade, the ACJM would be in the forefront of the Catholic Church's struggle against the anticlerical provisions of the Constitution of 1917.[7]

From 1917 to 1924, the ACJM underwent a period of rapid growth that transformed it into a genuine national organization. In 1913 the ACJM had consisted of only the Mexico City–based Centro de Estudiantes Católicos (CEC, Catholic Student Center) and eight study groups scattered throughout Mexico; by 1922, the ACJM boasted 125 centers containing four thousand members organized into eighteen regional unions, and two years later the number of ACJM centers had grown to 192.[8]

The Unión National de Damas Católicas (UNDC, National Union of Catholic Ladies), a Catholic lay organization founded in 1912, was an important factor behind the ACJM's successful development.[9] From its inception, the Union of Catholic Ladies served as patrons for Bergöend's group, donating the building that housed the Mexico City CEC and later providing a fixed monthly stipend to the ACJM's national headquarters to help cover their operating expenses.[10] The Union of Catholic Ladies was established in 1912 by the Jesuit priest Carlos María Heredia and shared the ACJM's ideological orientation, opposing the "perverse, destructive, anti-Christian, pernicious and antisocial doctrines" that threatened Catholic Mexico.[11] While the Union of Catholic Ladies' main sphere of action was within Catholic families, its general statutes obligated it to cooperate with the church hierarchy in promoting projects that sought to advance Mexico's "Christian social restoration."[12] The ACJM was one of these groups that enjoyed the Union of Catholic Ladies' patronage; the Union of Catholic Ladies and the Catholic Youth Association later formed—along with the Knights of Columbus, the National Parent's Association, and the National Catholic Labor Confederation—the core elements of the National Religious Rights Defense League, the Catholic umbrella group that confronted the federal government during the Cristero Rebellion of 1926–1929.

Catholic schools were prime recruiting grounds for Bergöend's ACJM, especially in Mexico City and other major urban centers.[13] These individuals, who had already been exposed to many of the basic elements of the Catholic social doctrine that Bergöend promoted, formed a natural constituency for the youth groups; however, the Catholic Youth Association did not limit itself exclusively to middle- and upper-class urban young men.[14] Bergöend sought to include the "select from every social class" within the ACJM, and this meant expanding the ACJM's social base to include members from Mexico's artisan class, with whom Bergöend had been in contact since 1907 when he first began organizing workers' circles in Guadalajara.[15] Night schools created for workers by the ACJM were potential recruiting grounds for new members, as was the National Catholic Labor Confederation. The ACJM's links to working-class Catholics were strengthened by events like the First Regional Catholic Labor Congress celebrated in Guadalajara, Jalisco, in 1919, which brought together Catholic labor organizations, Catholic clerics, and distinguished local ACJM members, some of whom later perished in the religious conflict of the 1920s.[16]

Study groups formed the heart of the ACJM locals and promoted an ideological perspective that was radically different from the secular orientation of the official schools. For example, Mexican history was presented with a strong pro-Catholic bias that denigrated great heroes of official histories, like President Benito Juárez, as agents of Protestant American imperialism and defended the recently overthrown dictator Victoriano Huerta as "an energetic, democratic, and upright man."[17] Catholic philosophy, literature, and the study of papal encyclicals rounded out the education that these young men received.

Bergöend had described the ACJM's study groups as serving the role of a surrogate Catholic university in a nation where political factors barred their existence; in reality they were much more than that.[18] They had the fundamental task of educating and indoctrinating these young men to become "action leaders" capable of fighting against Catholicism's ideological enemies: liberalism, anarchism, socialism, Protestantism, and materialism. Shortly after returning from exile in 1917, Bergöend wrote the following words in which he expressed the following beliefs concerning his student youth group: "The ACJM does not have as its ultimate goal the formation of young men dedicated solely to their studies, to inaction, once they are educated. If that was the ACJM's ultimate goal then I, its creator and its ecclesiastical assistant, would truthfully declare that it would have no reason to exist."[19] The ACJM's members put Bergöend's philosophy into effect by spreading the Catholic Church's social doctrine to the working class through actions like creating night schools for workers and establishing Catholic newspapers. But this call to action meant that young men of the ACJM found themselves on the front lines of the Roman Catholic Church's increasingly bitter struggle with Mexico's anticlerical revolutionary governing elite, with tragic consequences for the ACJM's membership.

The Asociación Católica de la Juventud Mexicana and the Cristero Rebellion

Political violence in Mexico continued to be a reality of Mexican society well after the ratification of the Constitution of 1917 brought the

Mexican Revolution to its symbolic conclusion. Bloody military revolts and aborted uprisings in the years 1920, 1923–1924, 1927, and 1929 shook the nation's political structure. Mexico was politically dominated by the strongman General Álvaro Obregón, who served as Mexico's president from 1920 to 1924. Obregón was anticlerical, but his distaste for the Roman Catholic Church did not reach the depths as that of his successor Plutarco Elías Calles (1924–1928).[20] Relations between the Catholic Church and the federal government reached a crisis when Calles sought to implement the anticlerical provisions of the 1917 Constitution. These articles gave state governments the authority to regulate the internal activities of the Catholic Church and closed down Catholic elementary schools, measures bitterly opposed by the church and its supporters.[21]

The ACJM's young "action leaders" were inevitably drawn into this growing conflict; in the process, they became radicalized and militarized by this atmosphere of political violence. In February 1921 Archbishop José Mora y del Río's palace in Mexico City was bombed; while the assailant or assailants remained unknown, Catholics immediately blamed Álvaro Obregón's government for the incident. The Mexico City–based CEC responded by establishing an armed guard to protect the archbishop's palace from additional attacks.[22] Later that year, they provided an armed security detail to protect the Basilica of Guadalupe, Mexican Catholicism's holiest shrine, from a feared assault by the government-supported Confederación Regional Obrera Mexicana (CROM, Mexican Regional Labor Confederation). However, this precaution failed to prevent a bomb from being detonated in front of the image of the Virgin of Guadalupe later that same year. The relic itself managed to survive the blast, a fact that was interpreted by the faithful as a miracle.[23] The following year, the CEC's local was sacked by workers of the anarchist Confederación General de Trabajadores (CGT, General Workers' Confederation) following a May Day rally, after the two sides had exchanged taunts.[24]

In 1924 Plutarco Elías Calles became Mexico's new president and church-state relations took a new turn for the worse. For Calles, members of the Mexican ecclesiastical hierarchy were the "eternal traitors of the fatherland"; he was determined to use "all the force that may be necessary" in order to force Mexican Catholics to comply with all the anticlerical provisions of the 1917 Constitution, something that his predecessors had not attempted to do.[25] The ACJM's leadership braced its members for the challenges that loomed on the horizon. This was

Miguel Palomar y Vizcarra's central message in his speech at the First National Eucharist Congress of 1924; the aristocratic Palomar y Vizcarra,[26] Bergöend's closest confidant, served as the CEC's study group director in Mexico City.[27] Palomar y Vizcarra riled the audience with an incendiary speech that called on them to confront governmental policies declared injurious to Catholic interests: "There is an infallible way of being defeated; leaving the field of battle to your enemy without a struggle: the sweetness of victory is granted only to those who have fought and know how to fight."[28]

In 1925, in response to the worsening political climate in Mexico, the Catholic Church hierarchy and its lay supporters created a Catholic umbrella resistance organization known as the Liga Nacional Defensora de las Libertades Religiosas (LNDLR, League for the Defense of Religious Liberty). The LNDLR was inspired by a project drawn up years earlier by Bernardo Bergöend but which had been shelved due to a lack of support from Mexico's ecclesiastical authorities.[29] The organization arose in opposition to the creation of a government-backed "Mexican Apostolic Catholic Church," a schismatic church that encouraged Roman Catholics to apostatize from their faith. The LNDLR also rejected Calles's efforts to put teeth into the constitutional articles that limited the church's educational role and that forced priests to register with the government in order to carry out their ministry.[30] The LNDLR was composed of the nation's key Catholic lay organizations: the UNDC, the ACJM, the National Catholic Labor Confederation, the National Parents' Association, and the Knights of Columbus. The ACJM's one hundred locals, established in towns and cities throughout Mexico, provided the LNDLR with an important grassroots network of support.[31] Bergöend's ACJM enjoyed additional influence in the LNDLR due to the fact that Miguel Palomar y Vizcarra served as one of the LNDLR's vice presidents and was one of its driving forces.

President Calles's determination to have Catholic priests register with the government led to a rupture in relations between the two parties. The LNDLR responded by formulating a plan for an economic boycott that they hoped would paralyze Mexico's economic and social life and force President Calles to reconsider his policies toward the church; Mexican Catholics were told not to purchase non-essential consumer goods, not to patronize public entertainment centers, and to refrain from purchasing newspapers friendly to the regime.[32] This civic action was scheduled to begin on July 25, 1926.

For their part, Mexican bishops put into effect an even more dramatic and provocative measure: the suspension of the celebration of the mass and the dispensation of the sacraments. By this measure, the clerics forced the faithful to focus on the church's confrontation with Calles's government; in fact, it served as the detonator for an armed Catholic uprising known as the Cristero Rebellion, which was waged primarily by peasants from central and western Mexico and claimed tens of thousands of lives.[33]

What position should the LNDLR and its component member groups assume toward this raging armed movement? That was the question facing the LNDLR's leadership, and their response was fateful and tragic. In November 1926 the LNDLR abandoned its campaign of peaceful resistance to the government's anticlerical policies and joined the Cristero Rebellion. The LNDLR's goals were to provide the Catholic fighters with a coherent political program and a political leader that could unify the movement. That month, the LNDLR sought and received an audience with the Mexican Bishops' Committee, whose secretary was the Bishop Pascual Díaz. The LNDLR presented to the bishops, for their consideration, a political program for the Cristero rebels and their candidate to become the Cristeros's political leader.[34] The bishops agreed not to block the LNDLR's decision to enter the armed conflict; they also ratified the LNDLR's political program and René Capistrán Garza, a former ACJM president, as the Cristeros's political leader.[35]

The LNDLR's entry into the armed struggle meant that the young men of the ACJM were now obliged to take up arms against the federal government. They had to face a battle-hardened army officered by veterans of the Mexican Revolution, and the results were almost always uniformly disastrous for the ACJM's young fighters. In January 1927 the ACJM's national leadership attempted its first major military action which consisted of a coordinated series of armed uprisings in several towns and cities in central and northern Mexico led by their local ACJM chapters. In the city of León, Guanajuato, the local ACJM leaders were arrested and shot before the uprising could get off the ground.[36] In Parras, Coahuila, the ACJM did manage to carry out attacks on the local police station and government offices; however, they were forced to flee when military reinforcements arrived the following day (January 4, 1927). They fled into the countryside to join Cristero rebel bands already operating in the area after losing nine of the original force of thirty-five men.³⁷ The Mexico City ACJM cohort decided to use the nearby Ajusco mountain region to carry out a guerrilla campaign under the leadership of a former Zapatista general, Manuel Reyes. On January 2, 1927, thirty-two Catholic Youth members left for the Ajusco; two days later, they were attacked by a unit of the federal army and were forced to run for their lives. Some survivors joined Cristero bands, but others simply slipped back into the city and went underground.³⁸ Those who fought with the government by engaging in written political activism were also treated brutally by the government, as was demonstrated by the case of Anacleto González Flores, the firebrand publisher of an underground Catholic newspaper and the ACJM's leader in Jalisco, who in April 1927 was arrested and executed by government security forces.³⁹

This unbroken chain of disasters highlighted how unprepared these young men were to engage in combat with professional soldiers. Nevertheless, the Catholic Youth Association leadership still insisted that its members militarily confront Calles's regime, no matter how hopeless the struggle, even though more and more members had lost their stomach for fighting and simply wanted to survive the conflict. When in 1927 the members of the Irapuato chapter of the ACJM decided to suspend their activities and go underground, they earned the ire of Manuel Dávalos Lozada, the Catholic Youth Association's general secretary, who blasted their decision in the harshest of terms:

> The General Committee has had the great disgust to learn that this group of our believed Association . . . has resolved to dissolve itself in view of the grave dangers that are hanging over Catholics throughout the nation, in order to reorganize it afterwards, when our cause triumphs. The Committee resists believing that you could have incurred in such cowardice, youths who have worn on their chests the glorious symbol of Catholic youth. . . . Today, as has been stated and ordered, every group member of the Association is obligated to work in the League, no matter at what [personal] cost, until we arrive at the triumph that with absolute confidence in God we await!⁴⁰

This confidence was misplaced, and, as the war dragged on, the likelihood of an outright Catholic victory became increasingly remote.

By 1927, the Cristeros's deteriorating military and political situation led the exiled secretary of the Mexican episcopal committee, Bishop Pascual Díaz, to begin working toward a negotiated end to the rebellion.⁴¹ Pope Pius XI eventually endorsed Bishop Díaz's efforts and made Díaz his sole intermediary with the Mexican ecclesiastical hierarchy.⁴² This critical papal support allowed Bishop Díaz to successfully overcome resistance to his negotiating efforts presented by hardline bishops and the LNDLR. Díaz's chief ally within the episcopal hierarchy was Leopoldo Ruiz y Flores, the archbishop of Morelia. Bishop José y Jesús Manríquez y Zarate of Huejutla, Hidalgo, was the Cristeros's main supporter within the ranks of the Mexican hierarchy; Francisco Orozco y Jiménez, the archbishop of Guadalajara, was another key hardliner. Bishop Díaz, who was being groomed by the Vatican to eventually succeed the aged Mora y del Río as archbishop of Mexico, used his new authority to pressure the LNDLR to abandon its military and political activities, a request that the LNDLR's leadership refused to accept.⁴³

Far from embracing Bishop Díaz's call for a negotiated peace settlement, radical elements within ACJM developed a terrorist plot to assassinate former president Álvaro Obregón, who was the front-running candidate in the 1928 presidential elections. Luis Segura Vilchis, a twenty-four-year-old electrical engineer, was the conspiracy's chief plotter. Segura Vilchis served on the ACJM's "Special Committee" in Mexico City, and in that capacity he was charged with organizing and coordinating military activities against the government, which he did with poor results.⁴⁴

Why was Obregón targeted instead of President Calles? Segura Vilchis gave this justification for his actions shortly before his own execution: "It is true that Calles is the one who occupies the presidency and has [led] the religious persecution. But Obregón is the true strongman [of Mexico], who has not impeded these calamities but rather has tacitly and specifically supported them. A single word from Obregón would have been sufficient to alter Calles's furious sectarianism. It is incumbent to begin with the strongman."⁴⁵ In addition, Obregón had been working, through Mexican and American intermediaries, to bring an end to the Cristero Rebellion on terms favorable to the government.⁴⁶ The Cristero leadership had some knowledge that these negotiations were taking place and feared that any agreement reached would be deleterious to their cause.⁴⁷ Assassinating Obregón would derail, or at least temporarily sidetrack, any negotiated settlement of the rebellion.

Segura Vilchis's assassination attempt was set for November 13, 1927. On that Sunday morning, an automobile containing Segura Vilchis,

Juan Tirado, Nahum Lamberto Ruiz, and José González approached Obregón's Cadillac as it traveled down the streets of Mexico City. The would-be assassins lobbed bombs and fired shots at Obregón's car, but the former president was only slightly wounded and his bodyguards managed to repel the attack. Obregón's men captured one of the conspirators, Nahum Lamberto Ruiz, who had suffered a severe head wound during the exchange of gunfire.[48] Segura Vilchis and Juan Tirado escaped immediate capture but were arrested within twenty-four hours; only González managed to elude the police.[49]

The police arrested two more men after Lamberto Ruiz, who lay blinded and dying in the hospital and inadvertently mentioned their names to a disguised police detective. These men were Miguel Agustín Pro, a Jesuit priest, and his brother, Humberto Pro. The authorities' suspicions against Humberto Pro were further aroused because he had formerly owned the Essex model automobile used in the attempt to take Obregón's life; in addition, Humberto Pro and Luis Segura Vilchis had also belonged to the same ACJM local, and Miguel Agustín Pro, SJ, had previously been arrested on a number of occasions for his pastoral activities during the Cristero Rebellion.[50] However, Calles was not interested in formally proving the defendants' guilt in a proper legal proceeding, and so on November 23, 1927, he had Luis Segura Vilchis, Juan Tirado, Miguel Agustín Pro, SJ, and Humberto Pro executed by firing squad.[51]

Obregón emerged victorious in a presidential campaign marred by political violence and accusations of electoral fraud; however, he did not live long enough to once again occupy the presidential palace.[52] On July 17, 1928, Obregón was shot and killed by the ACJM member José de León Toral during a political banquet at a restaurant in a Mexico City suburb; León Toral was motivated by both political factors and a personal desire to avenge the death of his close friend Humberto Pro.[53] Catholic militants applauded this act of political terrorism in pamphlets published by their underground press. One such document defended this act of terrorism using the following logic: "It is not a homicide because Obregón could no longer be considered a human being, given that he [had] trampled upon all the principles of humanity." León Toral was honored not as a terrorist but rather as the "avenging arm of divine justice" and a "soldier of Christ's phalanx."[54]

José de León Toral was executed on February 9, 1929, following a sensational trial that also included the Catholic nun María Concepción

Acevedo y de la Llata, better known as "Madre Conchita." Government prosecutors accused her of having manipulated León Toral into murdering Obregón. During the Cristero Rebellion, Madre Conchita had turned her Mexico City home into a center for clandestine religious services, attracting some radical young Catholics who hatched terrorist plots to assassinate President Calles and General Obregón. José de León Toral was one of these militants. Although León Toral had a close relationship with the Catholic nun, he maintained to the authorities that Madre Conchita was unaware of his plan to assassinate Obregón. The court did not accept León Toral's assertions about the nun's innocence and sentenced both Madre Conchita and Juan de León Toral to death; however, the authorities apparently did not have the stomach to execute a woman who was also a nun and eventually commuted her death sentence to twenty years in prison.[55] While León Toral's assassination of president-elect Obregón did not reverse the tide of war against the Cristero cause, it prolonged the conflict for another year and silenced Mexico's most outstanding political and military figure of the era.

The Arreglos of 1929 and the Asociación Católica de la Juventud Mexicana

On June 21, 1929, the Mexican government and the Roman Catholic Church signed an agreement that ended the Cristero Rebellion. This armistice was negotiated by Pascual Díaz and Leopoldo Ruiz y Flores with the assistance of the American Jesuit churchmen Father John Burke, SJ, and Edmund Walsh, SJ; Dwight Morrow, the US ambassador to Mexico, was another key intermediary between the two parties. Emilio Portes Gil, who became interim president due to the assassination of president-elect Obregón, stated to the nation's press that the "Arreglos" or agreement had clarified some "misunderstandings" that had divided the Catholic Church and the state.[56] While the government would continue with its intention of registering priests, this did not mean that the authorities would use this to appoint clerics not recognized by the ecclesiastical authorities. Although religious groups would still be barred from providing religious instruction in their schools, this did not mean that they could not impart religious instruction to children within temples. President Portes Gil also reassured the Catholic Church hierarchy that they, as Mexican citizens, could petition the Mexican congress to amend laws that Catholics felt to be offensive.[57]

Unfortunately, the terms of the armistice that ended the Cristero Rebellion did nothing to allay concerns entertained by Bishop Díaz's critics within the LNDLR. The registering of priests by the government, a key grievance that had sparked the Catholic Church's strike in 1926, was to continue, as was the provision stipulating that the Cristero fighters were to turn in their weapons, leaving them defenseless to future acts of government retribution against them. In return, the government allowed Catholic temples to reopen. To ease Catholic apprehension concerning the Arreglos, interim president Emilio Portes Gil stated that his government had no interest in interfering in the internal operations of the Catholic Church and granted a general amnesty to the rebels.

The government's promises failed to sway the hard-liners who saw in the Arreglos the ruin of the Roman Catholic Church and a betrayal of those who had died fighting for the Cristero cause.[58] Throughout the course of 1928, LNDLR members had become increasingly alarmed over the secretive nature of negotiations being carried out by Díaz and Ruiz y Flores and frustrated by their total lack of input in this process. Simply put, the LNDLR leadership feared that Díaz and Ruiz y Flores were going to reach an agreement based solely on "promises of men without honor" and who were, in addition, "moral degenerates."[59] They rejected Díaz's argument, transmitted by men like Alberto María Carreño, Díaz's future private secretary, that the Cristeros were doomed to failure because they lacked the two critical elements: adequate military resources and the diplomatic support of United States government.[60]

Pascual Díaz and Leopoldo Ruiz y Flores could discount the opposition from hard-liners because of the support that they enjoyed from the Vatican. This support was confirmed in 1928 when Pope Pius XI selected Pascual Díaz as the new archbishop of Mexico following Mora y del Río's death. The pope followed up this action the following year by naming Archbishop Leopoldo Ruiz y Flores as his apostolic delegate to Mexico. The new archbishop of Mexico also carried with him a critically important mandate from Pope Pius XI: to establish Catholic Action in Mexico, of which he, Pascual Díaz, would serve as its national president. Archbishop Pascual Díaz used this mandate to transform and tame the lay Catholic organizations that had, like the ACJM, become radicalized during the Cristero Rebellion.

Archbishop Díaz used Catholic Action to defuse organized resistance to the Arreglos from his critics within the LNDLR. This lay Catholic organization was characterized by the strict control that the ecclesiastical hierarchy exercised over its "lay apostles."[61] For the ACJM, this translated into a radical transformation of the organization and its goals. The UNDC, whose resistance to government policies had earned for some of its membership transportation to the Islas Marías penal colony, was another major target for Archbishop Díaz.[62]

News of the reforms that the church hierarchy proposed for the Catholic Youth Association reached the ACJM's executive committee. It prompted its president, Octavio Elizalde, to write a letter to Archbishop Díaz pleading with him to halt the reforms, arguing that they threatened to completely distort its social mission.[63] His central concern was that the ACJM's central goal of creating "action leaders" was now completely ignored in the proposed new statute; another issue that worried Elizalde was the new requirement imposing celibacy on its members, as it would drive away its older associates, many of whom were married.

Elizalde was also disturbed about the new process of selecting the ACJM's national and local leadership. Under the old regulations, the association's leaders had been democratically elected by the ACJM members, thus instilling within them a "conscience of responsibility" that Bergöend had sought to promote.[64] Under the authoritarian Catholic Action regime, the head of the local chapters were to be selected by the local parish priests, while the national leadership was to be appointed by the archbishop of Mexico. This granted Archbishop Pascual Díaz the power to marginalize the hard-liners within the ACJM by removing them from positions of authority and allowed him to put in their place those who would not challenge his authority or policies.

Having received from the archbishop a cold response to his letter, Elizalde and the ACJM's general committee decided to make a dramatic gesture that would show all that these reforms represented a rupture with the past. On December 31, 1929, they sent a circular to all of their regional committees and locals declaring that the ACJM was dissolved.[65] The ACJM General Committee justified their action by stating that the new statutes were so radically different from the old that they constituted an entirely new organization.[66] This measure angered and embarrassed Archbishop Díaz, who was forced to categorically state that he had not dissolved the ACJM and stated his continued support for the organization.[67] Díaz rebuked Elizalde and the ACJM leadership for spreading falsehoods.[68] Nonetheless, as a consequence of this act the ACJM entered into a period of hibernation that lasted almost two years.

Elizalde and his hard-line supporters refused to give up their struggle. In March 1930 Octavio Elizalde and fifty followers established a new organization, the "Civic Youth Group," using the historic CEC as its nucleus.⁶⁹ Elizalde took this measure in consultation with Bernardo Bergöend and was designed to put pressure on the archbishop.⁷⁰ They justified themselves by arguing that thanks to Archbishop Pascual Díaz's proposed reforms, the ACJM, as they knew it, would cease to exist. The Civic Youth Group promised to continue Bergöend's goal of forming activists who would advance Catholic interests in Mexico, something that the new ACJM would no longer seek to accomplish; however, this act of insubordination failed to deter the archbishop, and on August 1, 1930, he promulgated the Mexican Catholic Action's statutes.⁷¹ Archbishop Díaz's next step was to publish the definitive set of new regulations that would govern the ACJM.

At this critical moment, Bergöend emerged from the shadows and made a direct appeal to Archbishop Pascual Díaz in the hope of saving his creation. In a letter penned directly to the archbishop of Mexico, Bergöend strongly defended the ACJM's old statutes, arguing that these had created "a true army of youth" who had shown themselves willing to "shed their last drop of blood for their God and for their Fatherland."⁷² The proposed new statutes, Bergöend maintained, would only bring disunity into the ACJM's ranks. He urged Díaz not to blindly impose the Italian Catholic Action model in Mexico but to adapt it to the conditions existing within the country, and if the ACJM's old organization were retained, its members would "joyfully join Mexican Catholic Action."⁷³ To the sticky issue of how the ACJM national leadership should be selected, Bergöend suggested a compromise: the ACJM would draw up a list of three candidates, with the archbishop making his final selection from this field.

Archbishop Díaz's opponents did not simply rely on Bergöend's powers of persuasion in order to achieve their goals; they also went over his head and appealed their case directly to the Vatican. In the fall of 1930, Bergöend's associate Miguel Palomar y Vizcarra traveled to Rome in his capacity as the LNDLR's vice president to present before the papacy the dissidents' case against Archbishop Díaz; these grievances included Archbishop Díaz's intentions toward the ACJM. At first it appeared that

Palomar y Vizcarra had been met with success; Vatican officials stated that the ACJM would be allowed to retain its old codes.[74] Overjoyed, the rebellious CEC returned to the fold and the dormant ACJM locals began springing back to life; however, this victory proved to be short-lived. Archbishop Díaz continued to enjoy support in the Vatican, and so when he journeyed to Rome the following year he was able win papal approval for his policy toward the ACJM.

Having lost their struggle against Archbishop Díaz, the most committed of the dissidents decided that the only course of action left open to them was to walk out of the association. In July 1932 they established, with the CEC as its nucleus, a rival Catholic youth association named Nationalist Youth. Within a few months, they were joined by six more of the Mexico City ACJM's locals. However, although Nationalist Youth enjoyed the support of the dissident Catholic community, its lack of official recognition by the ecclesiastical authorities made it difficult to recruit new members. In 1935 Bergöend proposed to the Nationalist Youth's leadership an arrangement that would have Bergöend's ACJM provide Nationalist Youth with badly needed new members; in return, the Nationalist Youth organization would train Bergöend's followers to become political activists.[75] By the use of this ruse, Bergöend attempted to circumvent the limitations that Catholic Action had imposed on the ACJM, taking advantage of the fact that Nationalist Youth was an independent organization and thus free of ecclesiastical control; however, this project failed to prosper and Nationalist Youth disappeared by the end of the decade.[76] Bernardo Bergöend continued to serve as the ACJM's spiritual assistant until his death in 1943, but his organization never recovered the vitality it had enjoyed before the Arreglos of 1929.

Conclusion: The Asociación Católica de la Juventud Mexicana's Legacy

Bernardo Bergöend's youth organization, created in 1913 as a project to help refashion Mexican society according to the principles of social Catholicism, failed to achieve its lofty goals. This was not a surprising outcome given the strength of the contending visions of society held by many other Mexicans, particularly those held by its ruling elite.

But if the ACJM is examined from a broader perspective, its historical importance becomes evident. It helped the Roman Catholic Church reassert itself in Mexican society following the Revolution. The ACJM defended the Roman Catholic Church's interests in its confrontation with Mexico's post-revolutionary political leadership, and when the Cristero Rebellion broke out the Catholic Youth Association's members entered the fray against the government's security forces. They paid a heavy price for their lack of training and equipment.[77]

Ironically, the zeal with which the ACJM defended the Catholic Church's interests during the Cristero Rebellion became a major liability when the Catholic Church hierarchy decided to negotiate a political solution to the conflict. Its association with social Catholic hard-liners opposed to the Arreglos of 1929 put the ACJM on a collision course with the policies followed by Archbishop Pascual Díaz and endorsed by the Vatican. With the introduction of Catholic Action to Mexico, Archbishop Díaz gained the mechanism to bring radicalized lay Catholic organizations like the ACJM under the strict control of the church hierarchy. Archbishop Díaz's decision to deny the ACJM its traditional role of forming political activists provoked a bitter schism within the organization, and while Bergöend and the most militant elements within the ACJM made a spirited effort to defend the integrity of their institution, the archbishop's authority and determination prevailed.

Some former members of Bergöend's Catholic Youth Association went on to make important contributions to Mexican society, especially in the realm of Mexico's higher education system. For example, the former ACJM member Oswaldo Robles played an important role in the genesis of the institution that eventually became the Universidad Iberoamericana, which will be analyzed in chapter 4. In the 1920s Oswaldo Robles Ochoa had been a member of the same Daniel O'Connell ACJM local that contained José de León Toral and Luis Segura Vilchis and was imprisoned in Mexico City's notorious Santiago Tlatelolco prison for his political activities. In the 1930s Robles went on to become a distinguished neo-scholastic philosopher at the UNAM during the 1930s.[78] And as a university administrator in 1943, Robles was a key player in the complex process that produced the Centro Cultural Universitario (CCU, University Cultural Center), the forerunner of the Iberoamericana. The ACJM was also critical to the early development of the UNEC, an institution that directly contributed to the Iberoamericana's creation in 1943; the UNEC was also a major player in the world of university student politics, traditionally a training ground for national politics in Mexico and other Latin American nations.

Members of Bergöend's ACJM also made their mark on Mexican national politics. For example, ex-Catholic Youth members played a limited, but significant, role in the early development of one of modern Mexico's leading political institutions—the PAN. This will be analyzed in the next chapter. This organization, founded in 1939 by a coalition of businessmen, secular conservatives, and Catholic intellectuals, opposed the administration of President Lázaro Cárdenas (1934–1940). These Catholic and secular conservatives rejected Cárdenas's aggressive land-reform program, his establishment of government-affiliated labor unions, his nationalistic economic policies, and his administration's educational program. The figure of Efraín González Luna best illustrates the ACJM's influence within the embryonic PAN. In 1939 González Luna, a Catholic intellectual and former ACJM member, drafted the *Doctrine of National Action* at the PAN's founding congress. This document was infused with the Catholic social doctrine that González Luna had taught within the ACJM. It echoed the papal encyclicals *Rerum Novarum* (1891) and *Quadragesimo Anno* (1931) when it declared that "all socially useful work should be compensated so as to allow the raising of a family in dignity."[79] It also decried the liberal-capitalist concept that saw the commodification of human labor as an "assault against human dignity," while at the same time it denounced the Marxist concept of class warfare. Thirteen years later, Efraín González Luna served as the PAN's standard bearer in the 1952 presidential elections.[80] The PAN's second president, Juan Gutiérrez Lauscuraín (1949–1956), was another former ACJM member. For his part, PAN co-founder Efraín González Luna was closely associated with the establishment of the Universidad Autónoma de Guadalajara (Autonomous University of Guadalajara) in 1935. This private university, which today has one of Mexico's most prestigious medical schools and is known for its right-wing political orientation, was in opposition to the government's efforts to dictate the curriculum at the state-sponsored University of Guadalajara.[81] Through the efforts of men like Efraín González Luna, Oswaldo Robles, and Juan Gutiérrez Lauscuraín, Bergöend's Catholic Youth Association continued to influence Mexican society long after the original vision that the Jesuit cleric had for his organization had evaporated.

CHAPTER THREE

The Unión National de Estudiantes Católicos, the University of Mexico, and the Partido Acción Nacional

Student Politics, National Politics

> *It does not matter if they learn nothing and remain in monstrous ignorance. A generation of ignoramuses is worth more than an impious people. It is worth more to enter heaven poor, weak, and ignorant than to be hurled into hell with all the wisdom of the world.*
>
> —José de Jesús Manríquez y Zarate, Bishop of Huejutla, 1934

Introduction

The Unión National de Estudiantes Católicos (UNEC, National Catholic Student Union) emerged in 1926, during the darkest days of church-state conflict in post-revolutionary Mexico; it began as a grassroots movement by students from Mexico City's elite all-male *colegios* (preparatory schools) who felt that they were being discriminated against by officials of the Universidad Nacional Autónoma de México (UNAM, National Autonomous University of Mexico) because of their religious affiliation and organized themselves in order to protect their interests. This incipient group soon gained the attention of Bernardo Bergöend's Asociación Católica de la Juventud Mexicana (ACJM, Mexican Catholic Youth Association), which, with the church hierarchy's blessing, lost no time in gaining control of the organization's leadership positions. The UNEC was tasked with the responsibility of promoting the Catholic Church's doctrine among the nation's male university students, thereby promoting the church's position in an ideological war of ideas against their leftist and liberal adversaries. During the first years of the Student Union's existence, it was little more than an appendage to Bergöend's larger and more established organization, and its members followed the ACJM's lead in joining the Cristero cause, with equally disastrous results.

The Student Union emerged from the Cristero conflict in a shambles and with its continued existence in severe doubt; indeed, at one point Bergöend attempted to formally absorb what was left of the Student Union into his own ravaged organization. And so it is more than a little surprising that far from disappearing from the scene, the Student Union was about to enter the most dynamic phase of its history. Its revival in the early 1930s was due in large part to the support that it received from Mexico's most powerful cleric, the Archbishop of Mexico Pascual Díaz. There were several reasons why the archbishop took this decision, given the long list of pressing issues that he had to address in the post–Cristero Rebellion era. First, the Student Union recruited a highly desired element of the population—educated young men—who in the future would assume important roles in Mexican society. In addition, an independent Student Union would serve as a counterweight to the rebellious ACJM, whose members had loudly protested the modus vivendi that the archbishop had helped to draft; as a consequence of this and other issues, Bergöend and his ACJM became bitter enemies of the now-rival UNEC.

The UNEC prospered in the 1930s in large part because it took a leading position in opposing government-sponsored educational reforms to which the Catholic Church and other conservatives objected. As part of this effort, the Student Union became a major factor in the world of university politics, particularly at the UNAM, the country's leading institution of higher education. The Student Union's greatest legacy lay in the fact that it trained a generation of political activists that went on to assume leadership positions in the early years of the Partido Acción Nacional (PAN, National Action Party), an institution that went on to rule Mexico from 2000 to 2012.

The UNEC's decline was due in large part to yet another twist in the tortured and convoluted history of church-state relations in Mexico. After 1940, Mexico's ruling party moved sharply to the political right, embracing pro-business and anti-communist policies that created an opening for improved ties with its old advisory, the Roman Catholic Church. In these new conditions, the church hierarchy saw the controversial and highly politicized UNEC as a political liability; moreover, many elements of the church hierarchy had long disapproved of the Student Union's neglect of its pedagogical functions as it pursued political objectives. The church's solution to the conundrum that the Catholic Student Union had become, its transformation into the organization that became the Universidad Iberoamericana, will be analyzed in chapter 4.

Origins of the Unión National de Estudiantes Católicos

The UNEC's emergence in the mid-1920s was a direct consequence of the deteriorating state of the relationship between the Calles administration and the Catholic Church hierarchy. By that time, practicing Catholics in all walks of life were feeling the repercussions of the deteriorating religious climate in Mexico. These included the Catholic school students who attended exclusive Catholic all-male colegios in Mexico City. For years, these young men had been obligated to present their exams at official schools if they had any desire to attend government-operated schools of higher education. Then, in 1926 government education officials were not recognizing the courses students took at these colegios.[1] Not surprisingly, the affected students began to organize themselves against this threat to their academic future; within a brief period of time, 1,500 members from four Mexico City colegios had established the Union of Private School Students.[2]

The course of this embryonic student movement's development was permanently altered thanks to the concerted actions of a number of its members who also belonged to the ACJM. Oswaldo Robles, a Catholic student and ACJM member, was the bridge between the members of the fledgling student group and the ACJM.[3] He secured for the student group the use of the ACJM's main hall for their meetings; however, along with the use of this building came the Catholic Youth Association's rapidly growing influence within the student organization.

The ACJM's control of the student group is clearly seen by the time of its meeting on July 30, 1926. On that date, its members transformed the Union of Private School Students into the Confederación Nacional de Estudiantes Católicos de México (CNECM, National Confederation of Catholic Students), and Daniel O'Connell ACJM members were elected to key positions within the organization.[4] Archbishop Mora y del Río granted his official recognition to the CNECM and appointed Miguel Agustín Pro, SJ, the future martyred priest, as his representative within the student confederation.[5]

The CNECM's statutes dictated that the organization's goals were to promote Catholic social action in Mexico and to address the specific needs of its student members; its members were also tasked with the obligation to defend the cause of Catholic education and to establish contacts with Catholic student associations throughout Latin America and Spain.[6] However, in 1926 Mexico's political environment made it impossible for the CNECM to begin addressing any of these ambitious goals. The country descended into civil war, with Cristero guerrillas confronting Calles's security forces in a bloody, three-year conflict that left tens of thousands of Mexicans dead, wounded, or displaced.[7]

The CNECM's members played an active role in the fighting during the Cristero conflict, oftentimes with disastrous results. Luis Rivero del Val, the CNECM's president, became an active guerrilla fighter with the Cristeros.[8] Oswaldo Robles, the group's vice president, was imprisoned for a time in Mexico City's notorious Santiago Tlatelolco prison before escaping and fleeing into exile in the United States.[9]

The June 1929 accords between the Mexican government and the Catholic Church that ended the Cristero Rebellion ushered in a profound transformation of the relationship between the Catholic Church hierarchy and lay Catholic organizations. As noted previously, extremists within the Liga Nacional Defensora de las Libertades Religiosas (LNDLR, League for the Defense of Religious Liberty) bitterly opposed the terms of the Arreglos, viewing the agreement as a capitulation to the hated Calles and a betrayal of the Cristero cause.[10] While the LNDLR's executive committee officially stated that it had no option but to officially accept the Arreglos, conservative opposition to Archbishop Díaz and his policies remained strong, and he was obliged to make full use of the powers granted to him by the new Catholic Action organization to rein in lay Catholic organizations that had been radicalized during the Cristero Rebellion and were unhappy with the terms of the Arreglos.[11]

The Catholic Student Union in Post-Arreglos Mexico

The Catholic Student Union's position in 1929 could not have been bleaker. Its members were either in hiding, in exile, in jail, or had been killed by state security forces. Yet Archbishop Pascual Díaz considered the CNECM valuable enough to attempt its revival as a functioning organization. Why did Archbishop Díaz consider it a priority to rebuild the CNECM when the church had many other urgent matters to attend to? This question is answered in part by an internal Catholic Action memorandum that illuminates the concerns within the church on the need to address the needs of the Catholic student community. The document warned that the lack of an effective Catholic student organization made public university graduates victims of ideological influences that "perverted and disoriented them." Even Catholic school graduates became "apathetic, indifferent, and disconnected with other elements of the Church's living forces" due to the absence of a national student league.[12] Clearly, the church leadership was deeply concerned that Roman Catholicism was exercising a declining influence over the youths who, thanks to their education and social origins, could be expected to become the future leaders of an increasingly secular Mexican society.

Archival sources document the active role that Archbishop Díaz played in reviving the CNECM. For example, in 1930 Archbishop Díaz held a conference with Catholic school directors, telling them that the Catholic Student Union was "almost dead" and that their schools were crucial to its revival. He called on these Catholic schools to establish student communities that would be in regular communication with the CNECM's leadership.[13] Archbishop Díaz also provided financial assistance to the Student Union, providing the funds that allowed it to rent an old mansion in downtown Mexico City that served as its new national headquarters.[14] Mexican Catholic Action, which was under Archbishop Díaz's control, also appealed to the nation's Catholic school directors on the Student Union's behalf for a stipend in order to subsidize the CNECM's organizational activities.[15]

Ramón Martínez Silva, SJ, was the man with the direct responsibility of infusing new life into the Student Union. Born in 1890 in the historically pro-Catholic city of Zamora, Michoacán, the young Jesuit studied and ministered in Cuba, Spain, Belgium, and France as the Mexican Revolution raged back home.[16] Returning to Mexico in 1925, the stocky, thirty-five-year-old Martínez Silva briefly served as one of several Jesuit ecclesiastical advisors to the LNDLR's executive committee. When the ecclesiastical hierarchy grew estranged from the LNDLR due to policy differences, Martínez Silva's superiors ordered him to sever all contacts with that group.[17] In 1927 Archbishop Mora y del Río assigned him to be his representative to the CNECM, replacing the ill-fated Miguel Agustín Pro. Given the chaos of this time period, it is not surprising that Martínez Silva was unable to achieve anything of significance. To complicate things further, his superiors sent him out of the country in October 1928 for reasons that are unclear, although the issue of his personal security was likely a major factor, since prominent church figures were at risk from government-inspired violence.

Returning to Mexico the following year, Martínez Silva was shocked to learn that there were plans well underway to liquidate the CNECM as an independent organization. Eduardo Iglesias, a Jesuit priest left behind as the Catholic Student Union's caretaker, and the ACJM's leader Bernardo Bergöend (likely under his superiors' orders) had agreed to disband the Student Union in order to "avoid possible problems that could have arisen" between the two organizations.[18] However, the Student Union managed to survive thanks to the support it received from Archbishop Pascual Díaz.[19] Archbishop Díaz's support for Martínez Silva and the CNECM stood in contrast to the tough stance that the cleric assumed toward the ACJM, and this no doubt was a factor in the emergence of the rivalry between Bernardo Bergöend and Ramón Martínez Silva that blossomed into an intense antipathy that negatively affected the CNECM's development.

In 1931 the UNEC gave tangible proof of its recovered vitality when it hosted an international conference of Catholic students; this event coincided with other celebrations commemorating the IV Centennial anniversary of the Apparition of the Virgin of Guadalupe, Mexico's most important Catholic religious icon. The 1931 Iberoamerican Conference drew delegates from Central America, South America, Spain, and the Dominican Republic. The issues and conclusions reached at this congress served to define ideological positions that the student union, now re-baptized as the UNEC, would maintain in the coming decade. At this congress, delegates addressed the social and political issues facing Mexico and Latin America from a Catholic perspective.[20] The Roman Catholic Church's social doctrine, enunciated in Pope Leo XIII's encyclical *Rerum Novarum* (1891) and Pope Pius XI's *Quadraggessimo Anno* (1931) (which reinforced the message of the earlier encyclical), is clearly present in the congress' call for social reform in Latin America. The delegates called for an end to the exploitation of child labor, an eight-hour work day for laborers, guaranteed vacations for workers, and the establishment of profit-sharing programs.[21] Many of these provisions had already been adopted by Mexican revolutionaries in the 1917 Constitution but were not regularly enforced. The Iberoamerican congress delegates adopted paternalistic attitudes toward the issue of women in the workplace; they proposed restrictions on female employment, believing that women's "morality could be exposed to danger" by working with men in the factories. Mothers were also discouraged from working outside of the home for fear that it would interfere with their roles as child caregivers and homemakers.[22]

The congress also examined the question of land reform, an issue that had been at the heart of the Mexican Revolution. The delegates' analysis of the Mexican agrarian reform program up to 1931 was surprisingly positive in tone. Although the congress decried the use of land reform as a political tool, its legitimacy as a remedy to redress social ills was not reproached, as illustrated by the following statement: "Amongst the masses the reforms (in land-holding patterns) were inspired in a call for justice. The breaking up of the *latifundia*, the creation of small property holders, the restitution and distribution of the land became necessary."[23] These observations were indicative of the fact that the Catholic Church had had to at least begin to come to grips with the legacy of the Mexican Revolution.

The spread of socialism in Latin America and the proselytizing activities of Protestant ministers were of great concern for the delegates. The latter were dismissed as the "deliberate and irresponsible" vehicles of US capitalist penetration in Latin America. Delegates also rejected the Marxist doctrine of class warfare as suicidal for society and dogmatically stated that the problems of the working class "could not be solved outside of the Church."[24] The proposed solution to both threats was the same: the establishment of Catholic study groups. The cadre of Catholic activists that these study groups would produce would promote Catholic social doctrine and strengthen the Roman Catholic Church's position in Latin American society.[25]

The Catholic Church's celebration of the IV Centenary of the Apparition of the Virgin of Guadalupe (December 1931) occurred during the period of Mexico's history known as the Maximato (1929–1934), so named because the *jéfe máximo* of the Mexican Revolution, Plutarco Elías Calles, ruled the nation through a series of weak presidents whom he selected and controlled. Calles and his closest collaborators occupied key cabinet positions in these administrations and dictated the country's national and international policy. While the Arreglos had ended the government's military operations against the church's supporters, it did not end the antipathy that Calles and members of his circle entertained toward the Catholic Church and its component parts. Calles was convinced that the church's social influence was a barrier to Mexico's social, political, and economic development, and these convictions manifested themselves in many of the policies adopted by the federal government during the Maximato, including those dealing with the area of education.

Catholics vs. Federal Educational Policies in the 1930s

Narciso Bassols, the head of Mexico's the Secretaría de Educación Pública (SEP, Secretariat of Public Education) from 1931 to 1934, was the main architect of federal educational policies during the Maximato. Slight, balding, and bespectacled, Bassols was an intellectual and looked the part; a leftist who was a lawyer by training, the dynamic Bassols is associated with two highly controversial pedagogical initiatives: his attempt to introduce sex education into Mexican schools and his promotion of "Socialist Education."[26] Building on regional pedagogical experiments carried out in states ruled by populist governors, Bassols enacted policies that promoted a national civic culture that was critical of capitalism, in a country mired in the Great Depression and hostile to the interests of the Roman Catholic Church, in a nation that was overwhelmingly Roman Catholic. Under Bassols, the SEP carried out "defanaticization" campaigns designed to dramatically reduce the Catholic Church's hold over Mexican society. Federal schoolteachers also promoted notions of modern healthcare and hygiene among the nation's mostly impoverished rural population. In addition, Bassols mobilized schoolteachers to promote land reform and the incorporation of peasants into pro-government peasant associations; schoolteachers were also active in the efforts to promote the unionization of urban workers in government-controlled labor organizations. All in all, Bassols and the SEP made important contributions to the building of the corporatist one-party state that ruled Mexico until the end of the twentieth century.[27]

The Roman Catholic Church hierarchy and its lay supporters found much of Education Secretary Bassols's policies threatening and objectionable. They fumed when the Mexican congress, with Bassols's support and encouragement, voted to deny official recognition to students who graduated from Catholic middle schools. These institutions had long been a stronghold of Catholic education and the launching platform for the educational careers of elite boys. This action closed the doors of higher education to Catholic school graduates. At the same time, the SEP greatly expanded its own national secondary school system.

Mexican Catholics were also outraged by Bassols's sex education initiative, which emerged out of a recommendation made by the Mexican Eugenics Society. In 1932 this organization had urged the SEP to include sex education in its official plan of studies, arguing that proper sex education was fundamental in dealing effectively with such problems as births out of wedlock, venereal diseases, and sexual perversions.[28] Bassols and other supporters of sex education viewed it both as a scientific-biological matter and as a tool in undermining Roman Catholicism's lingering hold over the population; they sought to separate sexuality from any Christian notion of sin and in addition to inform children on the issues surrounding sexual reproduction: "The child should know that the act of pleasure is in itself neither bad or sinful, but that like any other act can be turned into something negative under certain circumstances. . . . There is no sin, there is only crime or the usurpation of rights."[29]

From their urban strongholds, the Catholic Church–affiliated Unión National de Padres de Familia launched a highly successful public relations campaign against Bassols's sex education proposal that fed on the ignorance, fears, and prejudices of Mexico's socially conservative parents. These efforts included the holding of an informal plebiscite in Mexico City that asked parents the leading question: "Do you accept that your children, and especially your daughters, are taught SEXUAL SECRETS at school?"[30] This highly effective public pressure campaign eventually forced the SEP to abandon its sex education program.

The uproar generated by sex education had not died down when an even more controversial educational initiative emerged: Socialist Education. While it was supported and promoted by Bassols, the genesis of this educational program was to be found in proposals made by the state legislatures of Tabasco and Veracruz, states ruled by populist and anticlerical governors. In 1933 the call for educational reform was embraced by Mexico's ruling Partido Nacional Revolucionario (PNR, National Revolutionary Party), and General Lázaro Cárdenas, its leftist candidate in the following year's presidential elections. The PNR's educational platform called for the termination of religious instruction in all

Mexican schools and the adoption of "scientific rational education based on the postulation of Mexican socialism."[31] This curriculum reform promised an intensified attack on the Roman Catholic Church's cultural influence in society; it also promoted collective action by workers and peasants in order to address the nation's grave socioeconomic problems that had been exacerbated by the onset of the Great Depression.[32] In 1934 a modified version of the PNR's educational platform was passed as an amendment to the Constitution of 1917 affecting all government and privately operated elementary, secondary, normal, and preparatory schools in the nation.

Roman Catholic Church officials were scathing in their denunciations of Socialist Education; Archbishop Ruiz y Flores, Pope Pius XI's exiled Apostolic delegate to Mexico, denounced Socialist Education as an effort by the state to wrest control of children from their parents and "tear away from the souls of children every religious belief."[33] Supported by the Vatican, the Roman Catholic Church in Mexico engaged in a determined and multifaceted opposition campaign designed to undermine the Socialist Education program that also drew on the support of secular conservatives.[34] Public reaction against Socialist Education in some quarters was so intense that it threatened to destabilize the nation and restart the terrible religious civil war of the 1920s.[35] Opposition to the government's educational polices was strongest in the countryside, where in Catholic strongholds government schoolteachers faced death or mutilation by the local population if they attempted to implement the Socialist Education program, with some one hundred educators killed and two hundred more mutilated.[36] This armed peasant opposition to Socialist Education, known in Mexican historiography as the Second Cristiada, was centered in the Catholic strongholds of Michoacán, Jalisco, and Durango and involved some 7,500 former Cristero fighters.[37]

The Cárdenas administration eventually withdrew support for the Socialist Education program as a consequence of the opposition that it had generated within the country. It is important to note that a significant amount of this opposition came from within the ruling PNR party, where many conservative governors simply refused to allow teachers to carry out policies that they deemed too politically radical.[38] Cárdenas also saw that it was to his political advantage to reach out to conservative Mexicans by retreating from Socialist Education's most anticlerical tendencies.[39] This was due to the fact that by 1935, Cárdenas had become engaged in a bitter power struggle against Mexico's strongman, Plutarco Elías Calles, who remained enemy number one in the minds of most Mexican Catholics. Under Cárdenas's administration, federal teachers downplayed the SEP's defanaticization campaign and focused on other key elements of Cárdenas's program: the promotion of land reform and the unionization of urban labor.

The Unión National de Estudiantes Católicos and Socialist Education

Martínez Silva's Catholic student group's rise to national prominence was intimately tied to the events that shook the privileged world of Mexican higher education in the early 1930s. The UNEC played a major role in the broad coalition of Catholics and secular conservatives that arose to oppose the introduction of a Socialist Education–inspired curriculum reform at the UNAM and other regional universities. The 1933 strike that engulfed Mexico's premier institution of higher education firmly established the UNEC as a major player in the turbulent world of student politics; more importantly, the young men of the UNEC became political actors of national importance as well, as they were in the vanguard of Catholic opposition to the federal government's educational policies. The Catholic Church hierarchy, while generally supportive of the UNEC's campaign against the government-supported Marxist curriculum reform in Mexico's universities, publicly maintained its distance from the Student Union for fear of government reprisals.

The effort to reform the privileged world of Mexican higher education began in 1933 under the leadership of Vicente Lombardo Toledano, a prominent Marxist labor leader and intellectual with strong ties to the UNAM. The grandson of an Italian immigrant who made his fortune in mining interests, Lombardo Toledano served as the director of the UNAM's National Preparatory School in 1933 and was on close terms with the college's rector. Lombardo Toledano could also count on the support of Education Secretary Narciso Bassols, who was a close personal friend, and that of Mexico's largest student organization, the pro-government Confederación Nacional de Estudiantes (CNE, National Student Confederation).[40]

The advocates of curriculum reform demanded a plan of studies that would make of each student a "useful and efficient worker capable of assuming the leadership of the national economy, employing the methods of modern science with a profound consciousness of collective responsibility ... an indispensable precondition for the coming of a state in the hands of the working classes."[41] Lombardo Toledano, convinced that the Great Depression spelled the collapse of capitalism, maintained that under these circumstances the UNAM had the obligation to "contribute to the substitution of a capitalist order to one that socializes the means of economic production through the [ideological] orientation of faculty members."[42] Lombardo Toledano and his supporters wanted faculty members who identified with the masses and not the "exploiting class" and who promoted the entrance of working-class youth into the elite stronghold of higher education.[43] Lombardo Toledano rejected the notion of academic freedom, the principle defended by the opponents of curriculum reform, as merely serving to produce anarchism and confusion in the minds of youth.

At first, an effort was made on both sides of the curriculum reform question to debate the issue in a rational manner within the university community.[44] Unfortunately, the conflict degenerated into violence when on October 10, 1933, pro- and anti-Lombardo Toledano forces clashed at the UNAM's Law School. Rodolfo Brito Foucher, the politically conservative director of the law school, had emerged as one of Lombardo Toledano's strongest opponents within the university, and on that day right-wing students carried out Brito Foucher's decision to expel leftist students from the law school. Appalled by the deteriorating situation within the university, the UNAM's faculty members staged a mass resignation. Faced with this major crisis, the university council held an emergency meeting where after a heated debate Brito Foucher was relieved from his post as director of the university's law school; however, Brito Foucher's ouster failed to end the conflict within the UNAM.[45] Law students loyal to Brito Foucher went on strike to protest his removal and attacked the offices of Lombardo Toledano and that of the university's rector, Roberto Medellín. Unable to reassert their authority or contain the violence, Rector Medellín and National Preparatory School director Lombardo Toledano had no choice but to resign their positions within the UNAM. The opponents of curriculum reform had prevailed, at least for the time being.

Martínez Silva's UNEC members were active players in this campaign against the Socialist Education and its advocates within the UNAM. From November 1932, when Vicente Lombardo Toledano was elected as the director of the UNAM's National Preparatory School, its members had engaged in a heckling campaign that mocked Lombardo Toledano whenever he made a public appearance. The UNEC also aggressively supported Brito Foucher during the October 1933 UNAM strike and organized a raid on October 13 against the CNE's headquarters in order to oust its leftist leadership.[46]

Having been purged of leftist students as a consequence of the fallout from the 1933 UNAM strike, the CNE became the vehicle that the UNEC used to extend its influence throughout Mexico. The UNEC provided the CNE with three consecutive national presidents, beginning with Armando Chávez Camacho in May 1934.[47] Claiming a national membership of 110,000 secondary, preparatory, and university students throughout Mexico, the CNE under the UNEC's tutelage waged a countrywide campaign against the Socialist Education curriculum under its different guises.[48] The CNE supported the wave of university strikes that irrupted across the country in August 1934. These actions were designed to pressure the Mexican national congress not to include higher education under the authority of the 1934 Socialist Education constitutional amendment. While this highly controversial amendment was passed by the national congress, it left higher education unaffected.[49]

The UNEC maintained generally positive relations with the rectors who led the UNAM following the 1933 strike. Manuel Gómez Morín (1933–1934), Rector Medellín's successor, was a distinguished technocrat and lawyer who enjoyed excellent contacts in both Mexico's conservative business class and the Catholic community; however, he was not able to adequately address the fiscal crisis that plagued the UNAM after an angry federal government cut off the institution's subsidy due to his strong relationship with the Catholic militants of the UNEC. That these links had been forged was clearly demonstrated five years later when Manuel Gómez Morín founded the conservative PAN and presented former and current UNEC members with leadership positions within his new political organization.

The UNEC also maintained close ties to Fernando Ocaranza, Gómez Morín's successor, and supported many of his initiatives. Rector Ocaranza followed Gómez Morín's policy of validating the educational achievements of students who had graduated from Catholic preparatory schools, a policy directly contradicting the Secretariat of Education's edicts. Catholic preparatory schools opposing the government's Socialist

Education curriculum sought and received the National Autonomous University's protection.⁵⁰ In addition, the UNEC endorsed Ocaranza's project to expand the National University's National Preparatory School educational cycle from two years to five. The purpose of this reform was to give the National University access to students not exposed to Socialist Education at government-controlled middle schools. The SEP, aware of the initiative's significance, nixed this plan. Undaunted, the UNEC successfully lobbied Ocaranza and the university council for the adoption of a university extension program that had the effect of establishing a de facto middle school free from the Socialist Education curriculum.⁵¹

The Unión National de Estudiantes Católicos and Catholic Action

By the mid-1930s, the UNEC was at the height of its success as an organization; however, it had not achieved its cherished goal to be an integral component of Mexican Catholic Action. This measure was essential for the UNEC's long-term viability.⁵² The UNEC faced two obstacles in achieving this goal: one was the feeling, widespread among Mexico's bishops, that granting the UNEC "fundamental" status within Catholic Action would bring the government's wrath down upon the Roman Catholic Church as a whole; another major obstacle was the ACJM, whose rivalry with the UNEC had grown stronger over the years. The ACJM's opposition to the UNEC's petition not only reflected self-interest but also the intense personal antipathy that the ACJM's spiritual advisor Bernardo Bergöend, SJ, and the UNEC's Ramón Martínez Silva, SJ, felt toward each other. Finally, the Catholic Action's leadership expressed doubt in the UNEC's dedication to the goals of Catholic Action and the viability of an urban university student organization in what was then a primarily rural nation that was both economically and socially underdeveloped. The debate over whether the UNEC would become a fundamental component of Catholic Action exposed fissures within both the church's and the ecclesiastical hierarchy's complicated relationship with this controversial organization.

In 1935 Archbishop Pascual Díaz communicated with the nation's bishops and the Catholic Action leadership, asking them for their opinions on the issue of granting the UNEC full status within Catholic Action. The responses that he received demonstrated just how polemical an organization the UNEC was perceived to be within the church. Catholic Action's director Luis Bustos was unequivocal in recommending that the UNEC's petition be rejected. Bustos labeled the UNEC as an organization "dedicated solely to politics" and with a poor record in working together with other Catholic Action organizations. He also noted the "chasm" that existed between the UNEC's ecclesiastical representative Ramón Martínez Silva, SJ, and the ACJM's Bernardo Bergöend, SJ. If the UNEC became a core organization within Catholic Action, Bustos predicted endless conflict between these two men and their rival organizations.[53] However, Bustos's reservations concerning the UNEC extended far beyond the issue of a clash of personalities between Martínez Silva and Bergöend. Philosophically, he believed that Mexico, then an impoverished agrarian nation, could not sustain an elitist organization like the UNEC.[54] Bustos noted that while the ACJM claimed a total national membership of twenty thousand young men in 1935, the UNEC had only a "few hundred" members and could only flourish in the few cities that boasted institutions of higher learning.[55]

Devastating as Luis Bustos's letter was to the UNEC's cause, the association did have its advocates within the Catholic Church hierarchy. Its position was defended by Archbishop Leopoldo Ruiz y Flores, the Vatican's representative to Mexico, who in 1935 was in government-imposed exile in the United States. He recommended to Archbishop Díaz that the UNEC be given full status within Catholic Action, but with the caveat that this not be publicly revealed under the "present circumstances" out of fear of government reprisals against the church.[56] To avoid the UNEC-ACJM conflict that so worried Luis Bustos, Archbishop Ruiz y Flores proposed to specify that in the future the UNEC would have the exclusive right to recruit its members from Mexico's universities, preparatory schools, and technical schools.[57] The Archdiocese of Guadalajara, another powerful voice within the church, also threw its support behind the UNEC and defended that organization from the criticisms that Luis Bustos leveled against it. The Vicario general of the Archdiocese of Guadalajara accepted Bustos's point that UNEC members were ignorant of Catholic Action regulations but argued that was due to the organization's marginal position within Catholic Action. Denying the UNEC full membership in Catholic Action would in fact intensify the feelings of alienation that the UNEC's members had toward Catholic Action. However, these pro-UNEC opinions were in the minority.

Archbishop Pascual Díaz rendered his decision in early 1936, shortly before his death in May of that year. While recognizing that the UNEC "possessed all of the requirements" to be "immediately recognized" as a full member of Catholic Action, he decided against this measure.[58] Díaz bluntly stated that is was the UNEC's highly public activities that led him to make this decision, and he repeated the concerns expressed by clerics like the archbishop of Monterrey[59] that publicly recognizing the UNEC as an element of Catholic Action would bring the government's wrath down on the church.[60] To ease the blow against the UNEC, Archbishop Díaz granted the UNEC exclusive recruiting authority in the nation's universities and normal and preparatory schools. The UNEC leadership later claimed that Archbishop Díaz's decision caused the sharp decline in the organization's fortunes, although their interpretation, as will be seen, was too simplistic and self-serving.[61]

The UNEC's failure to win full membership within Catholic Action heralded a year of reverses for the organization. First there came a crackdown on UNEC militants within the UNAM by the school's new rector Luis Chico Goerne, who was anxious to improve his university's relations with the federal government in order to reestablish the UNAM's governmental stipend; however, this goal was unlikely to be achieved so long as the UNEC retained its influence within the UNAM. Chico Goerne shrewdly used the continuing violence at the National University to carry forward with his goals. On June 2, 1936, the students from the UNEC-controlled CNE raided the offices of a rival organization, the Mexico City–based University Student Federation. Seizing the moment, Rector Chico Goerne called a meeting of faculty and students to deal with the unrest, eventually leading to the expulsion of the UNEC's most vocal activists within the UNAM: Armando Chávez Camacho, Luis Islas García, Antonio Aguirre, and Teodoro Schumacher.[62] Chico Goerne also placed the politically sensitive University Extension Program in the hands of an official who would avoid conflicts with the SEP.[63]

The year 1936 also witnessed the establishment of a government-supported rival to the Catholic-dominated CNE. Created from left-wing students expelled from the CNE after the 1933 UNAM strike, this new organization proclaimed itself as the true CNE and declared its support for President Lázaro Cárdenas's progressive social and political policies. Cárdenas reciprocated and provided assistance for this new organization, going so far as providing the use of a naval gunboat to ferry students to the new CNE's founding congress in Mérida, Yucatán.[64] The Catholic Student Union's hold over the national student movement was broken; it retained control of only a rump CNE.

The changing nature of church-state relations in the late 1930s was another critical factor in the UNEC's decline. Luis María Martínez, the new archbishop of Mexico, embraced a policy of seeking better relations with the administration of Lázaro Cárdenas and that of his successor, General Manuel Ávila Camacho. Although a leftist and an anti-clerical, President Cárdenas was nonetheless more of a moderate on church-related issues than his political mentor Plutarco Elías Calles, and he had publically lamented the destabilizing effects of the Maximato's defanaticization campaigns in 1936.[65] The improvement in church-state relations in the late 1930s can be seen in the Cárdenas administration's willingness to allow Archbishop Leopoldo Ruiz y Flores, the Vatican Apostolic delegate, to return to Mexico in 1937 after five years in US exile. The church hierarchy reciprocated by publicly endorsing Cárdenas's politically courageous decision to nationalize Mexico's foreign-dominated petroleum industry in 1938, which had created a major diplomatic crisis for Mexico with the United States, Great Britain, and the Netherlands.

The détente in church-state relations accelerated under Cárdenas's hand-picked successor Manuel Ávila Camacho (1940–1946), who initiated a sharp turn to the political right by Mexico's ruling party. In a gesture of conciliation to Mexico's majority Catholic population, candidate Ávila Camacho publicly announced to the nation his own Catholicism.[66] As president of Mexico, Ávila Camacho enacted a series of measures that won him the approval of both militant Catholics and secular conservatives. These included the purging of suspected Marxists from the SEP and the eventual elimination of the polemical Socialist Education program. In 1945 President Ávila Camacho allowed the Catholic Church and its followers to hold a public celebration commemorating the coronation of Mexico's greatest Catholic icon—the Virgin of Guadalupe.[67] To appease Mexico's conservative business community, whose cooperation he required to enact his pro-industrialization economic model, Ávila Camacho clamped down on independent and militant labor unions and reduced Vicente Lombardo Toledano's political influence and role as Mexico's main labor leader.

In order to exploit this opportunity in improving the Catholic Church's ties to the state, Archbishop Martínez needed to demobilize militant lay Catholic organizations, as these could upset the achievement of this goal. The highly politicized UNEC was one such organization. Happily for Archbishop Martínez, the UNEC's institutional weakness by the late 1930s eased his task considerably. In 1937 the controversial cleric Ramón Martínez Silva, SJ, was reassigned by his superiors to a new post in the United States, serving from 1938 to 1940 as the rector of the critically important Seminario Montezuma in New Mexico. This institution was created by the church hierarchy in order to educate future Mexican priests as seminaries in Mexico had been closed by the government.[68] Martínez Silva's replacement was the young, charismatic, and scholarly Jesuit priest Jaime Castiello, whose focus was to revive the UNEC's moribund pedagogical function of transmitting Catholic doctrine. The Mexican-born son of wealthy Spanish immigrants, Castiello enjoyed an elite education at an English public school before entering the Jesuit Order. Earning his PhD in Germany in 1934, Castiello taught at Fordham University in New York City and published *A Human Psychology of Education* in 1936 before being transferred to Mexico.[69] Castiello breathed new life into the UNEC's atrophied study circles that Martínez Silva had neglected during the organization's peak years of involvement in student politics.[70] However, these efforts were tragically derailed the following year when Castiello was killed driving his Mercedes-Benz automobile on a Mexican highway.[71]

Shortly after Castiello's untimely death, the UNEC was torn apart by the emergence of secret cells of extreme right-wing students in its Mexico City and Guadalajara chapters. The UNEC's new ecclesiastical representative Julio Vértiz, SJ, and other UNEC officials informed Archbishop Martínez that conspiratorial groups were attempting to wrest control of the organization for their own political purposes. For example, UNEC president Luis Calderón Vega, the father of Mexico's future president Felipe Calderón Hinojosa, accused the Catholic student activist Carlos Cuesta Gallardo of subverting the UNEC's authority over its Guadalajara chapter. Cuesta Gallardo was reportedly using his influence within the Universidad Autónoma de Guadalajara (Autonomous University of Guadalajara)—an institution founded in 1935 by Catholic and secular conservatives in the wake of the Socialist Education curriculum controversy that gripped the state-run University of Guadalajara in 1933—to achieve this goal.[72] Described by his detractors as an unabashed anti-Semite whose reading tastes included the notorious *Protocols of the*

Elders of Zion, Cuesta Gallardo's intentions were to transform the UNEC into a "Catholic Masonic order" that would "combat the omnipresent power . . . of the secret Jewish-Masonic organization."[73] Previously, Vértiz had informed Archbishop Martínez concerning the emergence of secret cells in the UNEC's Mexico City chapters. Vértiz singled out the activities of the Catholic student leader José Luis Curiel, whom he accused of undermining his authority over the organization and placing the UNEC's continual survival in doubt.[74] The damage that these secret groups inflicted on the Student Union's internal cohesion was seen by the UNEC's leadership as a key factor for the organization's demise.[75]

The UNEC's internal crisis provided Archbishop Martínez with the opportunity of politically neutralizing this organization, which was becoming increasingly out of step with the evolving political situation in Mexico. Using the occasion of the UNEC's 1940 national congress, Archbishop Martínez announced his decision to bar the Student Union's members from engaging in student politics in the future.[76] This was a crippling blow to an organization that had risen to national prominence precisely because of its high-profile political activism. Yet this measure was but the first step in the ecclesiastical hierarchy's dismantling of the UNEC. The following year, Archbishop Martínez stripped away from the UNEC its exclusive right to recruit university students that it had received from the late Archbishop Díaz. The ACJM was the primary beneficiary of this decision, which had already established a university student branch of its organization called the Professional-Student Movement.[77] By the early 1940s, the UNEC was a moribund institution without a clear raison d'être.

Conclusion: The Founding of the Partido Acción Nacional and the Unión National de Estudiantes Católicos's Legacy

The National Student Union had a brief but highly eventful and important existence, and it was an institution that continued to influence Mexican society long after it had passed from the scene. It emerged on the eve of a brutal and bloody religious war that cost the lives of tens of thousands of people and went on to play a major role in the world of university student politics during the turbulent decade of the 1930s. The Student Union created a generation of student activists who went on to graduate to the world of national party politics, becoming a pillar of the conservative PAN. This party, which for decades had to struggle in a political system dominated by the Partido Revolucionario Institucional (PRI, Institutional Revolutionary Party), finally broke the PRI's seventy-one-year hold on power during the 2000 presidential elections, which were won by its presidential candidate Vicente Fox. The PAN was founded in 1939 by a coalition of businessmen, secular conservatives, and Catholic intellectuals opposed to the Cárdenas administration's progressive labor, agrarian, social, and political policies.[78]

The man who gathered this disparate coalition together was Manuel Gómez Morín, who had served as the UNAM's rector in the chaotic period that followed the 1933 strike. Another key leader within the PAN during its early years was Efraín González Luna, a former member of Bergöend's Mexican Catholic Student Union and a well-known Catholic intellectual and activist. Gómez Morín and González Luna recruited many UNEC members into the fledgling political party using the links they had forged with these Catholic activists over the years. UNEC members, with their extensive experience in the bruising and sometimes brutal world of university student politics, provided the fledgling institution with an important cadre of dedicated political activists. The UNEC organizations scattered throughout the country provided an important organizational network for the PAN during its early struggling period as it tried to become an effective national political institution.

While not a Catholic party, the PAN was, especially in its early years, heavily influenced by the presence of the Catholic activists within its ranks. For example, one-third of the PAN's first national executive committee were members of the UNEC; these included such UNEC stalwarts as Luis Calderón Vega, Manuel Ulloa Ortíz, Daniel Kuri Breña, Luis de Garay, Armando Chávez Camacho, Luis Islas García, and Manuel Estrada Iturbide.[79] Catholic Student Union activists also sat on the party's important doctrine and political action committees and used this perch to promote the diffusion of Catholic social doctrine within the PAN's platform.[80] For example, Luis de Garay sat on the PAN's doctrine committee, which was headed by Efraín González Luna and which produced the PAN's "Doctrine of National Action."[81] This critically important document rejected the Marxist doctrine of class warfare as "false, inhumane, and contrary to the most fundamental laws of social life," while Catholic social doctrine, as defined by the papal encyclicals *Rerum Novarum* (1891) and *Quadregessimo Anno* (1931), was echoed in the PAN statement that declared that "all socially useful work should be compensated so as to allow the raising of a family in dignity."[82] The Doctrine of National Action also considered the liberal-capitalist view that human labor was simply a commodity to be "an assault against human dignity."[83] A UNEC member was also instrumental in the founding of the PAN official newspaper *La Nación*. Carlos Séptien García, a Catholic Student Union member, created the newspaper in 1941 and served as its editor until his untimely death in 1954; Séptien García was also credited with establishing the PAN's school of journalism.[84] Through these activists, the Catholic social doctrine that had been promoted by Jesuits like Ramón Martínez Silva was transferred to a national political organization that would steadily grow in national importance in the coming decades.

While the PAN has become ideologically more secular since the 1950s, the UNEC's legacy within the party can be seen in individuals like President Felipe Calderón Hinojosa (2006–2012), who is the son of the former UNEC leader Luis Calderón Vega. The UNEC's contributions to Mexico's system of private higher education, specifically how it contributed the material and human resources used in the creation of the Universidad Iberoamericana, were also of fundamental importance and are examined in the next chapter.

CHAPTER FOUR

The Revival of Catholic Higher Education in Mexico, 1943–1952
The Centro Cultural Universitario

> *Why is it that in the United States, where the majority of the population is Protestant and the minority is Roman Catholic, Catholics can have a Catholic university and in Mexico, where the great majority of the population is Catholic, they cannot have a Catholic university?*
>
> —Rodolfo Brito Foucher, 1967

Introduction

The establishment of the Jesuit-sponsored Universidad Iberoamericana was the result of the realization of a longstanding desire by the Catholic Church to reestablish a Catholic university in Mexico, something that the nation did not have since the New World's first university, the Real y Pontíficia Universidad de México (1551), was suppressed by liberals in the mid-nineteenth century and later reborn as the University of Mexico. The new Jesuit university advanced the fundamental goal of articulating and disseminating the Roman Catholic message in a manner congruent with the new era of church-state relations. With the change, the political militancy of the The Unión National de Estudiantes Católicos (UNEC, National Catholic Student Union) gave way to the more standard, but highly important, work of a university—educating the young people, who would then take a leading role in Mexican public and private life. The ideological work of the student union, promoting Catholic culture in its study groups, was transferred to the new Jesuit university, which promoted a strident, militant, xenophobic Roman Catholicism in contrast to an increasingly secular society. Indeed, the UNEC's legacy lived on in other ways, for its former spiritual directors played key roles in the Iberoamericana's early history. Other Student Union alumni served as faculty members and patrons of the Universidad Iberoamericana. And sympathetic Universidad Nacional Autónoma de México (UNAM, National Autonomous University of Mexico) faculty members and administrators, with connections to the defunct UNEC, used the university's resources to assist in the Iberoamericana's establishment.

The Iberoamericana's early history was a tortured one, as its development was constantly hampered by economic difficulties and by periodic conflicts with the UNAM. At the UNAM, there were strong elements that were either unsympathetic or overtly hostile to the Catholic-sponsored Universidad Iberoamericana. The Iberoamericana was incorporated into the UNAM, which meant that the UNAM decided which of Iberoamericana's programs it would recognize, and on more than one occasion an Iberoamericana major was denied recognition by the UNAM for reasons that appeared to be ideological or political. The modus vivendi of the 1940s opened a way around this roadblock, entailing the direct recognition of an academic major by the government's Secretariat of Public Education. The Iberoamericana's administrators waged a long and futile campaign to gain for the university "free-school" status from the federal government, and thus free it from the UNAM's control. In order to do this, the Jesuits legally relinquished overall control of the Universidad Iberoamericana to a board of trustees (1963) comprised of sympathetic laymen. The strategy was that with a non-Jesuit leadership, the government's granting of free-school status was more probable.

Lay Catholic businessmen and professionals covered the Iberoamericana's continual operating deficits and helped build its campus in the Mexico City suburb of Churubusco. Equally important, the Mexican business community helped to structure the Iberoamericana's curriculum, which offered new majors specifically designed to address the economy's human capital needs for a trained professional workforce; a number of these majors were also vehicles for promoting Catholic doctrine on labor-capital relations.

The Universidad Iberoamericana has gone on to become one of Mexico's premier educational institutions and the alma mater for many of Mexico's economic, cultural and political elite, ranking with the UNAM and the Instituto Tecnológico y de Estudios Superiores de Monterrey in its ability to attract elites from these three different realms.[1] This has been particularly the case for members of the Partido Acción Nacional (PAN, National Action Party), including former President Vicente Fox

Quezada (2000–2006), the PAN's 2012 presidential candidate Josefina Vázquez Mota, and the PAN's 1994 presidential candidate Diego Fernández de Cevallos Ramos.[2]

The Centro Cultural Universitario, 1943–1952

In the summer of 1942, Rodolfo Brito Foucher, the UNAM's newly elected rector, held a meeting in his downtown office attended by UNAM official Oswaldo Robles, the former Asociación Católica de la Juventud Mexicana (ACJM, Mexican Catholic Youth Association) and UNEC leader, and the polemical Catholic student activist José Luis Curiel. The meeting's purpose was to discuss the viability of a project long discussed in Catholic circles—the establishment of Catholic universities in Mexico. Brito Foucher's original idea was to create two institutions, one an all-female institution and the other an all-male university.[3]

Brito Foucher, a lawyer and a former director of the UNAM's law school, told Robles and Curiel that in his opinion a Catholic university was legally feasible. He based his opinion on the argument that while the 1917 Constitution barred the "Catholic Church, its ministers and the other religions from supporting elementary and secondary schools, normal schools and schools for workers," it made no mention of higher education, meaning there would be no legal impediment to such an institution.[4] However, this account of Jesuit school's genesis, which emphasizes the role of Brito Foucher as the catalyst for the Jesuit university, does not square with the information provided in Calderón Vega's history of the UNEC. Calderón Vega's work maintains that plans for the creation of a Catholic university were already being discussed by ecclesiastical hierarchy as early as 1941 and that this fact played a major part in the church hierarchy's decision to withdraw support from the Catholic Student Union.[5] While the availability of a friendly rector at the UNAM certainly assisted the enterprise, and he may have prodded the church hierarchy to seize the opportunity he presented to them, it is inconceivable given the rigid hierarchy of the Roman Catholic Church that such a project could have been initiated without Archbishop Martínez's blessing.

Brito Foucher claimed that his goal in creating a Catholic university was to strike a blow for academic freedom.[6] He maintained that his inspiration for the creation of a Catholic university came in the late 1930s when he lived in Washington, D.C., the site of the Catholic University of America. When he saw this institution's campus, he asked himself: "Why is it that in the United States, where the majority of the population is Protestant and the minority is Roman Catholic, Catholics can have a Catholic University and in Mexico, where the great majority of the population is Catholic, they cannot have a Catholic university."[7] Nevertheless, in judging Brito Foucher's motives for supporting the creation of a Catholic university, it is important to note that there were less noble factors that help to explain his enthusiasm for this project. In his 1942 bid to win the election as the UNAM's rector, Brito Foucher actively courted and received the support of Catholic student leaders on campus, including that of Jose Luis Curiel, as well as former UNEC activists who now lectured at the UNAM, like Manuel Ulloa and Luis de Garay.[8] While Brito Foucher was not solely dependent upon the political support of these Catholic activists, they comprised his hard-core of supporters during his stormy two-year term as rector.

Oswaldo Robles, Brito Foucher's principal collaborator within the UNAM on the Catholic university project, enjoyed extensive connections to the Jesuit order and its student organizations. The one-time vice president of the Confederation of Catholic Students had abandoned the study of medicine to become a distinguished lay proponent of scholastic philosophy in Mexico. At the UNAM, he became, along with his fellow scholastic philosopher Jesús Guiza y Acevedo, a core supporter of the Jesuit-led student union. In later life, Robles found it necessary to deny he was the "philosopher" of the controversial National Sinarquista Union, an accusation arising because several Sinarquista leaders had been his students.[9]

The establishment of an all-female Catholic university was relatively straightforward; it was based on an all-female preparatory school already incorporated into the UNAM, the Colegio Motolinía, founded and directed by Dolores Echeverría, aunt of Mexico's future president Luis Echeverría Alvárez (1970–1976).[10] The UNAM's recognition of the new Motolinía University was granted on February 18, 1943, and the ease of its establishment may have been due to women's political and social marginality, for female graduates would not be politically prominent in a country that still denied women the right to vote.[11]

Unfortunately, the plan to create an all-male Catholic university did not run so smoothly, with the project immediately running into serious difficulties. Robles and Curiel informed Brito Foucher that "according to canon law, it was imperative that the rector of the [Catholic] university be a bishop," and this was still politically impossible in the early 1940s. Brito Foucher summarized the objections to the plan which Robles and Curiel had collected from those they had consulted on the matter. The general message was that "it was premature... imprudent, [and] inconvenient to found a Catholic university with a bishop as its rector as it [would] produce inconvenient reactions in the anti-Catholic world."[12]

Undeterred, Brito Foucher refused to drop the idea of establishing a Catholic university and personally sounded out church officials on the subject. He approached the UNEC's current spiritual director, Enrique Torroella, SJ, who professed his ignorance of the project; this proved to be a fortuitous encounter. Torroella forwarded Brito Foucher's ideas to his superiors and there followed a series of conferences between church officials, UNAM officials, and the directors of the Catholic preparatory schools affiliated with the UNAM.[13] In order to build support for a Catholic university, a series of conferences were organized between the project's supporters and the directors of the privately operated Roman Catholic preparatory schools affiliated with the UNAM.[14] The goal of creating a single Catholic university, entertained by some of the project members, floundered because of the institutional rivalries between the different orders of the Roman Catholic Church, each of which insisted on the "defense of their autonomy."[15]

The Jesuit institution that finally emerged on March 7, 1943, was not the full-fledged university that Brito Foucher had originally envisioned. Rather, it was simply identified as the UNAM's Centro Cultural Universitario (CCU, University Cultural Center), a title that also provided it with valuable camouflage from its ideological adversaries. Nor was it an all-male institution; in fact, women dominated the CCU's student body throughout its brief history.[16] The CCU was also not considered to be a Catholic university under church canon law because it was not headed by an archbishop, and as a consequence the Jesuit school had to rely on lay Catholic donors, rather than the Roman Catholic Church itself, in order to finance its operations.

Gabriel García Rojas, a lay Catholic academic who had actively worked for Brito Foucher's election as the UNAM's rector in 1942, was the school's first director, but his was a figurehead position.[17] True authority resided in the Jesuit who served as the CCU's Private Director, a post that was first occupied by Enrique Torroella.[18] Ramón Martínez Silva, SJ, the UNEC's former spiritual leader, assumed the private director post in 1945. Making no effort to hide his authority, Martínez Silva identified himself as the CCU's director in his official communications with the UNAM; García Rojas, the nominal director of the CCU, was a forgotten figure.[19]

With the promotion of Catholic culture as the paramount goal of the CCU, the creation of its first major, philosophy, was justified as a measure designed to meet demands the UNAM could not satisfy: "This University Center was founded with the idea of receiving those students whose ever growing numbers made it impossible to accept them at the University."[20] This explanation is flatly rejected by the progressive Jesuit cleric and historian José Ignacio Palencia: "[The School of] philosophy was not, to be sure, a school which found itself 'saturated' with students at the UNAM."[21] The CCU's philosophy program was important because it offered a different orientation from the UNAM's Faculty of Philosophy, emphasizing leftist perspectives, especially the philosophical systems of Kant, Hegel, and Marx. The UNAM had Catholic neo-scholastic philosophers on its faculty, Oswaldo Robles and Jesús Guisa y Acevedo, but not surprisingly neo-scholasticism did not predominate at the UNAM's Faculty of Philosophy. Students entering the CCU's philosophy program recalled the warnings of their Catholic preparatory school teachers about the UNAM's School of Philosophy, controlled by neo-Kantians.[22] To all established churches, Immanuel Kant's assertion that morality was "an instrument inborn in man, who needed no guide but its own dignity," had presented a direct threat to their continued existence.[23] The Roman Catholic Church and its apologists saw Kant's philosophy as a prime promoter of extreme individualism, which encouraged moral chaos. For Catholic intellectuals, social and political anarchy were the natural consequences of this "cult of individualism." The promotion of neo-scholastic philosophy corresponded to the Roman Catholic Church's desire to create a new synthesis between reason and revelation as expressed in Pope Leo XIII's encyclical *Acerbi Animi*.[24]

The Center's master's program in history was the second major to be established. It was clearly a logical step; earlier Jesuit student groups had not only promoted neo-scholastic philosophy but also the teaching of ecclesiastical history, Mexican history, and Catholic "sociology."[25] The Center's history program focused on Mexico's colonial and pre-Hispanic past. At the center of its studies was Mexico's so-called spiritual conquest, the conversion of Mexico's indigenous population to Christianity.[26] At the head of this program was Mariano Cuevas, the nation's most distinguished Jesuit historian and author of the massive five-volume *Historía de la Iglesia en México*, completed in 1929.[27] In this work, Cuevas revealed himself as a strident, irredentist Catholic militant who was opposed not just to the historical perspective promoted by the Mexican state under Socialist Education but also that of great liberal historians of the nineteenth century—historians such as Justo Sierra, Vicente Riva Palacios, and Guillermo Prieto. Cuevas built upon Lucas Alamán's conservative historiography, seconding Alamán in defending Agustín de Iturbide and not Miguel Hidalgo y Costilla as the true father of Mexican independence and viewing Mexican liberals as pro–United States "agents" of Protestantism and Free Masonry.[28]

Cuevas's assessment of more contemporary historical events was equally biased and partisan. This was particularly true in his analysis of Victoriano Huerta's regime, in which he stated that Huerta's complicity in the assassinations of Francisco Madero and José María Pino Suárez was not proven. He described the murderous Huerta as "an energetic, democratic, and upright man" who would have brought "peace" to Mexico if not for the intervention of the United States.[29] Despite all this and with Cuevas at its helm, the CCU's history major program was officially recognized by the UNAM on April 15, 1944.[30]

Since Catholic students and intellectuals had fiercely defended the concept of academic freedom during the Socialist Education controversy, it is pertinent to examine how this principle was observed at the CCU. In fact, it is clear that the Jesuit school had a slanted view of how academic freedom should operate, reflecting the belief that "for academic freedom to function the instructors had to be carefully selected."[31] Not surprisingly, the Cultural Center observed a clear ideological bias in its selection of its non-Jesuit faculty members; many of the nonclerical instructors were former members of the Student Union or its predecessor, the National Catholic Student Confederation. These men included Oswaldo Robles, José Luis Curiel, Luis García Islas, Daniel Kuri Breña, Luis de Garay, Manuel Ulloa, and Rafael Aguayo Spencer.[32] Such ideological homogeneity defeated the spirit of academic freedom; it was safe to give free rein to instructors when they were all known to be reading from the same page. As will be seen later on, true academic freedom did not arrive at the Jesuit school until after the reforms ushered in by the Vatican II Council of the 1960s.

In July 1944 the Center's fortunes changed dramatically—and for the worse. In that month, the CCU lost its key ally at the UNAM, Rodolfo Brito Foucher, who was forced to resign as rector in the face of a bitter, divisive strike at the UNAM. After July 1944, the CCU found itself in a desperate struggle just to survive. The events of 1944 spotlighted the CCU's absolute dependence upon the UNAM, and the danger of this condition for the institution's future viability, and yet it was thirty more years before the Jesuit school was able to escape the UNAM's control.

The 1944 Universidad Nacional Autónoma de México Strike and the Centro Cultural Universitario

The events surrounding Brito Foucher's resignation as rector of the UNAM were as dramatic as those of the celebrated 1933 UNAM strike. From his first day as rector of the UNAM, Brito Foucher had been beset by determined opponents who actively sought his ouster from office. Leftists both within and outside the UNAM had vigorously opposed Brito Foucher's rectorship, remembering his notorious role in the 1933 university conflict. The political attacks on Brito Foucher were led by his old nemesis Vicente Lombardo Toledano, who harangued the UNAM's rector as a "cardboard Fuehrer" who led a "clerical-fascist clique" at the UNAM.[33] Lombardo Toledano, indulging in more verbal vitriol, denounced that the university had become a "valuable auxiliary of reactionary and pro-fascist politicians," and a "diminutive Nazi Empire" led by a "fascist megalomaniac."[34]

Ultimately, however, it was Brito Foucher's own incompetence and political intolerance, rather than the verbal barbs of his opponents, which proved to be the decisive factors in his removal from office. Brito Foucher relied on brutal authoritarian measures in order to deal with his political opponents rather than attempting to bridge the ideological divisions through consensus. Violent clashes between supporters and opponents of Brito Foucher had been frequent during his term of office, with both students and faculty members engaging in these skirmishes.

Brito Foucher was ousted in 1944 by a student-faculty strike called in order to protest the election of a pro-Brito candidate as the director of the UNAM's National Preparatory School. The rector's opponents accused him of vote buying and refused to accept the election's outcome; they seized the National Preparatory School building and staged a sit-in.[35] Using gangster methods, Brito Foucher unleashed a private force of armed thugs (*porras*) masquerading as students to break the strike, which had spread to other schools at the university; firearms were a component of the porras' arsenal and were used to kill a student at the UNAM's School of Veterinary Medicine.[36] Disgusted by Brito Foucher's policies, the faculty members at the UNAM's Law School, the School of Medicine, and the National Preparatory School resigned en masse as a high stakes gambit to pressure Rodolfo Brito Foucher out as rector.[37] This dramatic measure left Brito Foucher with no other alternative but to resign, which he did on July 27, 1944.[38] The events of 1944 transformed the UNAM; a new university organic law was drafted eliminating the role of faculty and students in electing directors of the university's schools. Student federations lost their seats on the University Council, and the Council itself lost the right to elect the rector, a privilege now transferred to a new governing board or Junta de Gobierno.[39]

Rector MacGregor and the Jesuit Centro Cultural Universitario

The revolution at the UNAM rapidly translated into trouble for the Jesuit-controlled CCU. The university's regulation on incorporated schools demanded that these schools had to reapply for their reincorporation every year, done on a major-by-major basis, a true bureaucratic nightmare, which opened the door to endless harassment of the incorporated institutions if UNAM officials were so inclined. The CCU now had to deal with UNAM officials who were far less sympathetic to their institution than the conservative Brito Foucher. The new political realities facing the Center in the post–Brito Foucher era became apparent in 1945 when the CCU applied for the reincorporation of its courses of philosophy and history, as the UNAM's regulations stipulated. The Jesuit school also sought to broaden its attraction to potential students by including two new majors designed to fulfill the needs of Mexican industrialization—economics and chemistry.[40]

To the CCU's regret, the UNAM's new rector, Fernando MacGregor (1945–1947), took a much sharper line toward the schools incorporated with the university, demanding that they strictly follow the regulations established by the UNAM's Statute of Incorporated Schools. MacGregor criticized the manner of the previous regime-authorized academic programs of incorporating schools without examining whether they complied with the regulations.

The Catholic-dominated Universidad Autónoma de Guadalajara (UAG, Autonomous University of Guadalajara) was an earlier victim of the new vigor that MacGregor brought to the regulation of incorporated schools. In a sharply worded directive, MacGregor stated his belief that the UAG's academic majors did not fulfill the requirements necessary to warrant the UNAM's recognition, but he decided in the end against removing UAG's recognition using the following arguments: "In the specific case of the Autonomous University of Guadalajara it is necessary, although painful, to accept that the National University of Mexico is partially responsible for its academic and administrative deficiencies, for having tolerated them for many years."[41]

MacGregor's stricter attitude toward incorporated schools impacted the CCU as well; no longer would the Jesuit institution have an easy time in gaining the UNAM's recognition for new majors. In fact, the CCU had to fight to preserve the majors it already offered. Initially, the UNAM agreed to grant the CCU incorporation of its courses in philosophy, chemical sciences, history, and economics; however, the UNAM's Commission of Incorporation then decided to solicit opinions from the directors of the UNAM's schools of chemistry, history, philosophy, and economics before rendering its final decision.[42] Given the academic rivalries that exist in even the most collegial universities, this step guaranteed trouble for the Center.

The CCU ran into strong opposition from within the UNAM regarding its expansion plans. Samuel Ramos, director of the UNAM's School of Philosophy, expressed his opinion that "reincorporation should not be granted to the University Center, and in addition any incorporation which was granted in its favor at the time should be nullified." Ramos objected strongly to the CCU's ideological orientation, arguing that "the aforementioned institution is not guided, nor is it willing to be guided, by exclusively university principles, given that its educational orientation is purely confessional, and, consequently the enemy of freedom of thought and of the principle of academic freedom."[43] Ramos also noted how the CCU played fast and loose with Article 4 of the UNAM's Decree on Incorporated Schools, which declared that all incorporated schools recognized by the UNAM had to adapt their curriculum to that of the UNAM. The CCU, he asserted, had subverted this principle, using it as a Trojan horse to teach materials quite different from those at the UNAM. Ramos provided clear examples to buttress his argument. The CCU required their philosophy students to take a course on the history of religion that did not form part of the UNAM's curriculum.[44] The CCU also offered a bachelor's degree in philosophy and advanced studies in religion that were not offered by the UNAM.[45] In spite of the apparent validity of Ramos's arguments, the UNAM's commission on incorporated schools overrode his objections and let the reincorporation of the CCU's philosophy major stand.

Not surprisingly, the UNAM's School of Economics recommended the denial of the CCU's petition to have its economics major recognized. The director of the UNAM's School of Economics, Gilberto Loyo, claimed that the creation of an economics major at the CCU was a poor utilization of resources, maintaining that it would be a waste of private sector resources to establish a new economics school at the CCU, which had a starting class of only eight students, when the UNAM's school had ample room for expansion.[46] The Incorporation Commission's initial response was to reject Loyo's recommendation, validating the Center's economics major in its Resolution #184 of October 24, 1945.[47] However, UNAM Rector MacGregor stepped in and pressured this body to reverse its decision, informing the CCU of this flip-flop in the following memorandum: "This Commission has had to suspend the implementation of its Resolution #184 of October 23 last, which granted the incorporation of the first year of the CCU's B.A. economics major program, as the Rector considers that that resolution violated the Regulation of Incorporated Schools, which stipulates that only entire majors can be incorporated and not fractions of these."[48] This explanation hides the real cause for the rejection of the CCU's economics major, which was ideological. Historically, the Center's previous majors had been incorporated in exactly this piecemeal fashion. The CCU's Jesuit leadership had no doubts about whom to blame for the failure of this project: "[The CCU's Economic School] failed to survive because it was persecuted by the [UNAM's] school directors and openly boycotted by the National School of Economics, infected above all by recognized communists."[49]

The Center suffered another blow when it failed to have its history major program reincorporated by the UNAM. No documentation is available at present explaining why, but it is reasonable to surmise that

Cuevas must have been a lightning rod for leftists and secular humanists at the UNAM's School of History.[50] Despite this major setback, the teaching of history at the CCU survived the disappearance of this program. History courses were incorporated into the philosophy major and a literature program which existed as well. Assuming the teaching burden was José Bravo Ugarte, SJ, author of the three-volume *Historia de México*.[51] Bravo Ugarte's work followed Cuevas's historical perspective, defending Cortés as the founder of the Mexican nation and defending Spain's cultural legacy in Mexico. This Hispanidad ideology contrasted sharply with post-Revolutionary *indigenismo*, emphasizing Mexico's Amerindian inheritance. During the late 1920s and 1930s, the concept of indigenismo became an anticlerical weapon, hence the strident defense of Hispanidad at the 1931 Iberoamerican Convention.[52] Bravo Ugarte's work at the CCU furthered the development of a distinctly Catholic perspective on Mexican history.

In contrast to these defeats, the CCU was successful in gaining the UNAM recognition of its chemistry major program. This can be explained by the inherently less ideological nature of the discipline as well as the political tack that the Jesuit demonstrated in selecting the head of the CCU's school of chemistry, known as the Berzelius Institute. This man was Rafael Illescas Friesbie, and his curriculum vitae bore no resemblance to those of other CCU faculty members. Illescas Friesbie had served on Lázaro Cárdenas's National Council on Higher Education and Scientific Investigation during the 1930s; this council had been bitterly opposed by both Catholic and liberal elements in academia and in civil society in general, for in it they saw an instrument for the destruction of academic freedom and the promotion of Socialist Education in postsecondary institutions.[53] Clearly, Friesbie was not a Catholic ideologue. Of critical importance was the fact that he was also the UNAM's National School of Chemical Sciences' director general. Friesbie's academic reputation and his political independence made it "easy to obtain the [Center's chemistry school's] incorporation to the National Autonomous University."[54]

Despite appearances, the Jesuit leadership of the CCU had not really backtracked ideologically when they selected Illescas Friesbie to be the head of their school of chemistry. In fact, Illescas Friesbie was nothing more than a useful figurehead with excellent connections at the UNAM; the true head of Berzelius Institute was the Jesuit priest Luis Verea.[55]

This type of political camouflage was a tactic that the Jesuit school repeatedly resorted to in these difficult years. And the gaining of the UNAM's recognition of the Berzelius Institute was absolutely essential for the CCU's survival. The chemistry major was aimed at training professionals for Mexico's rapidly expanding industries; this in turn would make the CCU more attractive to the Mexican business community and to a wider student population. The chemistry major project was also designed to correct what the Jesuits perceived to be a major problem within the CCU: the significant gender imbalance of its student body, which favored women over men.[56]

Not surprisingly, frustration with the UNAM's stranglehold over the CCU led its Jesuit administrators to seek its independence from that institution. But for its degrees to have any validity, the CCU needed to win recognition from the federal government's Secretaría de Educación Pública as a "free school." Having free school status would confer upon the CCU many privileges that it did not at that moment enjoy. The 1940 presidential decree on free universities granted these institutions the right to develop their own academic programs and guaranteed that the academic degrees they awarded would be legally recognized throughout Mexico.[57]

There were already two nationally significant free schools operating in Mexico at the time: the prestigious law school Escuela Libre de Derecho of Mexico City; and the Technological and Advanced Studies Institute of Monterrey, commonly known as the Tecnológico. The case of the Tecnológico is particularly relevant to the CCU. Created in 1943 under the patronage of the Monterrey industrialist Eugenio Garza Sada, the Tecnológico also had support from members of the Monterrey Catholic Cultural Center.[58] Garza Sada modeled the Tecnológico after his alma mater, the Massachusetts Institute of Technology. Jesuits served as faculty members and were students' spiritual counselors. These distinctly Catholic elements did not prevent the Tecnológico from having the federal government recognize its academic degrees during the presidency of Miguel Alemán (1946–1952), a conservative pro-business chief executive.[59]

In 1951 the CCU opened up its campaign to win free-school status under the leadership of the Jesuit cleric Félix Restrepo. Restrepo had been tapped by the Jesuit Order to lead this delicate task because he came from Colombia, and so he had no political history in Mexico to poison negotiations with the government. Had Restrepo been active in Mexico during the Cristero Rebellion or the anti–Socialist Education campaign, it would have made it difficult for Alemán, who was the son of a revolutionary general, to openly deal with him despite his own conservative political views. Restrepo's patient negotiating efforts came close to fruition, but ultimately Alemán's advisors managed to convince him that granting the CCU free-university status was politically still too delicate a measure to take.[60] The memories of the fierce religious controversies of the early post-revolutionary era were still too fresh for the government to publically recognize an openly Catholic university. Independence from the UNAM would take another twenty-five years. President Alemán's decision was a bitter disappointment to the CCU community, but rather than crippling the institution it merely served as a catalyst for a period of dynamic growth that transformed the institution into a true university.

Conclusion

The establishment of the CCU was the realization of a long-standing desire by Catholic Church officials to create a Catholic university in Mexico, something that the country had not possessed since the colonial-era Real y Pontíficia Universidad de México was closed down by anti-clerical liberals a century earlier. The CCU also solved the problem of what to do with the politically inconvenient UNEC. And so the CCU was established in 1943 by stripping the defunct UNEC of its resources, both material and human, to create the closest thing to a Catholic university that could be created in Mexico at that time.

At first the CCU enjoyed the patronage and protection of the administrators of the UNAM, which in 1943 was governed by Rodolfo Brito Foucher, whose election as the UNAM's rector had been secured in part by the support he received from Catholic faculty members and students activists. Using these powerful connections, the fledgling Jesuit-controlled CCU was able to initiate the process of developing its academic programs; however, these efforts were derailed in 1944 as the school's patron, Rector Brito Foucher, was ousted in a massive faculty-student rebellion against his authoritarian administration, ushering in a new administration that was unwilling to overlook the CCU's academic shortcomings and deviations from the UNAM's model. In addition, the CCU also had to face, in these post–Brito Foucher years, the ire and retribution of the elements of the larger UNAM academic community who were hostile to the CCU's ideological orientations and political connections. This new and hostile environment created a powerful impetus for the Jesuit-controlled CCU to seek independence from the UNAM by winning government approval for its legal petition to win free-school status, a privilege a few select secular private institutions of higher education had managed to achieve. However, the political realities of Mexican society in the early 1950s precluded this legal solution. Undaunted, the Jesuit college initiated a nearly thirty-year campaign to win this privilege while at the same time transforming itself into a genuine university that offered a complete and innovative curriculum, as will be seen in the next chapter.

CHAPTER FIVE

The "Mexican Economic Miracle" and Vatican II, 1952–1967

The Universidad Iberoamericana

> *Surround a man in an environment which accustoms him to always cultivate his two mentalities, scientific and religious, and you will never encounter conflict [between the two]. . . . What did Saint Thomas and Dante have around them which Goethe and the great philosopher of idealism did not have? A Catholic University.*
>
> —Julio Vértiz, SJ, 1953

Introduction

The 1950s and 1960s were years of curriculum development and institutionalization at the newly renamed Universidad Iberoamericana, and its success during this period was highly dependent on two key factors: the school received economic support from the Mexico City business community, and the institution found a way around the crippling roadblocks which the Universidad Nacional Autónoma de México (UNAM, National Autonomous University of Mexico) placed on its development. During the 1950s, the Iberoamericana started to develop an innovative curriculum oriented toward the needs of the economy's private sector during these times of "Mexico's Economic Miracle" as the nation rapidly expanded its industrial base by embracing the import-substitution-industrialization model: in return, the Mexican business community provided the economic and technical assistance that the school desperately needed. The school's administrators achieved government recognition for a number of its majors, a direct benefit of the improved relations between Mexico's one-party state, dominated by the Partido Revolucionario Institucional (PRI, Institutional Revolutionary Party) and the Roman Catholic Church.

At first the pitfalls of linking the Iberoamericana too closely with the Mexican business community were not apparent, while the benefits of such a relationship were symbolized by the private sector's financing of the Universidad Iberoamericana's modern new campus in the Churubusco section of Mexico City. It was only in the wake of the reforms emanating from the Vatican II Council of 1962–1965 that the dangers of this nexus became apparent. As the Universidad Iberoamericana's Jesuit leadership slowly introduced reforms inspired by the lessons of Vatican II, conflicts between the university and its business patrons increased, and the school became the target of the ire of traditional Catholics. Chapter 6 will analyze how these simmering tensions exploded into all-out conflict as the Universidad Iberoamericana became embroiled in the bloody Mexican Student Movement of 1968, a huge milestone in the history of modern Mexico that inspired a generation of activists determined to bring Mexico's one-party authoritarian political system to an end.

Fomento de Investigación y Cultura Superior Asociación Civil

Undeterred by its failure to win free-school status, in 1952 the Jesuit institution threw off its facade as a "cultural center" of the UNAM, changing its name to the Universidad Iberoamericana. In selecting this title, the institution was identifying with the concept of Iberoamericanism, embraced by the Unión National de Estudiantes Católicos (UNEC, National Catholic Student Union) during the 1930s, and this signaled the university's commitment to promote Catholic culture, which conservative Catholics saw as the unifying element of Latin America.

Members of the Jesuit Order retained control of the school, with a Jesuit always serving as the Iberoamericana's rector. However, the first two rectors were not recognized by the UNAM for reasons that are not altogether clear.[1] The Nicaraguan-born Manuel Ignacio Pérez Alonso, SJ, was the first rector whose authority was recognized by the UNAM (1956). The Iberoamericana's University Council was established in that same year and was comprised of the school's administrators along with the directors of its constituent schools; the Universidad Iberoamericana Asociación Civil (Iberoamerican University Civil Association), the body that legally represented Universidad Iberoamericana, had been constituted in 1954.[2]

In 1956 a financial board of trustees, officially called Fomento de Investigación y Cultura Superior Asociación Civil (FICSAC, Civil

Association for the Promotion of Investigation and Advanced Cultural Studies), was established by Mexican businessmen in order to "initiate, foment, found, and administer" educational, scientific, and cultural institutions at the Universidad Iberoamericana.[3] The need for this body was painfully clear as the Iberoamericana teetered on the brink of insolvency created by severe growing pains throughout the 1950s. The Universidad Iberoamericana's component schools were forced to move from site to site during the 1950s as they outgrew their old surroundings; this created a serious problem as the institution lacked the financial resources to construct the buildings that it urgently required. Moreover, as the Iberoamericana was not an official Catholic university according to canon law, the Roman Catholic Church refused to assume the primary economic burden of sustaining it. The Universidad Iberoamericana's economic problems became so severe that in 1957 it suspended payments to its faculty members after the school ran up a 200,000 peso deficit.[4] Academic majors with low enrollments, such as the Iberoamericana's Law School, were seriously threatened with being disbanded as a consequence of its economic crisis.[5]

The FICSAC's original board was comprised of seventeen members: one woman, Evangelina Rivas de La Chica, and sixteen men.[6] Rivas de la Chica was, ironically enough, the famous "Lady from Oaxaca" whose haunting image was painted (1949) in two beautiful portraits by the atheist, Marxist, and internationally celebrated Mexican artist Diego Rivera. Three of its male members were former presidents of the UNEC: Daniel Kuri Breña, Manuel Ulloa Ortíz, and Armando Chávez Camacho.[7] The heavy presence of former Student Union leaders was not accidental; the Jesuit cleric Julio Vértiz was responsible for selecting the FICSAC's founding board and he relied on "men whom he had formed during the difficult years of the 1930s," when he was the UNEC's spiritual director.[8] In addition to their ties to the defunct UNEC, these three men had been founding members of the Partido Acción Nacional (PAN, National Action Party). The connection between the PAN and the FICSAC did not end there, however. Adolfo Christlieb Ibarra, a founding member of the FICSAC, went on to become the PAN's national president (1961–1965) and Juan Manuel Gómez Morín, the son of founder Manuel Gómez Morín, also sat on the FICSAC's original board.[9]

In 1962 the FICSAC began construction of Universidad Iberoamericana's new Churubusco Campus in Mexico City, which gathered the Iberoamericana's schools together on one site, giving the university visibility and increasing its effectiveness. The financial board was the new campus' legal proprietor and collected the funds to carry out this major enterprise, whose initial phase cost 13.8 million pesos.[10] By 1966, the financial board had spent 46 million pesos on construction, equipment, and the purchase of the land for the Iberoamericana's new campus. The Iberoamericana's strong connections to the business community also allowed it to benefit from foundation and corporation money; for example, the Mexico-based Mary Street Jenkins Foundation, which was chaired by Mexico's leading banker—Manuel Espinosa Iglesias—gave the Iberoamericana 3.5 million pesos in order to establish the television and chemistry laboratories that would help provide the human capital needed for those growing sectors of the Mexican economy.[11] In addition, the Mexican subsidiary of the Italian business equipment firm Olivetti gave the Iberoamericana funds to establish a laboratory for its accounting school in order to provide accounts to a nation that was undergoing an economic boom.[12]

In 1963 the FICSAC took on a new responsibility when it became the school's Junta de Gobierno or governing board under the terms of a contract established between it and the Universidad Iberoamericana. The composition of the Junta de Gobierno was identical to that of the Board of Trustees and its authority superseded that of the Jesuit-dominated University Council. The Junta de Gobierno created a new legal wall of separation between the Jesuit Order and the Universidad Iberoamericana, a barrier that had been undermined by the public and official roles of Jesuits serving as rectors since 1952.[13] By distancing official clerical control over the university, it was hoped, vainly as it turned out, that the federal government would grant the Universidad Iberoamericana free-university status in the near future.[14]

One voice within the Iberoamericana's Jesuit hierarchy, Felipe Pardinas, SJ, called for an even more radical separation between the Jesuit Order and the university. In a March 1958 meeting of the Iberoamericana's University Council, Pardinas suggested that the Iberoamericana be handed over to lay Catholics with the Jesuit Order in a secondary role as instructors, advisors, and spiritual assistants.[15] In addition to solving the university's economic crisis, Pardinas saw this move as providing the Iberoamericana with "greater security vis-à-vis the state" in case the government initiated a new wave of anticlericalism.[16] The Council rejected Pardinas's bold proposal, but the seriousness with which the Jesuits addressed the possibility of new church-state conflict is revealing. The relationship between the Iberoamericana and the Junta de Gobierno soured in the late 1960s, affected by forces barely discernible in the early part of the decade. This rupture was part of fundamental changes within the Roman Catholic Church, which in turn transformed the Universidad Iberoamericana's mission in Mexican society.

Curricular Development: 1950s

The Universidad Iberoamericana's industrial relations major was one of the most significant academic programs the university developed during the 1950s; in fact, the Universidad Iberoamericana introduced this major to Mexico. The program adapted Catholic social doctrine to the practical managerial needs of a modern capitalist economy and was the brainchild of two Jesuit clerics—Emile Bouvier, of the Université de Montréal, and the Iberoamericana's José Sánchez Villaseñor. The French-Canadian cleric Bouvier was the director of the industrial relations section of the University of Montreal—a state-funded Canadian university—whom Sánchez Villaseñor heard lecturing in Mexico. Sánchez Villaseñor brought the program to the Universidad Iberoamericana and Bouvier became the director of the Iberoamericana's new School of Industrial Relations.[17]

Bouvier's views on industrial relations are encapsulated in his book *Neither Right nor Left in Labor Relations* (1951).[18] Bouvier's fear of communism permeates the work; he strongly believed that social institutions, especially labor unions and universities, were infiltrated by the agents of communism (even Catholic ones) and issued a warning to "keep our eyes open and stem the evil."[19] Bouvier saw Catholic social doctrine as the means to blunt Communism's influence among the working class: "The social teachings of the Popes hinder subversive activity and permit the solution of the social problem without resorting to revolution which alone can help the communists to seize power."[20] Bouvier argued that the Roman Catholic Church recognized a set of rights and responsibilities governing the relationship between labor and capital, with a need for *social engineers* who were well grounded in labor law, statistics, psychology, and sociology and in possession of a solid knowledge of Catholic social doctrine.[21] These professionals would assume complex responsibilities, including dealing with labor unions and negotiating collective labor agreements. Maintaining that professionals needed to have knowledge of complex legal regulations, statistics, and the social sciences (psychology and sociology), Bouvier considered a university education as the only way they could carry out their duties.

The Universidad Iberoamericana's industrial relations major was a four-year program; accounting, statistics, economic theory, commercial law, labor law, industrial sociology, and anthropology courses formed its curriculum, with Catholic social doctrine present in many of these courses. Anthropology dealt with the "problems of mankind" as well as "man as a conscious being; as a free being; and as a promoter of values."[22] The industrial sociology program gave a detailed presentation of the Roman Catholic Church's concept of the "common good," and the Iberoamericana's labor law course emphasized the mutual obligations between capital and labor.[23] The Mexico City business community played an active role in developing and shaping the Universidad Iberoamericana's industrial relations program, with executives from Mexico's leading enterprises in the fields of manufacturing, banking, insurance, retail sales, and transportation comprising the program's advisory committee.[24] Such a major fit perfectly within the Mexican economic and political elite's larger goal of transforming Mexico from an agrarian nation to an industrial nation while neutralizing Marxist influence and maintaining social peace.

In what was by then a familiar story, the UNAM once again attempted to roadblock the Universidad Iberoamericana's development by refusing to recognize the Iberoamericana's innovative new major; the UNAM authorities based their decision on the fact that the university's regulations governing incorporated schools demanded that these have a curriculum "the same as or similar to" that of the UNAM, and it did not offer this industrial relations major. The solution to the problem was found in applying directly to the federal government's Ministry of Public Education for recognition of this specific career; this path was also taken by the Universidad Iberoamericana's business administration major, established in 1957 by José Sánchez Villaseñor.[25] In making their case to the Secretaría de Educación Pública (SEP, Secretariat of Public Education), the Iberoamericana claimed that there was a high demand by the Mexican business community for the graduates of both its industrial relations program and business administration programs: "Industrialists and businessmen rush to offer our students positions as soon as they graduate, giving them preference over other applicants."[26] These majors were a success and by 1960 they attracted 14.4 percent of the 3,950 students that attended the Universidad Iberoamericana.[27]

The Iberoamericana's communications science major was another illustration of the Jesuit school's efforts to adapt its curriculum to the needs of private industry. Established in 1960, this major was designed to provide television networks, radio stations, and newspapers with "authentic professionals," and its advisory committee included the entertainment media mogul Emilio Azcárraga Milmo.[28] Its curriculum included courses in economics, statistics, and accounting, with classes in public relations, sociology, psychology, philosophy, and labor law rounding out the plan of studies. Its six-man advisory committee included two former UNEC stalwarts: Daniel Kuri Breña and Armando Chávez Camacho.[29] Their inclusion highlighted a long-standing interest of Catholic activists in using the media to disseminate ideas of Catholic culture, whose importance was recognized at the 1931 Iberoamerican Convention. The Universidad Iberoamericana offered the communications major without the recognition of either the federal government or the UNAM. Despite that, it was not a serious impediment to the program's success, since many of the potential employers of its students were on the major's advisory board. This major attracted 180 students in 1960 or 4.6 percent of the Iberoamericana's total student body.[30]

The Universidad Iberoamericana's industrial design major (1956) was yet another trailblazing program that the Iberoamericana introduced to Mexico. It was dedicated to serving the human capital needs of an industrializing nation. The goals of the industrial design program were to "prepare the student as to make him capable of resolving problems of not only a technical nature, but also those of a scientific and economic origin created by modern mass production [methods]."[31] The industrial design major was developed by Felipe Pardinas, SJ, who was also credited with founding the Iberoamericana's art history major (1953) and the School of Architecture (1955).[32] However, for reasons that are unclear, the industrial design program remained very small, with only twenty students enrolled in 1960.[33] It is possible that this was either due to the major's lack of recognition from either the UNAM or the Ministry of Public Education, or it could have been a consequence of the Mexican industry's dependency on imported technology, which reduced the need for students with a degree in industrial design. The Universidad

Iberoamericana's architecture school was, on the other hand, a success from the beginning, with five hundred students enrolled in 1960.[34] Two members of the Junta de Gobierno also served as faculty members at the Iberoamericana's School of Architecture: Augusto H. Alvarez and Enrique Corral, both architects by profession.[35] These men were later commissioned by the FICSAC to create the architectural plans for the Universidad Iberoamericana's new Churubusco Campus, which became an embarrassing fact and an issue of bitter contention when the campus was destroyed by an earthquake in 1979.[36]

The Iberoamericana's program in engineering was the university's most popular major in 1960, and its six hundred students constituted 15.2 percent of the university's total student body.[37] The cost for establishing this major was born in part by Mexican businessman Cresencio Ballesteros, a construction company owner who served as the president of Universidad Iberoamericana A.C., the university's legal association.[38] Ballesteros had attended the strife-torn Universidad Autónoma de Guadalajara (UAG, Autonomous University of Guadalajara) before it had been closed down by the state government of Jalisco in the 1930s.[39] At some point, Ballesteros established strong links to members of the Jesuit Order, and he made an offer to the head of the Mexican Province of the Society of Jesus, Roberto Guerra, to provide "the money necessary to purchase the indispensable equipment and instruments necessary to open the school of engineering."[40] Ballesteros's narrative goes on to highlight a fundamental point; the Iberoamericana's academic majors needed approval from the superior general of the Society of Jesus in order to be created.[41] In an obvious conflict of interest, Ballesteros's construction company built the Churubusco Campus and he was later embroiled in the controversy that followed the catastrophic collapse of Universidad Iberoamericana's campus in the 1979 earthquake, a seismic event that produced relatively little damage elsewhere in the city.[42]

In 1957 the Universidad Iberoamericana finally managed to have the UNAM recognize its history program, a goal achieved by following the plan of study of the UNAM's history major augmented "with some special materials" to fulfill the Iberoamericana's mandate to promote Catholic culture.[43] With this new major, the Jesuit university was targeting a very specific group of people: teachers at privately operated preparatory schools. According to a 1957 report by the Universidad Iberoamericana's rector Manuel Pérez Alonso to the University Council, there were some eight hundred instructors at private preparatory schools in Mexico, but only 15 percent of these had educational degrees recognized by either the UNAM or the SEP.[44] Pérez Alonso also informed the University Council that most of these preparatory school teachers were women; clearly, there was an educational need that the Universidad Iberoamericana's history program would satisfy. The Iberoamericana's history program would also serve male and female religious, who would enjoy a 50 percent tuition discount, although in order to avoid "unwanted attention" the female religious would attend the Iberoamericana without wearing religious clothing.[45] The Jesuit did not clarify whose attention he wanted the female religious to avoid, whether that of government officials or those of the Iberoamericana's male students.

First National Congress of Catholic Culture: 1953

An important window into the academic culture of the Universidad Iberoamericana during its early years is provided by the 1953 National Congress on Catholic Culture because of the significant participation of Jesuit Iberoamericana faculty members at this event. This assembly, held in Guadalajara in January 1953, brought together intellectuals, professionals, and students in order to "study and affirm Catholic thought in those fields which are currently most under assault in . . . [the] fatherland."[46] The assembly's letter of convocation painted an image of a Mexican society whose "traditional values and great fundamentals" were threatened by a "materialist interpretation of life and human destiny."[47] The presentations made by the Jesuit academics at the congress demonstrate ideological continuity with the doctrines of those promoted in previous decades by the Asociación Católica de la Juventud Mexicana (ACJM, Mexican Catholic Youth Association) and the UNEC.

The Universidad Iberoamericana's Jesuit faculty members at this congress were José Sánchez Villaseñor, Julio Vértiz, Eduardo Iglesias, and David Mayagoita. Sánchez Villaseñor's presentation was a reactionary assault on modern philosophical systems, blaming their human-centered perspective for Western society's "crisis."[48] Rejecting the course of Western intellectual development since the High Middle Ages, Sánchez Villaseñor traced the historical development of what he saw as the breakdown of Western civilization: "We attend the crisis of the false Renaissance humanism, which ripened during the Enlightenment, and the French Revolution, which in Kant found its genial systematizer, gave birth in the nineteenth century to the liberal individualist current and which finally culminated in its tragic antithesis: liberal capitalism vs. Soviet Marxism."[49] This historical process had produced, according to Sánchez Villaseñor, the "dehumanized and cruel man of our times," who "had lost . . . faith in spiritual values" because he had broken his ties to God.[50] The great Enlightenment philosopher Immanuel Kant was criticized for promoting "moral autonomy" and "individualism," which Sánchez Villaseñor saw as twin evils, but not surprisingly he saved his sharpest barbs for Sartrian existentialism, calling it "a true literary fad with its pretentious snobbism" that was "destructive and nihilistic."[51] Sánchez Villaseñor sarcastically paraphrased what he believed to be Sartre's message to society: "Man is nothing. He is a project condemned to be free, a useless passion. The human condition is revealed as being absurd . . . condemned to failure. He lacks any reason for being. God does not exist. Super temporal values are illusions."[52] He decried the "perniciousness" of contemporary, secular philosophical systems on Mexican youth and denounced their impact on Mexican society. Sánchez Villaseñor's discourse paints a picture of a Roman Catholic Church, in those pre–Vatican II Council days, still very much at war with the dominant values of contemporary Western society:

> What can these philosophies of transition and decadence offer of value to young people? What, besides taking from them the supreme values which give meaning to life? Faith in reason, in truth, in mankind, in God . . . if philosophy aspires to be something more than an transcendental topic, a fashionable topic or a literary exercise . . . then it is necessary to abandon the frivolous games of the imagination,[53] the cultural relativism, the insincere and pessimistic views of those [philosophers] in vogue[54] and begin to build on the immovable rock of truth.[55]

The promotion of Catholic culture was Sánchez Villaseñor's solution for Mexican society's crisis. He called on lay Catholics to contribute funds to establish "institutions of higher learning" (universities, libraries, journals) to promote this goal.

Julio J. Vértiz's presentation titled "Relations between Faith and Science" was a defense of both neo-scholasticism and Catholic universities.

Vértiz supported the thesis that the conflict between religion and science was "psychological" in nature and not based on logic.[56] The way this "psychological conflict" between religion and science could be avoided was, according to Vértiz, to establish more Catholic universities and thereby promote a more pervasive Catholic culture in Western society: "Surround a man in an environment which accustoms him to always cultivate his two mentalities, scientific and religious, and you will never encounter conflict [between the two]. The genius would not be Hegel, it would be Saint Thomas . . . the poet would not be Goethe, he would be Dante. . . . What did Saint Thomas and Dante have around them which Goethe and the great philosopher of idealism did not have? A Catholic university."[57] Taking Vértiz's words to heart, the Universidad Iberoamericana established additional mandatory courses in Catholic culture; on the horizon, however, were profound changes that upturned the discourse that these Jesuit clerics had promoted at this Catholic Congress, changes that buffeted the Roman Catholic Church, the Jesuit Order, and institutions like the Universidad Iberoamericana and whose fallout would affect these institutions for decades to come.

Vatican II and the Church Reform Movement

Pope John XXIII's groundbreaking reign as the spiritual leader of Roman Catholicism (1958–1963) ushered in an era of profound change in the church by moving toward ending its hostile relationship with the modern world: a world created by the Protestant Reformation, the Scientific Revolution, the Enlightenment, the French Revolution, and the Industrial Revolution. John XXIII's encyclical *Mater et Magistri* (1961) revitalized Catholic social doctrine by highlighting the needs of the poor, while *Pacem in Terris* (1963) addressed the right of all human beings to education, political participation, and the satisfaction of their basic material needs.[58] This message was echoed and strengthened in what was his greatest legacy—the Church Council known as Vatican II, which met in conclave from 1962 to 1965. In this historic assembly, the Roman Catholic Church affirmed that it was of this world and concerned with the issues and problems that it contained. Vatican II stated the need for Catholics to work toward the creation of more equitable societies and the elimination of poverty.[59] The Vatican II Council also promoted ecumenicalism by reaching out to its "separated brothers," in other words the Protestants and Jews, thereby promoting a healing process in the often-violent relationship between the Catholic Church and those respective religious communities. The Catholic Church also sought to bridge the chasm between the laity and the church hierarchy, proclaiming that the Roman Catholic Church was a "community of equals," in many ways a return to beliefs by the early Christians.[60] Tragically, Pope John XXIII's papacy came to an abrupt end in 1963 after his untimely death, but the boldness of his pontificate had permanently transformed the Roman Catholic Church and brought it into the twentieth century.

In his landmark 1967 encyclical *Popularum Progressio*, Pope Paul VI (1963–1978) continued and expanded the church reform program initiated by his predecessor and broke new ground by focusing on the needs and concerns of the developing world, rather than those of industrial Europe, the point of reference of earlier encyclicals on the social question. In so doing, the pontiff gave recognition to the critical importance of Latin America, Africa, and Asia to the future of Roman Catholicism. Paul's journeys to Latin America (1960) and Africa (1962) as Pope John XXIII's secretary of state powerfully influenced the future pope, as he acknowledged in *Popularum Progressio*. In Africa and Latin America, he came into contact with "the painful problems which afflicted continents full of life and hope."[61] Pope Paul VI believed that all humans entertained the aspiration "to see themselves free from misery, to find with greater assurance their protection from situations which offend their human dignity."[62] The pontiff recognized the brutal reality that "a great number of them are condemned to live in conditions which make these legitimate desires an illusion."[63] Paul VI blasted the extreme social inequalities present in the developing world in the following terms: "While in some regions oligarchies benefit from a refined civilization, the rest of the population, poor and struggling, are denied from almost all of the possibilities of personal initiative and responsibility, and living as well in living and working conditions unworthy of the human person."[64] As pontiff, Paul VI had to look to the church's future and was alarmed by the potential reactions to such conditions: "Who does not see the dangers in it, of the violent popular reactions, of the revolutionary agitation and the slide towards totalitarian ideologies?"[65] Cuba under Fidel Castro had become a Russian client state and revolutionary movements were active in Asia, Africa, and Latin America—all matters of extreme concern to Paul VI and the Roman Catholic Church as a whole.

The papal activism of John XXIII and Paul VI encouraged the development of a radical new theology in Latin America, liberation theology, in which European-trained Latin American theologians led by Peruvian Gustavo Gutiérrez used social science perspectives and Marxist class analysis in order to understand the realities of Latin America, to diagnose its problems, and to work for the region's betterment.[66] Embracing the lessons of the Vatican II Council, liberation theologians redefined the Roman Catholic concept of sin, no longer seeing it as a mere personal failing; rather, they emphasized the role which highly oppressive social structures played in condemning the poor to spiritual and physical degradation and advocated social policies that, in their view, would liberate the poor from their condition by transforming the structures oppressing them.[67] They also sought to free oligarchs from the sin they committed by oppressing those whom they should see as their Christian brothers and sisters. Furthermore, liberation theologians asserted that those who did not actively struggle to change the structures were in a state of sin. Liberation theology transformed the traditional relationship between the Catholic Church and Latin American elites and exposed members of the clergy to the extreme violence that so often had been used by the elites against the poor in their quest to maintain their social position.

Advocates of liberation theology dominated the 1968 Conference of Latin American Bishops of Medellín, Colombia, propelling this discourse to the forefront in Latin America. The influence of liberation theology and *Popularum Progressio* permeated the conference's denunciation of "structural sin" in its call for social justice and in the declaration that the Roman Catholic Church in Latin America would have a "preferential option for the poor."[68] The bishops soundly denounced economic development models that "contemplate possibilities only with the [social] sectors with high purchasing power" and which feed a lack of social "solidarity" (i.e., the unity of all Christians). These economic models had spawned the "unjust structures that characterize the Latin American condition."[69]

At the Medellín Conference, the Latin American bishops expressed a passionate belief in the power of education to "liberate" the great number of marginalized people living in Latin America from the oppression they suffered on a daily basis.[70] They were cognizant that conventional educational systems could not achieve this end, however, as these were designed to maintain "the existing social and economic structures rather than [seeking] their transformation."⁷¹ In its place, the progressive bishops of Medellín endorsed the pedagogical model of the Brazilian educator Paolo Freire, whose pedagogy of the oppressed sought not merely to teach basic literacy to the masses but also aimed to "prepare men and women to become conscious agents of their own integral development."⁷² To that end, the bishops at Medellín called upon Catholic colegios and universities to contribute the liberation of Latin America's poor; the Medellín Conference recommended that these institutions instill in their students a "healthy critical perspective on the social situation" and encourage the development of a social service vocation.⁷³

The promotion of Catholic culture was conspicuously absent in this post–Conciliar era document. Rather than waging war against modern society, the Latin American Bishops' Conference recognized that "in front of cultural change the Church has not always appreciated the new values of modern society nor has it developed a clear view of the new society in which it is living; a pluralist society in the process of secularization, a mass culture society."⁷⁴ The conference did not call on Catholic universities and schools to stem the advance of Protestantism in Latin America; rather, the Medellín Conference lamented that ecumenicalism was hampered by "Catholicism's traditional defensiveness" and its "official status in many of our [Latin American] nations," which offended the "principle of religious liberty."⁷⁵ These sentiments were diametrically opposed to Catholic religious orthodoxy and emphasize how profoundly the Roman Catholic Church in Latin America had changed from the time of the 1931 Iberomerican Convention and even from the 1953 Catholic Congress.

Church Reform and the Universidad Iberoamericana

The Universidad Iberoamericana was profoundly affected by the currents of change emanating from the church reform movement of the 1960s; this could not be otherwise, as this movement undercut what had been the Iberoamericana's original reason for being: promoting a pre–Vatican II definition of Catholic culture. The Jesuit Order's support for institutions like the Universidad Iberoamericana, which catered to the needs of Mexico's "living forces," was undermined by the Latin American church's new focus on the educational needs of the poor. The Jesuit Order's general superior, Pedro Arrupe,⁷⁶ expressed regret at the Jesuit Order's traditional emphasis on influencing "the ruling social classes and the education of the leaders thereof" at the expense of attending to the needs of the poor.[77] Arrupe wrote in a letter to the Latin American superiors of the Jesuit Order that "the Society [of Jesus] has a definite moral obligation to visibly make amends for what we Jesuits have failed and are failing to do to aid social justice and equity."[78] He further lamented the Order's failure to "seek social justice through the education of the poor."[79] In Mexico and elsewhere, Jesuits such as Bernardo Bergöend and Ramón Martínez Silva believed that the elites could be made agents of social reform by instructing them in Catholic social doctrine; however, by the end of the 1960s, the Jesuit Order in Mexico rejected this belief as a fallacy.[80] The tragic events of 1968, which will be analyzed and discussed in chapter 6, also served to shift the Mexican Jesuit Order's focus from servicing the educational needs of the elite to addressing the myriad needs of the poor.[81]

The prestigious Mexican Jesuit colegio, the Instituto Patria, became a victim of the Order's new educational policies. The Patria was Mexico City's most exclusive Catholic preparatory school, and its history mirrored the ups and downs of church-state relations in post-revolutionary Mexico. In the 1930s political repression had forced the Jesuit directors of the Instituto Patria to cede formal control of the school to a group of pliant lay Catholics; this arrangement lasted for a decade until the conservative Manuel Ávila Camacho administration's arrival to the presidency allowed the Jesuit Order to drop this subterfuge. The Patria prospered in this new political environment, and by the late 1960s the school had a student body of 2,500 students and the demand for admittance was such that the school's Jesuit administrators imposed rising academic and tuition requirements in order to keep the student population stable; many Patria students went on to the Universidad Iberoamericana.[82] Then in January 1971, the Patria's Jesuit directors announced the school's closure. This totally unexpected announcement left the Patria's students and parents in stunted disbelief. After recovering from their initial shock, the parents launched a storm of protests against the decision, but the Jesuit authorities refused to reverse their decision.[83] Using the proceeds from the sale of the Instituto Patria's assets, the Jesuits created the Fomento Cultural y Educativo (1972), whose goal was to sponsor new educational and social projects for the urban and rural poor; these projects were located in the slums of Ciudad Netzahualcóyotl, which borders Mexico City, the Bachajón Mission in the highlands of Chiapas, and in the central state of Hidalgo and the Gulf state of Veracruz.[84]

The case of the Instituto Patria graphically demonstrated the Jesuit Order's determination to embrace the needs of the poor over of its old practice of servicing the interests of the rich. The Universidad Iberoamericana, the Jesuit Order's crowning educational institution in Mexico, also had to deal with the new Jesuit Order's orientation. In the coming years, this would lead to strained relationships between the Iberoamericana and many of those groups who in previous decades had been its most ardent supporters.

The "University of Christian Inspiration"

After a few years of digesting the changes generated by the church reform movement, the Jesuit leadership at the Universidad Iberoamericana produced the *Ideario de la Universidad Iberoamericana* (1968), which was promulgated by the University Council on the eve of the Medellín Conference. The Iberoamericana's *Ideario* stated that the Universidad Iberoamericana was not a Catholic institution of higher education, but rather one of "Christian Inspiration" that would have "as a fundamental norm respect for the freedom of all persons and the diffusion of the spirit of service within its faculty, its students, and its collaborators."[85] The *Ideario* served as recognition that the ideological straitjacket that the Universidad Iberoamericana had imposed on its faculty members and student body in earlier years, which had been loosened in recent years, was to be completely removed.

The *Ideario* also put the Universidad Iberoamericana on the path of "serving Mexico by collaborating in the promotion of changes in accordance with the [principle] of social justice."[86] As a consequence, the Iberoamericana would "attempt to instill in all of its members a living and working consciousness of Mexico's social problems, and of the consequent responsibility of cooperating in resolving these."[87] To further this goal, the Iberoamericana would seek to put its students "in direct contact with the nation's realities, and establish as an element of its curriculum an authentic social service which benefits the community."[88] This goal became a reality when its Jesuit rector Ernesto Meneses (1968–1976) instituted a mandatory social service program for the Iberoamericana's students. These young men and women were sent to Mexico City's poor neighborhoods to aid the local residents and to gain a sense of social consciousness, largely absent in the Iberoamericana's privileged student body.[89] The Universidad Iberoamericana's social service program was intended to open students' eyes to the plight of the large numbers of ordinary Mexicans who had been denied the benefits of the so-called Mexican Economic Miracle of the post–World War II era. Anticipating protests from conservative parents of the Iberoamericana's student body, the University Council justified their actions by stating that it was the university's obligation to become an agent in Mexico's transformation into a more just society.[90]

The Universidad Iberoamericana's 1968 *Ideario* articulated changes to be made in the institution, a reflection of the spirit or reform emanating from Vatican II. Another manifestation of this process was the founding of the journal *Comunidad*, or Community, in 1966; this scholarly periodical, edited by Felipe Pardinas, SJ, was attached to the Iberoamericana's School of Social and Political Sciences, which had been created in 1964 by that same cleric. The Iberoamericana's School of Political and Social Sciences reflected the Jesuit university's commitment to face the modern world—in their view, to make incarnate the spirit of Vatican II.

In the decade of the 1960s, Pardinas, along with the faculty and students of the disciplines of anthropology, sociology, and political science, were at the forefront of the Iberomerican University's ideological transformation. A new level of student activism, heretofore nonexistent at the Iberoamericana, was expected from the students of this new school. The issue was raised at a June 24, 1965, University Council meeting, in which students' right of expression was discussed.[91] The issue, as encapsulated by Councilor Héctor González Uribe, SJ, was the need to

> maintain on the one hand the apolitical position of the Iberoamerican University and on the other develop the capabilities and activities of the political science student, of course seeking [at the same time] to develop in them a high scientific level. It is intended that the students understand and interpret political phenomena. For that reason it is necessary for them to know the diverse political currents, [both] national as well as international. The student should not only know them but should also try to study and discuss these, and this explains why some type of conflict can be generated.[92]

The statute that emerged from the University Council specified that the School of Political and Social Sciences would be autonomous from all political parties, favoring no political party in its curriculum, activities, or publications. Furthermore, the University Council disavowed all positions and declarations emanating from the School of Political and Social Sciences not approved beforehand by the school's director.[93] Future events were to prove that the University Council was correct in anticipating difficulties for the university from student activism, as the Universidad Iberoamericana found itself involved in the dramatic events of the Mexican student movements of 1968 and 1971, episodes that altered the nation's political development.

Pardinas's "Letter from the Editor," published in the first issue of *Comunidad*, is a document that uneasily attempted to combine pre-Conciliar perspectives with those emanating from Vatican II.[94] Echoing traditional Mexican Catholic discourse, Pardinas criticized the French and Mexican Revolutions for their spread of the "virus" of individualism, while faulting the Russian Revolution of 1917 for creating new "social responsibilities without individual or social liberties."[95] However, the Jesuit cleric rejected the East-West dichotomy of the Cold War and in this he drew on the Conciliar Reform Movement. Pardinas affirmed that Christianity "inspired in the Second Vatican Council" sought to "serve human society and not to isolate itself from it, to contribute efficiently to the fomentation of peace and solidarity between all of the different cultures of the world. From the social anthropological point of view, it can be said that this orientation tends to strengthen the sense of brotherhood between Christians and non-Christians and to weaken the traces of sectarianism that some groups of Christians could give to their religiosity."[96] The views presented in the journal *Comunidad* were not necessarily those of the Universidad Iberoamericana but were intended to present to the outside community the notion that "the Iberoamerican University is the place where the small light of social humanism and world Christianity burns brightly."[97]

The spirit of Vatican II, of the Roman Catholic Church wishing to engage itself in the world, shines through many of the articles published in *Comunidad*. Raúl Olmedo's article "El Estructuralismo y las Teorias de Althusser, Debray y Gunder Sobre el Funcionamiento del Capitalismo Actual" (February 1968) is reflective of this new intellectual openness at the Iberoamericana. The article's purpose was to explain, not condemn, intellectual currents within the New Left of the 1960s. Like it or not, Olmedo explained, structuralism had become "the most debated, the most important theory amongst the Latin American Left" that sought to do away with a "mummified Marxism which was closed to all new ideas."[98] In 1967, in a series of articles published in *Comunidad*, Raúl V. Duarte raises the possibility of Marxist-Christian dialogue; specifically, he commented on the French Marxist philosopher Roger Garaudy's invitation to initiate dialogue with old and bitter ideological enemies, Christians and Marxists. Duarte reasoned that as one-third of the population (1968) professed the Christian faith and one-third followed the doctrines of Karl Marx, "the future of humanity could not be constructed against [the interests] of the believers and the non-believers."[99] In an article published by Raymundo Ozanam de Andrade in 1967, the author expressed the belief that "believers and non-believers . . . can break down the wall which separates them and begin together a genuine reflection, without any sentimental or intellectual concessions, on the necessity and possibility of constructing a tolerant world that effectively respects the philosophical and religious options of each and every one."[100] Given the Catholic Church's previous leading role in the struggle against world communism, these calls for dialogue reflected the sea of change that was taking place within the Catholic Church during the 1960s.

The Universidad Iberoamericana contributed to this process of Christian-Marxist dialogue by giving some of Mexico's most influential leftists a forum for expressing their views. The Iberoamericana invited the ancient Catholic nemesis Vicente Lombardo Toledano to deliver a presentation at the school, as well as Carlos Madrazo, the former 1930s Marxist student leader and scourge of the UNEC who in the 1960s had led an unsuccessful reform of the PRI, Mexico's ruling party.[101] To those who founded the Jesuit university in 1943, it was inconceivable that these two men, who had led the Socialist Education campaign during the 1930s, would one day be invited to speak at the Universidad Iberoamericana.

It is important to acknowledge that the church reform movement was not universally approved within Mexico's larger Catholic community. Traditionalists, both within the clergy and among lay Catholics, were outraged by the ecumenical movement, the church's new focus on the needs of the poor, liturgical reform, and a host of other issues. The editor of *Comunidad*, Felipe Pardinas, SJ, was often singled out by conservative Catholics for attack, especially by the reactionary, anti-Semitic Mexican Jesuit priest Joaquín Saénz y Arriaga. This cleric articulated the fantastically bizarre belief that the church reform movement was part of nefarious plot by "international Jewry" to seize control of the Roman Catholic Church, a plot led by none other than Pope Paul VI: "Is Giovanni B. Montini [Pope Paul VI] a real Catholic or an infiltrate, a Jew who is being remotely controlled by the mafia? In the beginning this was only suspicion; now there is almost evidence that Paul VI is no legitimate Pope, but an anti-Pope, a Jew trained by the mafia to climb, using despicable means as well as time, money, and evident cunning, for the benefit of those who have always dreamed of dominating the world."[102] It is hardly surprising that Saénz y Arriaga's vicious beliefs and statements ultimately led church officials to defrock and excommunicate him.

Saénz y Arriaga placed Pardinas in his crosshairs because of Pardinas's involvement in what became known as the Lemecier Affair. This controversy arose when the Benedictine Abbot Gregorio Lemercier used psychoanalysis at his Santa María de la Resurrección Monastery (Cuernavaca) in the "selection of the religious vocations and in the spiritual perfection of the souls consecrated to God."[103] Lemercier's use of psychoanalysis was eventually condemned by the Holy Office [of the Inquisition] in a 1965 ruling, a decision later modified by a special Tribunal of Cardinals appointed by Pope Paul VI (May 18, 1967).[104]

The Tribunal of Cardinals, while prohibiting Lemercier from using psychoanalysis in the selection for process of future novices, did reinstate him as the Abbot of the Santa María de la Resurrección Monastery. However, the story did not end there. Lemercier then informed the French newspaper *Le Monde* of his intention to transform the monastery into a new community called the "House of Emmaus," which would no longer be affiliated with the Benedictine Order. Going even further, he stated that in the House of Emmaus, monastic vows would be abolished and its members would no longer be bound to any vow of celibacy.[105] Psychoanalytical principles and practices were to be a prominent element of the new community. In keeping the ecumenical spirit of the Vatican II Council, the House of Emmaus was to be open to all, "without distinction to ideology, religion, or race," and as such would no longer be an institution under the authority of the Roman Catholic Church.[106]

Progressive Jesuit clerics like Felipe Pardinas refused to condemn

Lemercier's experiment out of hand. Pardinas identified Lemercier's movement as a "Christian challenge" in a television program he hosted (June 18, 1967) and pleaded that before the Catholics "pass a judgment" they should consider "this moment in the Church's transformation."[107] Pardinas implied that Lemercier's experiment was derived from this spirit of change when he stated that "my action does not pretend to be either a defense or an attack on Lemercier. I feel that inspiration of the [Vatican II] Council and [Pope] John XXIII on Christianity's future life is irreversible. [I also believe] that public opinion, of which I feel I am a humble spokesman of, is a right of all Christians, made more so when it was something Vatican II exhorted us so energetically [to express]."[108]

The Lemercier episode absolutely enraged conservative Mexican Catholics. Saénz y Arriaga blasted Lemercier as a "betrayer of God" and as a rebel against the authority of Rome, and he labeled Pardinas as Lemercier's "fellow traveler."[109] Saénz y Arriaga also denounced Pardinas as an "advocate of violence" for his promotion of liberation theology at the 1968 Medellín Conference.[110] René Capistrán Garza, another prominent Catholic conservative, the one-time president of the ACJM during the Cristero Rebellion of the 1920s and a staunch admirer of the reactionary Saénz y Arriaga, maintained that the church reform movement had created a "false church" juxtaposed with the pre-Conciliar traditions defended by conservatives.[111]

Conclusion

The early history of the Universidad Iberoamericana deepens our understanding of Catholic institutions during the modus vivendi between the Mexican State and the Roman Catholic Church. Large-scale persecution of the Roman Catholic Church had ceased, but as demonstrated, the Iberoamericana was still adversely affected by the legacy of this conflict. The Iberoamericana's main difficulties did not come from the state, but rather from non-Catholic elements at the UNAM who were unsympathetic to the Universidad Iberoamericana's efforts to Christianize Mexico through the education of its "living forces." The Iberoamericana's reliance on a network of old National Student Union members and Mexican businessmen to deal with the university's economic and political difficulties proved to be a double-edged sword. At first, this arrangement appeared to be completely beneficial for the Iberoamericana. Private enterprises' patronage of the Iberoamericana allowed it to build a modern, new campus and cover its operating deficits. In return, the university helped to resolve the private sectors' needs for trained professionals in specific fields. The granting of formal control of the Iberoamericana to a lay board of trustees was designed to accrue political benefits vis-à-vis the Mexican state. The pitfalls of this strategy became apparent only later, after the advent of reform within the Roman Catholic Church as a consequence of the Vatican II Council (1962–1965). As will be seen in chapter 6, the Iberoamericana's lay Catholic Junta de Gobierno sparred with its academic community as a consequence of ideological differences. These differences emerged out of Vatican II and from the newly articulated liberation theology. These currents permeated Iberoamericana through the vehicle of the Jesuit Order. The Iberoamericana's social mission changed dramatically as a consequence of this, and these changes alienated the Junta de Gobierno from the Iberoamericana's academic community. Chapter 6 places Iberoamericana's internal conflict within the context of a larger crisis within the Mexican Right of the 1960s—one which spelled the end of the anti-Communist consensus.

CHAPTER SIX

Tlatelolco, the Corpus Christi Massacre, and the Transformation of the Universidad Iberoamericana, 1968–1979

> *For the Christian of today the greatest sin is that of non-participation.*
> *... the participation of the Christian in the social process of liberation is not optional. It is essential for Christians to reject injustice.*
>
> Carlos Palomar, SJ, 1968

Introduction

The years from 1968 to 1979 were the most dramatic and important in the history of the Universidad Iberoamericana; during this decade, the university was engulfed in the Mexican Student Movement of 1968 and its corollary the 1971 Corpus Christi Massacre, which were two of the most important episodes in the history of post-revolutionary Mexico. The university also experienced an internal conflict that pitted the school's politically conservative board of trustees against leftist faculty members and students with the end result being the creation of a new system of university governance that was more democratic than what had existed previously and which better protected academic liberties and freedom of expression within the university.

The Mexican Student Movement of 1968, which reached its climax with the Tlatelolco Student Massacre on October 2, 1968, was a milestone in the history of modern Mexico. These young men and women had organized themselves in the hope of transforming Mexico's authoritarian political culture and narrowing its extreme social inequalities; the government of President Gustavo Díaz Ordaz (1964–1970) responded to their demands with an act of violence that has haunted Mexico to this day. These horrible events were also a milestone in the history of the Universidad Iberoamericana and showed to the society at large how much the school had changed as a consequence of reforms inspired by the Second Vatican

Council; during the Mexican Student Movement of 1968, the Universidad Iberoamericana's faculty members and students assumed political positions that were unimaginable a decade earlier, and as a consequence of this activism the institution became the target of the ire of the government and its supporters as well as those religious conservatives opposed to the reforms emanating from the Vatican II Council.

The political activism displayed by elements of the university community during the Mexican Student Movement of 1968 also angered the school's politically conservative business patrons, who lost no time in using their control of the Iberoamericana's finances in order to punish the institution. Eventually, the heavy-handed tactics of the Universidad Iberoamericana's patrons sparked a successful campus revolt against their influence over the college led by leftist faculty members and students, which was an act that would have been both inconceivable and outrageous to those who had created the school in the 1940s. These estranged parties came together, however, to rebuild the Universidad Iberoamericana following a devastating 1979 earthquake that destroyed most of the school's infrastructure and which put the university's future existence in grave doubt. And in the midst of all of this turmoil, the Universidad Iberoamericana was finally able to liberate itself from the Universidad Nacional Autónoma de México (UNAM, National Autonomous University of Mexico)'s control by winning the federal Ministry of Public Education's official recognition, in large part because the Jesuit school's original goal of promoting a Catholic culture in Mexico had been abandoned for others in the post–Vatican II era.

The Mexican Student Movement of 1968

Mexican leftists, revitalized and electrified by the example given by the Cuban Revolution of 1959, were the driving force behind the Mexican Student Movement of 1968. The growth of left-wing forces in Mexico was manifested in the emergence of the National Liberation Movement (1961), a network of Marxist student associations on Mexico's university campuses, and in the rise of first rural and then urban guerrilla organizations. The National Liberation Movement brought together figures from the Old Left—Lázaro Cárdenas, Vicente Lombardo Toledano, and the Mexican Communist Party—in support of Fidel Castro and the Cuban Revolution; although internal differences doomed the National

Liberation Movement, it did serve to spread the message of the Cuban Revolution to Mexican society.[1]

Mexico's first Cuban-inspired guerilla movement emerged in 1965 in the rugged mountains (sierra) of the northern state of Chihuahua, a region dominated by cattle barons who possessed huge estates that were often in violation of Mexico's agrarian laws. In a clear echo of Fidel Castro's historic attack on the Moncada Barracks, on September 23, 1965, a small group of fighters led by Arturo Gámiz, a twenty-four-year-old rural schoolteacher and leftist activist, attacked an isolated army garrison of Madera. The action was disastrous; eight fighters of the thirteen-man guerrilla force comprised of rural school teachers, students, and landless peasants were killed along with five federal army soldiers. In the wake of the attack, the survivors of the Chihuahua-based guerrilla group established the "23 of September" movement and eventually joined forces with Lucio Cabañas's insurgent forces in the impoverished southern state of Guerrero. Cabañas was, like Gámiz, a leftist rural school teacher and his "Partido de los Pobres" (Party of the Poor) had emerged in 1967 following a massacre of striking teachers and their peasant supporters by pro-government forces. The Partido de los Pobres was finally crushed in 1974 by the Mexican Army and Lucio Cabañas killed the government's security forces.[2]

Pro-Castro Marxist groups also made important inroads in Mexico's universities (and other Latin American universities) during the early 1960s. In 1963 the Mexican Communist Party established a new student confederation called the National Center of Democratic Students that quickly became a major force in organizing students at universities throughout the country.[3] Student actions in regional universities often began over non-ideological but pressing matters, such as the federal government's woefully inadequate funding of provincial universities.[4] The Center of Democratic Students took these protests to a higher level, incorporating political demands as well; however, Marxist agitation was not the only factor fueling this wave of student unrest. President Díaz Ordaz's repressive policies were absolutely critical in galvanizing student opposition to the government, eventually spreading to a broad-based movement including major elements of the Mexican urban-dwelling middle classes.

Díaz Ordaz had already given ample evidence of his political inflexibility and his penchant for using state violence against dissidents prior to the events of 1968, a lethal combination that was to come to full flower during the Mexican Student Movement of 1968 crisis. An example of Díaz Ordaz's political rigidity was his sacking of Carlos Madrazo, the one-time student activist of the 1930s who in the mid-1960s served as president of the ruling Partido Revolucionario Institucional (PRI, Institutional Revolutionary Party).[5] Madrazo's political offence was his attempt to introduce a measure of democracy to the PRI's candidate selection process and thereby undermine the authority of political bosses within the party, of whom the president was the most powerful. Not surprisingly, Madrazo's initiative was met by powerful resistance from the entrenched interests within the ruling party, and the episode ended with Madrazo's fall from power. Díaz Ordaz's ouster of Carlos Madrazo as the PRI's president was a clear signal to all of Mexican society of the regime's intention to preserve the status quo at all costs. The administration had also indicated that it would not tolerate any anti-government activism on university campuses when it sent in the army to brutally crush university strikes at regional universities in the states of Michoacán and Tabasco.[6] The government's strong reaction to this student unrest was no doubt related to the fact that these states were the strongholds of the two strongest left-wing critics of Díaz Ordaz within the PRI. Michoacán was, and remains to this day, the powerbase of the Cárdenas family, which in the 1960s was still led by former president Lázaro Cárdenas, whose progressive policies had made him an icon of the Mexican political left, while Tabasco was Carlos Madrazo's political fiefdom.[7]

The Mexican Student Movement of 1968 began inauspiciously enough on July 23 as a street brawl in Mexico City between overly aggressive and immature teenage students from rival schools: the UNAM and the Instituto Politécnico Nacional (IPN, National Polytechnic Institute). At the time, Mexico City was governed by an ex-military man named Alfonso Corona del Rosal, who had been picked personally by President Díaz Ordaz for this sensitive position and was cut from the same conservative, authoritarian political cloth as the president. Corona del Rosal had no patience for hormone-fueled student high jinks as the city prepared to host the 1968 Summer Olympics and sent in the *granaderos*, Mexico City's notoriously brutal riot police, to put an end to the melee with unwarranted violence.

The painful thrashing that the students received at the hands of the granaderos spurred them to put aside their petty differences and to concentrate on their true enemy: Mexico's authoritarian one-party state and the economic policies that it embraced, which while generating sustained economic growth had also fostered growing social inequality.[8] On July 26, 1968, the fifteenth anniversary of Fidel Castro's assault on the Moncada Barracks, students from the UNAM's National Preparatory School staged a protest march through the streets of Mexico City against the granaderos, converging with a separate march carried out by the communist Center of Democratic Students.[9] These two marches came together at Mexico City's *zócalo*, the historic central plaza where both the seat of state and church power, the Presidential Palace and the National Cathedral, have been located for centuries. This public demonstration challenged the law of social dissolution, which was initially created in 1944 to curtail the activities of Axis spies and saboteurs during World War II and had morphed over the years to become the centerpiece of Mexico's authoritarian system; for decades the hated law of social dissolution had been used by the PRI to crush legitimate anti-government protests and movements against the one-party state.

Corona del Rosal was beside himself at this public challenge to this authority and once again called the granaderos into action; he hoped that simply clubbing the students into submission would end the escalating political crisis. Far from intimidating the students, however, the incipient movement became increasingly radicalized as a consequence of the government's heavy-handed policies. The Center of Democratic Students' entry into the conflict widened the parameters of the embryonic public protest movement; not only did the Center of Democratic Students demand the abolition of the hated riot police, but they also sought the release of political prisoners and the abolition of the law of social dissolution. The release of the Marxist railroad leader Demetrio Vallejo became a specific demand of the Mexican Student Movement of 1968; in 1958 Vallejo organized a celebrated railroad strike that the army broke up, and he had been languishing in jail ever since, yet another victim of the notorious law of social dissolution.[10] Gustavo Díaz Ordaz, as the interior minister of then-president Adolfo López Mateos, was instrumental in the crushing of the 1958 railroad workers' strike and of Demetrio Vallejo's subsequent imprisonment.

Unable to contain the growing student unrest, which had now spread to include a strike at the UNAM's National Preparatory School, an exasperated Corona del Rosal appealed to the federal government for support; the hard-line president did not hesitate in giving his affirmative response. On July 29th President Díaz Ordaz sent the national army into the fray and by doing so turned a smoldering conflict into a full-blown political conflagration. Not only did the army violate the UNAM's jealously guarded autonomy by moving into the National Preparatory School, they did so by using a maximum level of violence, employing a powerful anti-tank weapon to blast down the ancient wooden doors of the colonial-era building that housed the National Preparatory School without consideration for loss of human life or damage to the building's world-famous Diego Rivera murals.[11] Díaz Ordaz's thuggery turned Mexico City into a battleground as he treated these dissident Mexican youth as if they were an invading enemy force that had to be militarily crushed.

The *bazukazo*,[12] as the military's attack on the National Preparatory School was popularly called, radicalized Mexico City's university students, sparking strikes at the UNAM and the IPN, the nation's two largest and most important public universities. A National Strike Committee was created on August 2, 1968, dominated by Marxist students of the Center of Democratic Students, which organized the largest anti-government demonstrations that any post-Revolution government had ever had to confront; the August 27, 1968, demonstration brought together 400,000 people, while 250,000 persons participated in the "Silent March" of September 13. These marches drew not only students but also workers and middle-class Mexicans united in their desire to change Mexico's authoritarian political culture. Díaz Ordaz's government was incensed that these huge protests were overshadowing the public relations buildup to the 1968 Summer Olympics, due to be held in Mexico City in October of that year, and tarnishing his government's international image and reputation.

Unaccustomed to such public demonstrations of dissent, Díaz Ordaz's government lashed out against its perceived enemies with ever-increasing levels of violence; one step was the army's occupation of the UNAM (close to the main Olympic site) on September 18 and the IPN three days later. The government's goal was to decapitate the movement by arresting its leadership, which was based at these schools. In response to these actions, the National Strike Committee members still at liberty transferred their headquarters to the Tlatelolco Housing Project and called a mass meeting at Tlatelolco's historic Plaza of Three Cultures for October 2, 1968, to protest the government's use of military force. The spiral of governmental repression reached its apocalyptic climax on the rainy evening of October 2, when at the signal of an overflying military helicopter the Mexican Army opened fire point-blank on the unarmed, defenseless crowd of young men and women huddled among the Pre-Cortesan ruins and the colonial-era temple of Santiago Tlatelolco; among the pitiful images recorded after the massacre were the scores of women's high-heeled shoes abandoned by their terrified owners as they fled for their lives. The Díaz Ordaz government admitted that fifty-seven people had been killed, but independent analysts calculated that the true death rate ran in the hundreds, and in the days and weeks that followed many activists were arrested and tortured by the security forces, with young people hiding or destroying their student identification cards in order to escape arrest.[13] The government held their now-blood-tainted Olympic Games and tried to pretend to the outside world that stability had been restored in Mexico; however, this was not the case. The Tlatelolco Massacre was a defining moment in the history of modern Mexico, creating a generation of activists who would struggle in the coming decades, mostly through peaceful means, to bring down Mexico's one-party state.

The Universidad Iberoamericana during the Mexican Student Movement of 1968

The Universidad Iberoamericana was profoundly affected by the events of 1968, with the students of the social science majors, whose disciplines were most directly affected by the Roman Catholic Church's renewed emphasis on helping the poor, being those most active in the movement. The Iberoamericana's transformation, under the impact of the church reform movement, was also publically demonstrated by the Mexican Student Movement of 1968.

The first public demonstration of the Universidad Iberoamericana's involvement in the student movement came on August 15, 1968, when an assembly of sociology, political science, and social anthropology students published a manifesto in the leading Mexico City newspaper *Excélsior* in which they articulated their solidarity with the student movement and its goals. The document highlighted the deep level of students' social and political awareness and the responsibilities that they as university students felt they had toward the larger Mexican society: "In the present day the role which university students are playing forms a call to the people's conscience and a real collaboration in the transformation of a deficient social order. There exists in Mexico few civic groups as capable as university students in raising their voices and both demanding and collaborating in the acceleration of the changes in the social structures which are indispensable to the realization of a dignified life for all Mexicans."[14] Believing that conflict was deeply rooted in Mexico's social inequalities, the students went further, stating that "It is our conviction that this is not a passing social crisis, but rather a manifestation of great national problems that are non-resolved or poorly addressed."[15] Unequal income distribution, racial discrimination against the indigenous population, and unbalanced economic development policies that did not benefit the bulk of the population were, according to the Iberoamericana's students, Mexico's gravest social failings.[16] They also made specific demands that addressed the needs of the moment, including the freeing of all political prisoners, the reform of the granaderos, and the abolition of the law of social dissolution in order to "avoid [becoming] legal instruments of oppression."[17] Putting their words into action, the Universidad Iberoamericana students sent representatives to the National Strike Committee and participated in the brigades carrying out the grassroots work of mobilizing student support.[18]

The Universidad Iberoamericana's administrators took a cautious and conservative approach to the mushrooming student movement; for instance, they decided not to cancel the 1968–1969 academic year in spite of the ongoing student strike at the major public institutions. Conditions were far from normal, however, and there was a constant and well-founded fear by students, faculty, and administrators that the Iberoamericana's campus would be stormed by the army in reprisal for the participation of elements of its university community in the movement. This fear was fueled by the military's seizure of the campuses of both the UNAM and the IPN and the fact that Iberoamericana students were among 1,500 persons arrested in these raids.[19] The Universidad Iberoamericana's rector, Ernesto Meneses, SJ, did temporarily close down the college on September 23, after the army's seizure of the UNAM and IPN campuses, in response to the university student body's pleas to "avoid falling into a police trap" that would give the government the pretext to occupy the Universidad Iberoamericana as well.[20]

Until the events of September unfolded, the Iberoamericana's

University Council had avoided taking any public stands on the Mexican Student Movement of 1968; it was only after the UNAM was occupied by the military that the University Council finally felt compelled to act. As the University Council's minutes show, however, this body was extremely reluctant to take any measure that might possibly bring down the government's wrath on the university. While Meneses did send a series of telegrams to Javier Barrios Sierra, the rector of the UNAM, expressing his university's support for Barrios's stand against the government, the issue for the Iberoamericana's council was whether a statement expressing support for the broader student movement should accompany these telegrams.[21] The Universidad Iberoamericana's Judicial Commission recommended that the university not take an official stand vis-à-vis the student movement "because the problem had become too muddled, there were too many political interests involved."[22] Ultimately, the University Council accepted this recommendation and voted to reject the inclusion of any sort of declaration to Meneses's telegrams to Barrio Sierra, defending their decision by arguing that such a measure would appear "opportunistic."[23] The reality was, of course, that the Universidad Iberoamericana's University Council was cognizant of the political realities of living under Díaz Ordaz's authoritarian regime and reached a politically cautious, rather than a courageous, policy decision; the Universidad Iberoamericana's administrators were simply not interested in engaging in an act that could very well mean political martyrdom for themselves and their institution.

In the aftermath of the October 1968 Tlatelolco Massacre, the University Council expressed major concern that anti-government statements made by the school's faculty and students would be taken as official declarations by the university; the councilors feared that these unofficial statements could "reverberate in many diverse forms, uncontrollably, and [could] seriously damage the university."[24] Given the historically fractious church-state relations in Mexico and the volatile political climate of the late 1960s, the councilors' caution is entirely understandable. The Council called on the students not to make "isolated decisions" and resolved to invoke the university's Disciplinary Council for those students attempting to make declarations in the name of the Universidad Iberoamericana as a whole.[25]

The University Council was also concerned about the possibility of attacks by "outside groups of students" against the Universidad

Iberoamericana, such as the notorious ultra-right-wing student organization known as Movimiento Universitario de Renovadora Orientación (MURO, University Movement for Restored Orientation), which on August 30 had already conducted a raid involving some sixty hooded thugs on the IPN's Vocational School #7.[26] If the university came under attack, the University Council determined not to call in governmental security forces as this would constitute "an unbearable humiliation and a provocation." Enormously complicating the whole matter was that these shock forces usually operated with the tacit approval if not the outright direction of the authorities. The University Council eventually decided that the mandatory evacuation of the university was the most viable course of action in case of a large-scale assault, an event that fortunately never occurred.[27]

It is unfortunate that the University Council's official documents do not record the private thoughts of the councilors on the horrendous events at Tlatelolco; someone who did address the deeper meaning of the events of 1968 was Ángel Palerm, the director of the Universidad Iberoamericana's Institute of Social Sciences since its founding two years earlier. Palerm's position on the Iberoamericana's faculty exemplified the changes in the institution since the early 1960s. Palerm was a Spanish Republican refugee, a member of the Spanish Diaspora that fled to Mexico following the defeat of the Republic in the Spanish Civil War (1936–1939) to escape the murderous political repression unleashed by General Francisco Franco's victorious regime. In Spain, Palerm had been a member of the Iberian Anarchist Federation and fought in the Spanish Civil War against Franco's Nazi-supported Fascist army, winning the Spanish Republic's highest award for bravery—the Medal of Valor—for his wartime heroics.[28] Palerm's employment at the Universidad Iberoamericana reflected that institution's greater commitment to genuine academic freedom and highlighted the depth of the reforms underway in the Roman Catholic Church in the 1960s. Palerm's employment at the Universidad Iberoamericana would have been unthinkable in the pre–Vatican II era, regardless of his unquestioned professional qualifications; he simply would have been vetoed by the Iberoamericana's Jesuit leadership on purely ideological grounds.

In 1969 Palerm published a series of four articles in *Comunidad* that provide valuable information on Iberoamerican student participation during the Mexican Student Movement of 1968. Palerm's most poignant and eloquent passages came when he described seeing the Iberoamericana students who attended the October 2 Tlatelolco Assembly and had somehow managed to escape death or imprisonment; observing these emotionally crushed students sent Palerm's mind racing back to the terrible images that he had witnessed in the 1930s as a combatant during the Spanish Civil War and which had haunted him for decades: "In my days of war I saw young soldiers scattered and terrified after an aerial bombardment or a tank assault. They had the same expressions on their faces as the young men and women who arrived [at the Universidad Iberoamericana] the day after Tlatelolco, attempting to relate their experiences, yet without being able to do so."[29] The shattered young people described by Palerm became the targets of an intense government manhunt; Díaz Ordaz's regime filled the notorious Lecumberri Penitentiary with students and left-wing intellectuals, subjecting them to torture and privation and denying them the right to habeas corpus.[30] In response to these measures, the jailed dissidents staged a hunger strike from December 1969 to January 1970 with the goal of forcing the government to grant them their constitutional right to legal due process, to either bring them to trial or else allow them to be freed on bail; this dramatic action by the dissidents sparked yet another wave of student mobilization at the Universidad Iberoamericana and other Mexico City universities.[31] Several, but not all, of the Universidad Iberoamericana component schools suspended academic activities in support of the Lecumberri hunger strikers. Student assemblies, organized by separate schools, were held at the Universidad Iberoamericana in order to decide whether to strike in support of the Lecumberri hunger strikers. The results of this internal democratic experiment at the Iberoamericana served to demonstrate that not all members of the Universidad Iberoamericana's student body were politically active or sympathetic to the plight of the Lecumberri prisoners.

Those Iberoamericana schools most active in the Mexican Student Movement of 1968—anthropology, political science, sociology, history—supported the hunger strikers.[32] The Universidad Iberoamericana's School of Philosophy, a bastion of neo-scholasticism on campus, was, not surprisingly, among those components not joining the student action, and students in schools associated with business either refused to go on strike or did not even bother to hold an assembly to discuss the matter.[33] Students refusing to go on strike were in the departments of architecture, business administration, mechanical engineering, communications, and industrial relations. The School of Civil Engineering and the School of Industrial Design neither held assemblies nor supported the academic strike.[34] The reasons for the decisions that these students made were no doubt varied, but the fact that they were looking for future employment by Mexico's politically conservative business community no doubt played a role in their considerations.

Jesuits and the Mexican Student Movement of 1968

The Mexican Student Movement of 1968 had a radicalizing effect on some members of the Jesuit Order, with a number of Jesuits actually directly participating in the movement. Some of these experiences were recorded by the Jesuit priest José Ignacio Palencia in the Jesuit periodical *Pulgas*. Palencia's 1968 article detailed how he and other Jesuits worked for the National Strike Committee, painting political graffiti on public buildings and distributing flyers, all in support of the student movement.[35] Palencia explained that the decision of "not a few Jesuits" to participate in the Mexican Student Movement of 1968 was made after a series of meetings between the Jesuits who felt committed to the UNAM. Palencia maintained that not joining the movement "would have been a comfortably bourgeois desertion [of responsibilities], which they would hardly have forgotten."[36] The activist Jesuits were "not only tolerated but accepted" by the members of the student movement.[37] Importantly, Palencia and his colleagues maintained the Jesuit tradition of discipline, soliciting and receiving "the support and advice of the Province"[38] for their actions.[39] Palencia blasted the communist label applied to the student movement by the government and its supporters; while portraits of Che Guevara were found in the marches and left-wing groups participated in the movement, Palencia believed that "beyond the diverse and antagonistic ideologies [within the movement] there exists a collection of aspirations and demands which encompasses us all."[40] Palencia expressed his belief that the presence of priests or Catholic institutions, such as the Universidad Iberoamericana, in the student movement "has not come to compromise the Church, in the bad sense of the term."[41]

The Universidad Iberoamericana faculty member Carlos Palomar was another Jesuit priest involved in the student movement; Palomar expressed his views in the Jesuit journal *Pulgas*, writing a provocative article titled

"I Wish to be Arrested for the Crime of Social Dissolution."[42] Palomar saw the student movement as part of a greater effort to redeem Mexico's impoverished popular classes, declaring that little by little more people were discovering their complicity with the defenders of the status quo who "[under] the pretext of order, economic stability, [and] international prestige achieved prosperity, [and now] attack an entire generation who manifest their demands to create a more just and viable future for all."[43] Palomar asserted that the students leading the fight against governmental authoritarianism were the "most sensitive sector of the generation which in the future will be [the leaders of] Mexico" and condemned those who refused to take an active role in the movement.[44] An advocate of Liberation Theology, Palomar saw his involvement in the student movement as an inescapable moral obligation for all those who called themselves Christians: "We must recall that the participation of the Christian in the social process of liberation is not optional. The essence of the Christian is to reject injustice."[45]

The boldest Jesuits went so far as to publically criticize the conservative political stance taken by most of the church hierarchy during the Mexican Student Movement of 1968. For example, Enrique Maza, SJ, editor of the Jesuit publication *Christus*, offered a biting post-Tlatelolco analysis of the student movement, its meaning and purpose, and the Catholic hierarchy's reaction to it.[46] Maza saw the movement as the "vague but true expression of non-conformity with the political structures of Mexico and with the social and economic inequalities from which our society suffers. The persistence and growth of the movement manifested the inherent weaknesses of our political system."[47] Maza's article highlighted many failures of the Mexican society. He believed, with good reason, that the nation was ruled by a party dictatorship in which an authoritarian bureaucracy operated in place of popular representation, that Mexico's judicial system was not only deficient but corrupt, that the nation suffered from a government-controlled press, that its organized labor and peasant movements were corrupt and subservient to the State, that Mexico's agrarian reform movement had failed, and that society was marked by an unjust distribution of wealth.[48] Maza believed that the Mexican Student Movement of 1968, which began as "a rock-throwing fight" between rival bands of students, had acquired "social-political dimensions" and had raised the political consciousness of an entire generation.[49] Furthermore, he maintained that the process of politicization would have important consequences in future political conflicts, an observation that proved to be correct.

Not one to mince words, Maza's criticism of the Roman Catholic Church hierarchy was as harsh as that directed toward the Mexican state. He chastised the Roman Catholic Church for historically failing to promote social reform, in spite of the papal encyclicals addressing the social question, arguing that while *"Rerum Novarum* has been there for 77 years," Mexican Catholicism "has taken other paths."[50] Maza's comments on the actions of the Mexican bishops, or rather their inaction, were the essay's core message; the Jesuit cleric launched a blistering, emotional attack against the church hierarchy for their lack of leadership during the 1968 crisis: "We lived two and a half months of violent transcendence for Mexico's destiny: without the bishops. They were not with us. The young fought, died, were imprisoned, took positions, wrote, and were defeated in a struggle they considered to be just without even knowing their pastor's thoughts, without finding a light to guide them—without their presence."[51] The Jesuit cleric maintained that the student movement forced the Catholic clergy to take sides, to determine whether they would stand with the "side of capital or with the side of those who suffered injustice."[52] The only bishop escaping Maza's criticism was the bishop of Cuernavaca, Sergio Méndez Arceo; Maza praised "Don Sergio" for his "dedication as a pastor" for which he had been "attacked and slandered."[53] Bishop Méndez Arceo, a proponent of the goals of Vatican II, had been alone among the Mexican Catholic hierarchy in voicing public support of the goals of the Mexican Student Movement of 1968.[54]

The Roman Catholic Church's official position on the Mexican Student Movement of 1968 was presented by Ernesto Corripio Ahumada, the archbishop of Oaxaca and the future archbishop of Mexico, in his capacity as the president of the Episcopal Council of Mexico. His pastoral message focused its criticism not on governmental repression but rather at the students; indeed, Corripio Ahumada stated that the bishops had sympathy for the government's position and criticized the tactics employed by the student protesters: "We understand very well the difficult task of governing and we cannot approve the destructive impulse nor the criminal taking advantage of . . . the admirable qualities of youth in order to induce them to violence, to the anarchical struggle, to the disproportionate confrontation, even if their motivations were noble."[55]

This pastoral message, written when the blood of the massacred students of Tlatelolco had barely dried, reflected the bishops' monumental lack of comprehension of the student movement and of its historical importance. Although the modus vivendi with the Mexican government continued to influence the majority of the Mexican ecclesiastical hierarchy, that view was at variance with the beliefs of a vocal minority of clergy, many of whom were Jesuits.

The Universidad Iberoamericana and the Corpus Christi Massacre of 1971

For all its violence, the Tlatelolco Massacre of October 1968 failed to completely halt student anti-government movements; the Autonomous University of Nuevo León, located in Mexico's third largest city, Monterrey, became the new epicenter of student militancy in post-Tlatelolco Mexico. Since the late Porfiriato, Monterrey has been one of Mexico's leading industrial centers, whose powerful and well-organized business class had long exerted a dominate political force over the city and the region. However, in the wake of the Mexican Student Movement of 1968 leftist students in Monterrey had been challenging the established order; from 1969 to 1971 the Autonomous University of Nuevo León, the state's top public institution of higher learning, was wracked by unrest as student activists and the state government, the latter highly influenced behind the scenes by the powerful Monterrey industrialist class, fought each other for control of the institution.[56] A parade of rectors tried and failed to govern the university during this period; each, however, fell afoul of either Governor Eduardo Elizondo or the student militants, and the situation at the highly politicized Autonomous University of Nuevo León became completely chaotic.

By April 1971, the institution found itself with two rectors, one supported by university leftists and the other by the governor. Elizondo attempted to resolve this schism by expelling the dissidents from the university, an act that resolved nothing and simply produced more violence at the strife-torn school. Mexico's new president, Luis Echeverría (1970–1976), who had directed the 1968 Tlatelolco Massacre as Díaz Ordaz's interior minister, finally decided to directly intervene in order to put an end to the chaos. President Echeverría sent his secretary of education, Víctor Bravo Ahuja, to Monterrey on June 4, 1971, and secured the resignation of both Governor Elizondo and the government-supported rector from their respective posts.[57]

The events of Monterrey did not go unnoticed in the nation's capital. The Mexico City–based National Council of Struggle (successor to the 1968 National Strike Committee) mobilized students in support of the Monterrey movement and called for a massive protest march to be held in Mexico City on June 10, 1971, to promote a list of demands that included the defense of the University of Nuevo León's autonomy, the liberation of political prisoners, labor democracy, and greater student representation in university government.[58] Students from the Universidad Iberoamericana,[59] the UNAM, the IPN, the National School of Agriculture of Chapingo, the National School of Anthropology and History, and the Superior Normal School participated in the march.[60] They were also joined by dissident labor activists as well as members of an urban poor league, the Poor People's Organization of Nezahualcóyotl, that represented some of the inhabitants of this huge working-class urban center that borders Mexico City.[61]

The Mexico City riot police attempted to halt the march, but when the activists pressed onward, the authorities appeared to retreat; however, this was just a ruse because when the protesters reached Mexico-Tacuba Boulevard they were suddenly attacked by civilian-dressed thugs armed with firearms, bats, and clubs.[62] These attackers were members of the notorious Halcones (hawks), a paramilitary group trained by the Mexican Army that had been already used on previous occasions to deal with student protests.[63] The attack of the Halcones on the unarmed protestors killed sixteen people and left twenty-six severely injured, while the police arrested 159 persons.[64] Questions were raised in the country as to whether the use of the Halcones had been authorized by Echeverría or if their use represented a plot by Monterrey industrialists and Echeverría's enemies to embarrass the president and his government for his involvement in the University of Nuevo León crisis. This second theory is supported by scholars like Donald C. Hodges, who maintain that the violence of June 10 was provoked by Monterrey industrialists seeking revenge against Echeverría's administration because of his decisive intervention in Nuevo León's affairs, which they sought to exclusively control.[65]

This act of violence, which is known today as the Corpus Christi Massacre because it took place on that Catholic feast day, had grave repercussions for the Universidad Iberoamericana; it put the university in the crosshairs of right elements in the government and in society as a whole, factions not at all sympathetic with the course that the Universidad Iberoamericana had taken since the advent of the 1960s church reform movement. The Universidad Iberoamericana's turmoil began when the pro-government and right-wing Mexico City newspaper *El Día* launched a smear campaign against the school. The government alleged that the student marchers were responsible for the violence of June 10 rather than any government-controlled paramilitary force, and *El Día* built on this farcical charade by accusing the Universidad Iberoamericana of having served as a clandestine arsenal that had provided the weapons supposedly used by the students.[66] The accusation was totally without merit, predicated on the falsehood that the marchers had opened fire, but the delicacy of the political situation obligated Rector Meneses to take some action to clarify the activities of Iberoamericana students during the event, and so he established a commission to collect the testimonies of Iberoamericana students and faculty present at the march.

Rector Meneses selected Professor Ángel Palerm, a trained anthropologist, to head this commission that was comprised of three faculty members and three students. The testimonies collected by the commission were consistent with each other; all of the informants insisted that the march was proceeding in an orderly fashion until the marchers were attacked by groups of armed young men who descended from gray vehicles located near the police lines. The Iberoamericana witnesses also made it clear that the marchers were completely unarmed, except for the sticks used to display the protest banners; according to the Iberoamericana informants, the marchers only used these sticks to defend themselves after they were set upon by the paramilitary Halcones.[67] The Mexico City police's complicity in the violence of June 10 was strongly suggested by the multiple testimonies of the Iberoamericana students who emphasized the police's passivity at the events unfolding in front of them and their refusal to rescue student marchers being beaten to death literally before their eyes.

The Corpus Christi Massacre also detonated an internal crisis within the Universidad Iberoamericana, as student anger at the political activities of Mexico's business community was brought home to the university. The 1971 crisis exacerbated relations between the university community and its business patrons that had been deteriorating since the advent of

Vatican II–inspired reforms at the Universidad Iberoamericana. The conservative businessmen who dominated the Fomento de Investigación y Cultura Superior Asociación Civil (FICSAC, Civil Association for the Promotion of Investigation and Advanced Cultural Studies) were not sympathetic to the radicalism that elements of the Iberoamericana had demonstrated in the Mexican Student Movement of 1968 and in subsequent protests, and they used their economic clout to express their displeasure with the university community. The FICSAC's actions in turn alienated more and more members of the Universidad Iberoamericana from that institution and sparked one of the gravest institutional crises in the university's history.

The origins of the conflict between the FICSAC and the university date back to 1963, when the Universidad Iberoamericana's Jesuit leadership signed a contract with the FICSAC whereby the financial board agreed to assume the additional responsibility of being the Iberoamericana's Junta de Gobierno or governing board. The Junta de Gobierno and the FICSAC, which in effect were one and the same, had the authority to appoint the Iberoamericana's rector and directors of the university's component schools and drew up the Iberoamericana's budget.[68] The original purpose of creating the FICSAC-controlled Junta de Gobierno was to facilitate the long-cherished goal of winning the federal government's recognition of the Universidad Iberoamericana as a free (autonomous) university. The Iberoamericana's logic for taking this measure was that federal government officials would look at their case with more sympathy if they created a secular authority superior to the Jesuit-dominated University Council; in addition, by creating a Junta de Gobierno the Universidad Iberoamericana would bring its internal structure closer to that of the UNAM.[69] In reality, however, the Jesuit Order intended to retain control over the selection process of the Universidad Iberoamericana's rector, with the nominee's final confirmation being made not by the Junta de Gobierno but by the Jesuit's Superior General in Rome; the governing board was intended by the Jesuits to simply rubber-stamp the decisions that they had already made.

That the Jesuit leadership fully intended to remain in control of the Universidad Iberoamericana is clearly seen in the 1968 Xavier Mesa Affair. Francisco Xavier Mesa, SJ, had been named the rector of the Iberoamericana by the Superior General of the Jesuit Order in 1964 following the accidental drowning death of his predecessor, Carlos

Hernández Prieto, SJ, despite the fact that this authority was supposedly reserved for the Iberoamericana's Junta de Gobierno.[70] For reasons that remain unclear, Xavier Mesa soon fell afoul of the college's Jesuit community, and so the head of the Jesuit Order in Mexico at that time moved to replace Xavier Mesa as rector as punishment for his hidden transgressions.[71] Unfortunately for the Jesuit leadership, things became complicated when Xavier Mesa refused to step down quietly from his post; with the encouragement of his key ally within the university's Jesuit community, Felipe Pardinas, Rector Xavier Mesa decided to appeal his cause to the Junta de Gobierno, since by statute only could that body remove him. The Junta de Gobierno's president, the prominent businessman Carlos Trouyet, initially supported Xavier Mesa, but eventually he and his fellow board members came to accept the Jesuit hierarchy's arguments that it needed to discipline one of its members. Nonetheless, this episode hinted at a growing friction between the Iberoamericana community and the FICSAC-controlled Junta de Gobierno that quickly mushroomed under the weight of the events of 1968.

Evidence that the Junta de Gobierno/FICSAC was not happy with the attitude assumed by elements of the Universidad Iberoamericana during the Mexican Student Movement of 1968 came to light the following year when the body sent the school into a severe fiscal crisis by unexpectedly refusing to pay off a 580,000-peso deficit that the Universidad Iberoamericana had run up in 1968 and the 4 million–peso debt the university incurred in the construction of its School of Engineering laboratories.[72] The FICSAC's actions produced an economic crisis that was addressed at the University Council's February 27, 1969, meeting; most suggestions offered by the councilors on how to deal with the crisis merely centered on efforts to pressure the student body to pay their tuition payments more promptly and appeals to the parents for money beyond their children's normal tuition and related fees. Ángel Palerm, however, addressed the fundamental question behind this fiscal crisis, openly stating what must have been on the minds of his colleagues: was the financial board (FICSAC) punishing the Universidad Iberoamericana for the political activism of some of its members?

> I wish to ask a question, a little bold perhaps, but as they say *there are no indiscreet questions, only indiscreet answers*, and it is this: To what point can this attitude assumed by the University's Board of

Trustees be interpreted as a [negative] policy it has assumed towards the university, or is it simply the unfortunate product of accidental circumstances? If unfortunately it is the former, I dare suggest to the Council and [this] university's authorities a reexamination of the entire university's financing. There exist other formulas for financing universities apart from a Board of Trustees [model].[73]

Palerm called for "democratic" solutions to the Iberoamericana's economic problems, solutions which would better safeguard against what he believed were "improper pressures over the university's life," in a clear allusion to the FICSAC-dominated Junta de Gobierno.[74]

Palerm's statements clearly hit a nerve; Rector Meneses tried to ignore Palerm's statement, going on instead to discuss and endorse a modest proposal put forward by another councilor to help alleviate the crisis. Council member Luis González finally requested that Meneses answer Palerm's "indiscreet" question, and Meneses responded by saying that the financial board's decision was based on economic rather than political factors and that "they do not want hear more about this at the moment." To make up for the FICSAC's lack of support, the Universidad Iberoamericana was obliged to take difficult measures: solicit commercial banks for 2.5 million pesos worth of loans, raise tuition rates by 20 percent, and dramatically reduce operating expenses.[75]

Faculty and student activists at the Universidad Iberoamericana were not swayed by Meneses's statements and did firmly believe that the Junta de Gobierno/FICSAC was using its control of the purse to politically punish the college. And the dissent within the Universidad Iberoamericana against their Junta de Gobierno was not an isolated phenomenon: by 1971 there existed a generalized antipathy in Mexico among the student activists against the Junta de Gobierno model of university governance, which, as in the case of the UNAM, had been created after the chaotic rectorship of Rodolfo Brito Foucher in order to deny students any active role in the decision-making process that had produced the highly charged university politics of the 1930s and 1940s. The disappearance of these authoritarian university governing boards was a key student demand among activists at many different educational institutions by the early 1970s.[76]

The Iberoamericana's Junta de Gobierno did not escape the attention of the Mexico City student activists; in a meeting held three days after the tragic events of June 10, the Iberoamericana student leaders announced their intention to "emancipate the [Universidad Iberoamericana] from the group of businessmen who control it."[77] Not surprisingly, it was progressive students and faculty from the Universidad Iberoamericana's social science programs who led the movement against the Junta de Gobierno, handing out campus flyers calling for the abolition of this group of "bankers and industrialists."[78] These left-wing dissidents held an assembly on August 16 to formulate their plan of action, presided by the Iberoamericana's leading left-wing faculty member, Ángel Palerm. This assembly proposed the creation of three commissions, each tasked with a specific duty; one would ask the Junta de Gobierno to cede its authority to the University Council, a second group would examine the university's economic condition "and [find] the possible solution [of its fiscal problems] so as to guarantee the [Iberoamericana's] autonomy," and the third would seek an audience with President Luis Echeverría to ask for his support for the Universidad Iberoamericana's free-university status bid.[79]

Alarmed by this campus activism, the Jesuit-controlled University Council moved to take the lead of this university reform movement and channel it into more moderate positions by reaching a separate agreement with the FICSAC whereby the University Council and the financial board agreed to dissolve the Junta de Gobierno and replace it with a Senate comprised of representatives from all sectors of the university community. The University Council presented a lengthy rationale for making this radical change in the school's structure. It acknowledged that change was needed as a consequence of forces unleashed during the 1960s, Vatican II and the Mexican Student Movement of 1968, which had had an enormous impact on the Universidad Iberoamericana and Mexican society at large. The Vatican II Council, the university officials stated, had "pointed out new paths for lay Catholic[s]" and had "removed the Church's paternalistic attitude towards [the laity]."[80]

With this document, the Jesuit-dominated University Council was justifying the creation of a new relationship between laity and the Jesuit Order at the institution, one more faithful to the Vatican II's affirmation of the equality between the laity and clergy within the community of the faithful. The student movements of the 1960s, which had broken out in Mexico (as well as in other countries) had "highlighted students as an essential component of the university."[81] The University Council, in short, was recognizing that change was needed at the Iberoamericana in the governance of the school. The shape that this reform took was determined by the events taking place in the broader world of university politics.[82]

The University Council formulated these "basic considerations" in developing plans for the creation of a Senate. Of fundamental importance was the issue of university autonomy, understood as the right of the Iberoamericana to govern itself. As the university community had an innate right to self-determination, it would name the representatives to the Senate.[83] No longer would a non-elected body like the FICSAC select the members of the Universidad Iberoamericana's supreme governing body.

The new University Senate addressed many of the faults and weaknesses of the old governing model. The authority to approve the Iberoamericana's operating budget was taken away from the financial board, FICSAC, and placed in the hands of the Senate.[84] This prevented incidents like the FICSAC's refusal to pay the university's 1968 operating deficit, which left-wing elements at the university had blamed on political factors. Moreover, the Senate was specifically entrusted with "transmitting society's needs and worries to the university [community]," as well as promoting the school's 1968 *Ideario*—responsibilities which the businessman-controlled Junta de Gobierno did not assume.[85] The Senate also addressed the issue of student participation and non-Jesuit faculty in university governance; previously, the Universidad Iberoamericana's students and secular faculty members had had no say in the operation of the Junta de Gobierno. Conversely, the Senate represented the entire Iberoamericana community; it contained, in addition to the rector, two representatives from each of the following corporate bodies at the university: the student body, faculty members, school directors, and the financial board.[86] However, anger over the student rebellion, which was directed at the financial board, prompted the FICSAC's refusal to send representatives to the Senate; this boycott lasted until 1973.

The Destruction of the Universidad Iberoamericana Campus: 1979

At five o'clock on the morning of March 14, 1979, the reformed Universidad Iberoamericana was put to the ultimate test of its strength as an institution when an earthquake that registered a 7 on the Mercalli scale destroyed 60 percent of the university's campus.[87] Fortunately there were no injuries, but if the earthquake had taken place during class hours hundreds of students, faculty, and staff would undoubtedly have been killed or injured; photographs contained in the Universidad Iberoamericana's Historical Archive grimly illustrate how many of the university's multi-floor buildings completely collapsed to form layered pancakes of cement, iron, and bricks. Any human beings trapped in these structures would have been crushed to death by tons of fragmented building materials and office furniture. The destruction of the Iberoamericana's campus placed in jeopardy the future the school's continued existence as well as the academic future of its 6,300-person student body.

Mexico City universities that were unaffected by the earth tremor flooded the Universidad Iberoamericana's administration with offers of assistance, mostly in the form of promises to accept limited numbers of Iberoamerican students at their institutions. Not surprisingly, the Iberoamericana's leadership did not want to disperse its student body among several institutions, as this would destroy any sense of a university community among the students, faculty, and staff of the Universidad Iberoamericana. Rector Enrique Portilla Osorio, SJ, and the Iberoamericana Senate decided to accept the offer made by the IPN to allow the Iberoamericana to use two new and as yet unused buildings at its Escuela Superior de Ingeniería Mecánica Eléctrica in Culhuacán, a ten-minute drive from the Iberoamericana's Churubusco district campus.[88] The fact that it was the IPN that came to the Universidad Iberoamericana's rescue is ironic, as this institution was an educational centerpiece of President Lázaro Cárdenas's administration and was created, in part, in response to the 1933 UNAM strike.

The long-term solutions to the Universidad Iberoamericana's crisis were provided by the school's estranged financial board and by the Mexican business community, many of whose executives were Iberoamericana alumni. This tragedy eventually served to reconcile the Iberoamericana community with its business patrons; at first, however, the earthquake merely served to increase tensions between elements of the FICSAC and the university administrators. The Universidad Iberoamericana's campus had been built by a construction company owned by the prominent businessman Crescencio Ballesteros, a key member of the FICSAC and the head of the Universidad Iberoamericana Asociación Civil (Iberoamerican University Civil Association), who were legally the owners of the campus; Ballesteros's son Jorge Ballesteros was also a member of the Iberoamericana Senate.[89] In the immediate aftermath of the earthquake, there were university and city officials who were eager to investigate whether shoddy building materials contributed to the collapse of so many of the Iberoamericana's buildings with a view toward seeing if Ballesteros's firm would face criminal charges.[90] Nothing, however, came out of these allegations; the official explanation for the catastrophic failure of the Universidad Iberoamericana's buildings was that they were built on a fault line in a notoriously seismically active urban center, although it must be noted that Ballesteros was a politically well-connected businessman whose company had recently constructed the Mexican army's new military academy on the outskirts of the nation's capital.[91]

The FICSAC waged a successful fundraising campaign that collected funds for the temporary buildings that allowed the Universidad Iberoamericana to use its shattered campus the next academic year. These buildings, nicknamed the *gallineros* (chicken coops) by the members of Iberoamericana community, were eventually replaced by a brand-new campus in an entirely new location in Mexico City's now-exclusive Santa Fé district, which in the twenty years since its construction has been joined by an impressive number of ultra-modern office buildings housing multinational and domestic corporations and exclusive residential developments—the winners of Mexico's post-NAFTA process of globalization.

Conclusion

In 1974 the Universidad Iberoamericana finally gained what it had sought for twenty years—independence from the UNAM. The Ministry of Education issued a decree by which it recognized the titles emitted by the Iberoamericana.[92] The Iberoamericana was, however, a profoundly different institution from that which had first applied for governmental recognition in the 1950s. By 1974, in addition to being a mature institution with well-developed academic programs, the Iberoamericana had entered, thanks to the church reform of the 1960s, into the mainstream of Mexican intellectual life. The participation of the Iberoamericana community in transcendental political issues of the day—the 1968 and

1971 student movements—is testimony of the institution's relevance to Mexican society.

The Jesuit Order promoted radical changes within the Universidad Iberoamericana. Under Superior General Pedro Arrupe, SJ, the Jesuit Order moved away from its historic strategy of influencing society through the education of society's elites to one favoring the satisfaction of the social needs of the popular classes. This forced a fundamental reevaluation of the Iberoamericana, from an institution dedicated to promoting an exclusionary and authoritarian set of values to one which promoted greater academic discussion and which scientifically addressed Mexico's social, economic, and political weaknesses. The conflict, in 1971, between the Iberoamericana's Junta de Gobierno and progressive elements of the university community highlighted the conflict between those who championed and those who were unsettled by this process of change. The Junta was comprised of pious businessmen who were wedded to the values which the Jesuits and the Iberoamericana had historically promoted. Those faculty members and students who wished to abolish the Junta were the fruit of the Iberoamericana's transformation and the progressive's victory was a fitting culmination of the reform process.

CONCLUSION

On May 11, 2012, the Partido Revolucionario Institucional (PRI, Institutional Revolutionary Party)'s telegenic presidential candidate Enrique Peña Nieto arrived at the Universidad Iberoamericana's Santa Fé Campus in Mexico City for a stop on his ongoing campaign to win the Mexican presidency. Enjoying favorable press coverage from many media outlets, especially from the critically important television duopoly *Televisa* and *Televisión Azteca*, Peña Nieto had skillfully capitalized on the widespread horror that President Felipe Calderón's bloody and militarized campaign against traffickers had generated among all levels of the Mexican population. There was also a broadly felt sense of deep-seated frustration that twelve years of Partido Acción Nacional (PAN, National Action Party) administrations had failed to enact the political and fiscal reforms that Mexico desperately required. Peña Nieto had built an apparently insurmountable lead in the polls against a weak PAN candidate in Josefina Vázquez and the highly polarizing leftist candidate Andrés Manuel López Obrador. Yet on that day, Peña Nieto's well-oiled political machine suffered a rude awakening when the PRI's presidential candidate was vociferously challenged by Iberoamericana students. The key issue raised on that day was Peña Nieto's treatment of the rebellious community of San Salvador Atenco in 2006 during his term as governor of the state of Mexico. The villagers of Atenco exploded on the national political scene in 2002 when they waged a successful campaign to block the construction of a new international airport for Mexico City, earning this peasant community the enmity of powerful political and economic forces. The 2006 police action ordered by the then governor Peña Nieto had resulted in a large-scale police action that ended in widespread human rights violations. In many ways, the Iberoamericana students' fierce questioning of Peña Nieto's actions at Atenco in 2006 were a reflection of the larger concern felt by many Mexicans at the prospect of the return to power of the PRI, a political party that had governed the nation in an authoritarian manner for seventy years until its electoral defeat in 2000 and that seemed destined to return to power in the 2012 elections. A video of this political confrontation between the 131 Universidad Iberoamericana students was uploaded to the Internet and became an instant national sensation.

Seeking to minimize the damage generated by this bungled political event, Peña Nieto's political handlers publically dismissed the students as operatives of his leftist rival López Obrador; this trivialization of the Iberoamericana students' concerns generated outrage and led to the creation of the #YOSOY132 (I am 132) movement, whose supporters expressed their solidarity with the original 131 protesters. Using social media, the #YOSOY132 activists launched a national campaign that hounded the PRI's candidate and called out the two major television networks for their perceived slanted news coverage in favor of Peña Nieto's campaign. In the closing weeks of the campaign, López Obrador closed the gap against the frontrunner and finished much closer to Peña Nieto than what *Televisa*- and *Televisión Azteca*–commissioned polls had indicated before election day. While certainly not the only factor behind López Obrador's momentum, the outbreak of the #YOSOY132 movement eliminated some of the triumphalist tone of Peña Nieto's presidential campaign which had at that time had seemed more of a coronation than a highly competitive contest between three well-established political parties.

The political activism demonstrated by the Iberoamericana students in the #YOSOY132 movement in the 2012 presidential campaign was an echo of previous generations of political activism by Iberoamericana students. And despite their deep ideological differences, it also marked a continuation of the legacy of activism that the #YOSOY132 movement inherited from their forbearers in the Asociación Católica de la Juventud Mexicana (ACJM, Mexican Catholic Youth Association) and the The Unión National de Estudiantes Católicos (UNEC, National Catholic

CONCLUSION   141

Student Union). The #YOSOY132 movement contributed to placing the issue of Mexico's monopolistic media industry as an important part of the national agenda, which the current president Enrique Peña Nieto was politically clever enough to partially address in his own recently passed telecommunications reform law. The #YOSOY132 movement has been the latest example of the Iberoamericana students' ability, along with the abilities of its ACJM and UNEC predecessors, to help influence and shape Mexico's political agenda even if they lacked the ability to completely determine its final outcome.

The Roman Catholic Church's goal of promoting Mexico's Christianization, which had been the main goal of the ACJM, the UNEC, and the Jesuit and lay Catholic founders of the Universidad Iberoamericana, did not succeed. Throughout the twentieth century, Mexico's dominant political ideology remained firmly secular. More to the point, the Jesuit's historical strategy for maximizing their influence in society—by cultivating the education of elite men—was deemed a mistake within the Order itself by the 1960s in the wake of Vatican II. But while the creation of the Universidad Iberoamericana did not lead to Mexico's Christianization via Catholic-educated elites, it nevertheless had a highly significant impact on Mexico. The transformation of the Universidad Iberoamericana's basic mission, from a promoter of Catholic culture to an agent for the resolution of Mexico's social, economic, and political ills, was testimony to the university's vitality and to the Jesuits who kept that institution in the forefront of education in the post–Vatican II era. The open intellectual debate sponsored by the Iberoamericana in the 1960s contributed to the process by which the Roman Catholic Church opened itself to the larger world. And in so doing, the Iberoamericana became not only a mainstream Mexican educational institution but one of the elite Mexican educational institutions. The new, critical perspective on Mexico's social, economic, and political development since the 1940s was reflected in the positions taken by its social science students in the Mexican Student Movement of 1968. That movement, and the Iberoamericana's role in it, pushed lay Catholics (and some elements of the clergy) far beyond the Catholic paternalism for the poor advocated in past decades.

The establishment of the Universidad Iberoamericana contributed greatly to the development of Mexican private higher education by paving the way for the creation of later Catholic universities: institutions such as the Salesian Order's La Salle University and the Jesuit Instituto Tecnológico y de Estudios Superiores del Occidente. It also tested the limits of the modus vivendi in church-state relations in the post-Cárdenas era, in which the two major institutions of Mexico embarked on an uneasy but nonetheless significant path toward coexistence, if not cooperation. Twenty years of effort to gain for the Iberoamericana free-university status is testimony to the limitations of modus vivendi. Conversely, when it finally achieved its goal in 1973, it was a landmark of the first order in church-state relations in post-Revolutionary Mexico. The final achievement of this goal involved both traditional church-state issues as well as President Luis Echeverría's "carrot and stick" policy toward opponents of his regime.

A key contribution of the Universidad Iberoamericana was the development of academic programs new to Mexico; students trained in industrial relations, industrial design, and communication sciences were needed by both the public and private sectors during the years of rapid economic expansion after 1945. The Universidad Iberoamericana's innovative curriculum attracted the patronage of Mexico's most powerful business interests, who with their economic support and technical advisory assistance gave the strongest endorsements for the Jesuit institution's importance. Although the Universidad Iberoamericana did not succeed in achieving Catholic cultural hegemony in Mexico, it did offer its students not only a distinctive historical and philosophical perspective, in this fashion continuing the work of Jesuit-led student organizations of the early twentieth century, but also access to networks of economic power via contacts made at the Iberoamericana. The study of the evolution of the student body and its subsequent roles in Mexican society deserve additional research.

Evidence for the importance of Catholic doctrine and organizations for the Mexican Right in post-Revolutionary Mexico is overwhelming. Church-state conflict provoked the largest civil insurrection in Mexico since the Revolution—the Cristero Rebellion of 1926–1929. That uprising was coordinated by a collection of lay Catholic groups. Catholic associations led the civil society resistance campaign against governmental-instigated changes in educational policies in the 1930s, which proved ultimately successful. Perhaps most important was that Catholics, as well as Roman Catholic doctrine, played a fundamental role in the PAN's founding and in the development of its party platform. While the Roman Catholic Church remained, legally and politically, officially marginalized, Mexico's political elite tacitly recognized its importance when it reestablished a modus vivendi in church-state relations in the 1940s. Making peace with the Roman Catholic Church hierarchy was a fundamental political achievement of Mexico's ruling party—one that allowed it to retain power for decades.

The Jesuit-led, Catholic student associations analyzed in this work—the ACJM and the UNEC—had mixed legacies. They certainly failed to halt or reverse the secularization of Mexican society, which is what the "Christianization" process attempted to accomplish. These organizations were the early training ground for Catholic activists who helped shape twentieth-century Mexico, in ways both positive and deleterious. As highlighted in chapter 2, the ACJM was a major player in the Liga Nacional Defensora de las Libertades Religiosas (LNDLR, National League for the Defense of Religious Liberty) during the Cristero Rebellion. José de León Toral, a Catholic Youth Association member, changed the course of Mexican history when he assassinated Mexico's strongman Álvaro Obregón in 1928. León Toral dashed Obregón's aspirations to become Mexico's new Porfirio Díaz and inadvertently aided the creation of Mexico's one-party state in 1929. Efraín González Luna, the co-founder of the PAN, represents a more constructive legacy of Bergöend's Catholic Student Association. In addition to his involvement in the founding of Mexico's oldest opposition party, González Luna participated in the creation of two private universities: the Universidad Autónoma de Guadalajara (UAG, Autonomous University of Guadalajara) in the 1930s and the Instituto Tecnológico y de Estudios Superiores del Occidente (Western Institute of Technology and Higher Learning) in 1957.

The Catholic Student Union also provided the UNEC with its initial nucleus of membership. As detailed in chapter 3, the Catholic Student Union had an important role in the 1930s controversy of Socialist Education. The principal at stake in this controversy was how much autonomy the Mexican middle class would have in the corporatist political structure being constructed by Lázaro Cárdenas. As Soledad Loaeza asserts in her *Las Clases Medias en México*, education is the gateway to middle-class status in Mexico; thus the importance of who controls the education. The UNEC was instrumental in the movement to deny the state in its attempt to control the educational and ideological formation of Mexico's movers and shakers. Even though the UNEC's members were promoters of an intolerant ideology, they nonetheless contributed to the maintenance of political and ideological pluralism which benefited Mexican society in the long term and contributed to the PRI's loss of the presidency from 2000 to 2012. The return once more of a supposedly now-chastened PRI to the presidency opens a new chapter in Mexico's political life whose outcome remains to be determined.

NOTES

Introduction

1. David J. Mabry, *The Mexican University and the State* (College Station: Texas A&M University Press, 1982).

Chapter One

1. Obregón's policy toward the Roman Catholic Church had its corollary in his policy toward the thorny petroleum controversy. As with the issue of the Roman Catholic Church, Obregón chose to avoid a conflict instead of enforcing the 1917 Constitution.

2. Alan Knight, "The Mentality and Modus Operandi of Revolutionary Anticlericalism," in *Faith and Impiety in Revolutionary Mexico*, ed. Matthew Butler (New York: Palgrave MacMillan, 2007), 24.

3. By supporting the intervention of external forces, the Roman Catholic Church and its Conservative Party allies vainly sought to reverse the outcome of the "Guerra de Reforma," which had stripped the church of its great material wealth and had broken its virtual monopoly over education and other social services.

4. While Catholic resistance to Lerdo de Tejada was not the determining cause for the overthrow of the regime, it did prevent the liberal president from consolidating his hold on power.

5. John Frederick Schwaller, *The History of the Catholic Church in Latin America: From Conquest to Revolution and Beyond* (New York: New York

University Press, 2011), 174–75; Edward Wright-Rios, *Revolutions in Mexican Catholicism: Reform and Revelation in Oaxaca, 1887–1934* (Durham, NC: Duke University Press, 2009), 18; and Knight, "Mentality and Modus Operandi," 24.

6. Jean Meyer, *La Cristiada: 2-el conflicto entre la iglesia y el estado 1926–1929* (Mexico City: Siglo Veintiuno, 1973), 45. Because of these changes, the Roman Catholic Church in Mexico became increasingly "Mexicanized," shaking off its dependence on foreign-born clerics. The number of priests increased over 25 percent during this period.

7. Manuel Ceballos Ramírez, *El Catolicismo Social: Un Tercero en discordia (Rerum Novarum, la "cuestión social" y la movilización de los católicos mexicanos [1891–1911])* (Mexico City: El Colegio de México, 1991), 46.

8. Wright-Rios, *Revolutions in Mexican Catholicism*, 10.

9. Lillian Parker Wallace, *Leo XIII and the Rise of Socialism* (Durham, NC: Duke University Press, 1966), 270.

10. Schwaller, *History of the Catholic Church*, 208; and Parker Wallace, *Leo XIII and the Rise of Socialism*, 270.

11. Stephen H. Haber, *Industry and Underdevelopment: The Industrialization of Mexico, 1890–1940* (Stanford, CA: Stanford University Press, 1989), 44–62. Breweries, textile mills, and cigarette production are examples of the nature of light consumer manufacturing created during the Porfiriato.

12. Manuel Ceballos Ramírez, "Rerum Novarum en México: cuarenta años entre la conciliación y la intransigencia (1891–1931)," *Revista Mexicana de Sociología*, 49.3 (July–Sept. 1987): 154.

13. Knight, "Mentality and Modus Operandi," 24.

14. Ceballos Ramírez, *El Catolicismo Social*, 175.

15. Ibid., 166.

16. However, the Puebla Congress did not address the problem of alcoholism among the elite or the middle classes. See John W. Sherman, *The Mexican Right: The End of Revolutionary Reform, 1929–1940* (Westport, CT: Praeger, 1997) for more on these Catholic congresses during the late Porfiriato.

17. Ceballos Ramírez, *El Catolicismo Social*, 193, 197.

18. Ibid., 211.

19. Ibid., 212.

20. José Bravo Ugarte, SJ, *Historia de México: Independencia, Caracterización Política e Integración Socia*, vol. 3 (Mexico City: Editorial Jus, 1962), 407; and Ceballos Ramírez, *El Catolicismo Social*, 313–18. Edward Wright-Rios analyzes the complex motivations of clerics like Oaxaca's influential cleric Bishop Eulogio Gillow in supporting the church reform movement and how this movement fit into the larger picture of post-independent, church-state relations in his work *Revolutions in Mexican Catholicism*.

21. Bravo Ugarte, *Historia de México*, 407.

22. Ibid., 408.

23. The War of the French Intervention (1862–1867), which was a continuation of the War of the Reform (1858–1861), ended with the catastrophic defeat of the clerical-backed Conservative Party.

24. "Letter from José Elguero to Lic. Miguel Palomar y Vizcarra," August 31, 1906, File #293, Box #38, Miguel Palomar y Vizcarra Collection, *Archivo Histórico de la Universidad Nacional Autónoma de México*.

25. Ibid.

26. Ceballos Ramírez, *El Catolicismo Social*, 313–18.

27. Antonio Rius Facius, *La Juventud Católica y la Revolución Mejicana: 1910–1925* (Mexico City: Editorial Jus, 1963), 22.

28. Bravo Ugarte, *Historia de México*, 426. Gabriel Fernández Smollera was a veteran Catholic activist, having founded the Círculo Católico Nacional in 1909. This organization had sought to promote the political organization of Mexican Catholics.

29. Ceballos Ramírez, *El Catolicismo Social*, 399.

30. Wright-Rios, *Revolutions in Mexican Catholicism*, 70; and Bravo Ugarte, *Historia de México*, 426.

31. Francisco Banegas Galván, *El Porque del Partido Católico Nacional* (Mexico City: Editorial Jus, 1960), 50.

32. Sherman, *Mexican Right*, 8.

33. National Catholic Party political literature, 1911, File #317, Box #40, Miguel Palomar y Vizcarra Collection, *Archivo Histórico de la Universidad Nacional Autónoma de México*.

34. Ibid.

35. The greatest controversy that surrounded the contests for the federal Chamber of Deputies was that the PCN claimed seventy-five seats in the new legislature. Pro-Maderista forces, led by the noted journalist and intellectual Luis Cabrera, utilized "political criteria" in disqualifying forty-six of these contenders.

36. National Catholic Party political literature, 1911, File #315, Box #40, Miguel Palomar y Vizcarra Collection, *Archivo Histórico de la Universidad Nacional Autónoma de México*.

37. Knight, "Mentality and Modus Operandi," 27–28.

38. Bravo Ugarte, *Historia de México*, 429. The PCN's candidate Francisco León de la Barra became the governor of the state of Mexico in the election held on March 20, 1913, and toward the end of Huerta's administration Rafael Ceniceros y Villarreal, the PCN leader of the state of Zacatecas, was elected that state's governor.

39. The document brokered between the coup leaders that laid out how political power would be divided among them.

40. A prominent intellectual, Gamboa was also a freemason. This was a curious choice for the PCN given the historical conflict between freemasons and the Roman Catholic Church in Mexico. General Maas was the nephew of General Huerta, so it is clear that the PCN's nomination bid to Maas was merely an attempt to ingratiate the party into the Huerta regime.

41. At the very least, federal recognition of the degrees conferred by Catholic schools would have been expected with a member of the PCN as the head of public instruction in the nation.

42. A small parliamentary faction called the "Liberal Renovators" was especially vocal in their opposition to Huerta's measure. Two members of this group, Félix Palavicini and Manuel Puig Casauranc, played important roles in defining educational policies in the post-Huerta era. The breaking of the Roman Catholic Church's monopoly over education, a legacy of colonial New Spain, had been a defining issue for liberals during the nineteenth century. The passions surrounding this issue are understandable given the violence of the liberal-conservative struggle in the previous century, climaxed by the War of the French Intervention.

43. Jorge Vera Estañol, *La Revolución Mexicana: Orígenes y resultados* (Mexico City: Porrúa, 1957), 337. Huerta utilized the Tamariz case in the proclamation to the nation issued in order to justify the closure of the national congress.

44. Rius Facius, *La Juventud Católica*, 56. Two weeks before the elections, while the controversy over the closure of the national congress was unfolding, Huerta let it be known to his cronies in the political structure that he would not be adverse to his name being placed on the ballot, while, confusingly, he stated publicly that he was not interested in seeking an extension of his office. Huerta's Secretario de Gobernación reported that the standing president had won a plurality of votes, but the Chamber of Deputies declared that the legal formalities had not been met and declared the elections void.

45. These included the congressional as well as the presidential and vice-presidential candidates.

46. The same fate befell the director of the *La Nación*.

47. "Letter from Rafael C. Contreras to Miguel Palomar y Vizcarra," February 16, 1914, File #325, Box #41, Miguel Palomar y Vizcarra Collection, *Archivo Histórico de la Universidad Nacional Autónoma de México*.

48. These acts must be placed, however, in the context of the generalized violence of this period. The Zapatista agrarian revolutionaries did not generally engage in anticlerical actions. Folk Catholicism played a far more important role in the society of the Indian peasants of Morelos than in the north, which produced most of the Constitutionalist revolutionary leaders.

49. This ambitious and talented Constitutionalist general was already positioning himself to replace Carranza as Mexico's strongman.

50. Roderic Ai Camp, *Crossing Swords: Politics and Religion in Mexico* (New York: Oxford University Press, 1997), 10.

51. Schwaller, *History of the Catholic Church*, 192. These articles were, in order, the following: Articles 5°, 24°, 27°, and 130°. In addition to regulating the internal activities of religious corporations, Article 130° paradoxically denied them legal recognition and denied the members of these organizations the political rights of other Mexican citizens. The clerics objected to Article 5° because it barred monastic vows, Article 24° because it barred public religious ceremonies, and Article 27° because it denied religious associations the right to "acquire, own, or administer" property. Felipe Tena Ramírez, *Leyes Fundamentales de México* (Mexico City: Editorial Porrúa, 1957), 827–28.

52. The 1917 Constitution built upon earlier liberal federal legislation on the issue of education. Article 3 of the 1857 Constitution specified that education in Mexico was to be "free." This vague wording was altered by President Sebastian Lerdo de Tejada in 1874 in order emphasize the secular nature of Mexican education under the liberal regime. The *Adiciones y Reformas a la Constitución de 1857* of December 14, 1874, stated that religious instruction and official practices of any religion are prohibited in the educational establishments of the federation, states, and municipalities. Collectively, the 1857 Constitution and the *Adiciones y Reformas* . . . marked the official termination of the Roman Catholic Church's monopoly over education. With the expansion of Catholic educational institutions during the Porfiriato, many Constitutionalists were convinced that moving against Catholic educational institutions was absolutely necessary, even if that meant compromising traditional Liberal values of tolerance and freedom. José Bravo Ugarte, SJ, *La Educación en México: (. . . –1965)* (Mexico: Editorial Jus, 1966), 136.

53. Leonardo Gómez Navas, "La Revolución Mexicana y la Educación Popular," in *Historia de la Educación Pública en México*, ed. Fernando Solana, Raúl Cardiel, and Raúl Bulanos (Mexico City: Secretaría de Educación Pública/Fondo de la Cultúra Económica, 1981), 141.

54. Ibid.

55. Bravo Ugarte, *Historia de México*, 136.

56. Palavincini was also the founder of the leading Mexico City daily newspaper *El Universal*.

57. Gómez Navas, "La Revolución Mexicana y la Educación Popular," 144–45.

58. Ibid.

59. *Diario Oficial* (November 21, 1918).

60. Ibid.

61. Rius Facius, *La Juventud Católica*, 104.

62. Ibid., 105–6.

Chapter Two

1. Adrian A. Bantjes, "The Regional Dynamics of Anticlericalism and Defanaticization in Revolutionary Mexico," in *Faith and Impiety in Revolutionary Mexico*, 115.

2. Andrés Barquín y Ruíz, *Bernardo Bergöend, S.J.* (Mexico City: Editorial Jus, 1968), 17–42.

3. Benjamin F. Martin, *Count Albert de Mun: Paladin of the Third Republic* (Chapel Hill: University of North Carolina Press, 1978), 63. Bergöend's letter to Miguel Palomar y Vizcarra indicates that the initiative for establishing the ACJM came from Bergöend and not Archbishop Mora y del Río, who had to be sold on the project ("Letter from Bernardo Bergöend, S.J. to Miguel Palomar y Vizcarra," November 6, 1912, Miguel Palomar y Vizcarra Collection, Section: *Organizaciones Católicas*, Series: *A.C.J.M.*, File #330, Box #46, *Archivo Histórico de la Universidad Nacional Autónoma de México*).

4. "Letter from Bernardo Bergöend, S.J. to Miguel Palomar y Vizcarra," November 6, 1912, Miguel Palomar y Vizcarra Collection, Section: *Organizaciones Católicas*, Series: *A.C.J.M.*, File #330, Box #46, *Archivo Histórico de la Universidad Nacional Autónoma de México*.

5. Rius Facius, *La Juventud Católica*, 44.

6. The Catholic Church in Mexico, under the leadership of Archbishop José Mora y del Río, took advantage of the greater political freedom created by the Díaz dictatorship's collapse in 1911 in order to strengthen its presence in Mexican society. The Catholic Church hierarchy promoted the creation of the PCN (1911), the Union of Catholic Ladies (1912), Catholic labor unions, as well as the ACJM (1913).

7. Sherman, *Mexican Right*, 9. The details of Bergöend's escape from Mexico, his exile, and his return to his adopted country remain unknown and are an important lacuna in the history of the Jesuit's life and ministry. Archival information preserved by the Society of Jesus on Jesuits working and living in Mexico during the twentieth century is currently inaccessible to lay scholars. This archive could possibly fill in this gap in Bernardo Bergöend's life.

8. "Quinta Asamblea General, Informe Presidencial 1938–1940, Asociación Católica de la Juventud Mexicana," October 17, 1940, Miguel Palomar y Vizcarra Collection, Section: *Organizaciones Católicas*, Serial: *A.C.J.M.*, File #332, Box #46, *Archivo Histórico de la Universidad Nacional Autónoma de México*; Antonio Rius Facius, *De Don Porfirio a Plutarco: Historia de la A.C.J.M.* (Mexico City: Editorial Jus, 1958), 285; and Barquín y Ruíz, *Bernardo Bergöend*, 82.

9. Sherman, *Mexican Right*, 10. The Union of Catholic Ladies was originally known as the "Asociación de Damas Católicas Mexicanas."

10. Barquín y Ruíz, *Bernardo Bergöend*, 64; and Rius Facius, *De Don Porfirio a Plutarco*, 172, 220, 262.

11. Barquín y Ruíz, *Bernardo Bergöend*, 63.

12. "Estatutos Generales de la Unión Nacional de Damas Católicas Medicines," in *Primer Congreso Nacional Unión de Damas Católicas, noviembre de 1922* (Tlalpam, Mexico: Imprenta Patricio Saenz, 1922), 16–17.

13. Miguel Jiménez Rueda, "El Padre Bergöend S.J. y el Centro de Estudiantes Católicos," No date, Miguel Palomar y Vizcarra Collection, Section: *Organizaciones Católicas*, Serial: *A.C.J.M.*, File #333, Box #46, *Archivo Histórico de la Universidad Nacional Autónoma de México*.

14. Gerardo Decorme, SJ, *Historia de la Compañía de Jesús en la República Mexicana durante el Siglo XIX: Restuaración y Vida Secularizada 1848–1880*, vol. II (Guadalajara: J. M. Yguiniz, 1921), 264; and Manuel Ceballos Ramírez, *El Catolicismo Social. Un Tercero en discordia (Rerum Novarum, la "cuestión social" y la movilización de los católicos mexicanos [1891–1911])* (Mexico City: El Colegio de México, 1991), 164. Since 1870, Jesuit schools in Mexico had been seats for Marian Congregations, a sixteenth-century institution whose goal was to "collect isolated energies; group together the healthiest and purest elements of Mexican youth, create a nucleus of men of faith and of profound convictions. . . . In short, prepare a vigorous and dignified generation." These groups existed in eight Mexican cities by the end of the Porfiriato.

15. Joaquín González, "Don Bernardo Bergöend," *Excélsior*, October 20, 1943.

16. Pbro. Librado Tovar, *Crónica y Trabajos Principales de Primer Congreso Católico-Regional-Obrero Celebrado en Guadalajara, Jalisco, en Abril de 1919* (Guadalajara: Tip. C. M. Sainz, 1920).

17. Mariano Cuevas, SJ, *Historia de la Iglesia en México*, vol. 5, appendix 1 (El Paso, Texas: Editorial *Revista Católica*, 1928), 423.

18. "Letter from Bernardo Bergöend, S.J. to Eduardo Hernández," June 15, 1917, reproduced in Rius Facius, *De Don Porfirio a Plutarco*.

19. Barquín y Ruíz, *Bernardo Bergöend*, 215.

20. The Constitution of 1917 prohibited the reelection of all officeholders. This was in response to Porfirio Díaz's practice of standing for reelection during his long hold on the presidency (1876–1880; 1884–1911).

21. The 1920s was also marked by the entry of organized labor into the world of formal politics. The government affiliated CROM and the anarchist CGT both used violence against each other in order to win control over the Mexican organized labor movement. They also targeted the National Catholic Labor Confederation, with whom they competed for adherents.

22. Rius Facius, *De Don Porfirio a Plutarco*, 179.

23. Ibid., 183–84.

24. "Los Acontecimientos del 10 de Mayo," May 3, 1922, Miguel Palomar y Vizcarra Collection, Section: *Organizaciones Católicas* Series: A.C.J.M., *Archivo Histórico de la Universidad Nacional Autónoma de México*.

25. "Telegram from the President of the Republic, P. Elías Calles, to Juan Federico Philippi," July 28, 1926, Pascual Díaz Archive, File #192, Box #5, *Archivo Histórico del Arzobispado Primado de México*.

26. Miguel Palomar y Vizcarra's family had held the title of Marquis of Pánuco during the colonial era (*Diccionario Porrúa de Historía, Biografía, Geografía de México* [Mexico City: Editorial Porrúa, 1986], 2188).

27. "Letter from the 'Centro de Estudiantes Católicos Mexicanos' to Miguel Palomar y Vizcarra," May 21, 1918, Miguel Palomar y Vizcarra Collection, *Archivo Histórico de la Universidad Nacional Autónoma de México*. Bergöend appointed Palomar y Vizcarra to head the ACJM's Mexico City study groups in 1918.

28. "Speech of Miguel Palomar y Vizcarra to the First National Eucharist Congress," October 9, 1924. Miguel Palomar y Vizcarra Collection, *Archivo Histórico de la Universidad Nacional Autónoma de México*.

29. Andrés Barquín y Ruíz, *Luis Segura Vilchis* (Mexico City: Editorial Jus, 1967), 80–82.

30. "El pueblo mexicano se organiza para defender sus libertades," *El País*, March 22, 1925.

31. "Letter from Ramón Ruiz to Andrés Barquín y Ruíz," December 13, 1927, Miguel Palomar y Vizcarra Collection, *Archivo Histórico de la Universidad Nacional Autónoma de México*. The League was inspired by a proposal Bergöend had made years earlier for the creation of a "Civic League of Civil Resistance" in order to combat the influence of "American Protestantism" in post-revolutionary Mexico and the "antireligious hostility of the [Mexican] state" (Barquín y Ruíz, *Luis Segura Vilchis*, 80–83).

32. "Programa de Boycott," July 7, 1926, Pascual Díaz Archive, File #192, Box #5, *Archivo Histórico del Arzobispado Primado de México*.

33. Sherman, *Mexican Right*, 11.

34. They also petitioned the bishops to provide the Cristero guerrilla bands with chaplains in order to provide spiritual comfort. Finally, they wanted the bishops to appeal to wealthy Catholics for the money needed to sustain the armed movement. The bishops did turn down their request for chaplains, and they informed the LNDLR leadership that, in their opinion, it would be "very difficult, almost impossible, and particularly dangerous" for them to appeal for money from wealthy Catholics for the Cristero cause.

35. Untitled document, May 13, 1929, Miguel Palomar y Vizcarra Collection, Section: *Organizaciones Católicas* Series: *L.N.D.L.R.*, File #348, Box #47, *Archivo Histórico de la Universidad Nacional Autónoma de México*.

36. Antonio Rius Facius, *Méjico Cristero: Historia de la ACJM 1925 a 1931* (Mexico City: Editorial Patria, 1960), 194–95. Unfortunately, Catholic peasants recruited by the ACJM did not know that the plot had been uncovered and walked into a trap when they attacked the city on January 3, 1927.

37. Ibid., 212, 214–15.

38. Ibid., 222, 224.

39. Miguel Palomar y Vizcarra Collection, Section: *Hemerográfica* Series: *Colección Traslosheros*, File #161 Box #110, *Archivo Histórico de la Universidad Nacional Autónomo de México*. González Flores's newspaper *Gladium* was a self-described "combat journal" dedicated to "killing and burying tyrants."

40. "Letter from Manuel Dávalos to the 'Secretario del Grupo Local de la ACJM Irapuato, Gto,'" April 20, 1927, Miguel Palomar y Vizcarra Collection, *Archivo Histórico de la Universidad Nacional Autónoma de México*.

41. Robert E. Quirk, *The Mexican Revolution and the Catholic Church: 1910–1929* (Bloomington: Indiana University Press, 1973), 201–2. These clerics included Father John J. Burke, the National Catholic Welfare Conference general secretary, and the Vatican's Apostolic Delegate to the United States Monsignor Pietro Fumasoni-Biondi.

42. Ibid., 212.

43. Ibid.

44. Segura Vilchis had helped to organize the ill-fated Ajusco campaign earlier that year. Controversy surrounds the inspiration for the attempt on Obregón's life. Andrés Barquín y Ruíz, a friend of Segura Vilchis, claimed in his friend's biography that Segura Vilchis had acted without the approval of his superiors. However, Antonio Rius Facius adamantly states in *Méjico Cristero* that Segura Vilchis had been commissioned by the LNDLR's directors to carry out the plot. It should be remembered that Barquín y Ruíz had a strong motivation not to implicate him or others in this plot, even though he wrote his biography of Luis Segura Vilchis some forty years after the attempt on Obregón's life, given the general's icon status within the Mexican Army.

45. Barquín y Ruíz, *Luis Segura Vilchis*, 155.

46. Quirk, *Mexican Revolution*, 209–10.

47. "Letter from Miguel Palomar y Vizcarra to Bishop Manríquez y Zarate," July 5, 1928, Miguel Palomar y Vizcarra Collection, Section: *Organizaciones Católicas*; and Series: *L.N.D.L.R.*, *Archivo Histórico de la Universidad Nacional Autónoma de México*.

48. John W. F. Dulles, *Yesterday in Mexico: A Chronicle of the Mexican*

Revolution, 1919–1936 (Austin: University of Texas Press, 1961), 313; and Rius Facius, *Méjico Cristero*, 317.

49. Rius Facius, *Méjico Cristero*, 317.

50. Dulles, *Yesterday in Mexico*, 312–13.

51. In 1988, sixty-one years after his death, Miguel Agustín Pro was beatified by Pope John Paul II as a martyr of the Roman Catholic Church and his canonization is pending. The Society of Jesus Order in Mexico has named their human rights organization in Father Miguel Agustín Pro's honor (Camp, *Crossing Swords*, 79).

52. The 1928 electoral campaign witnessed the government's assassination of Obregón's two main rivals—General Francisco Serrano and General Arnulfo Gómez—after federal agents uncovered their plot to kidnap both Obregón and President Calles in order to seize control of the country.

53. Luis Rivero del Val, *Entre las Patas de los Caballos: Diario de un Cristero* (Mexico City: Editorial Jus, 1953), 171, 214; Rius Facius, *Méjico Cristero*, 366; and Dulles, *Yesterday in Mexico*, 364. León Toral had been a close personal friend of Humberto Pro, one of the men executed the previous year following the first attempt on Obregón's life.

54. "La muerte de Obregón no fue un asesinato," July 1928. Miguel Palomar y Vizcarra Collection, Section: *Conflicto Cristero*, Series: *Persecución Religiosa*, File #517, Box #63, *Archivo Histórico de la Universidad Nacional Autónoma de México*.

55. Dulles, *Yesterday in Mexico*, 403.

56. "Declaraciones que Hizo Anoche a la Prensa el Señor Presidente," *Excélsior*, June 22, 1929.

57. Ibid.

58. "Letter from Daniel Tello to Miguel Palomar y Vizcarra," June 27, 1929, Section: *Organizaciones Católicas*, Series: *L.N.D.L.R.*, File #378, Box #51, *Archivo Histórico de la Universidad Nacional Autónoma de México*. Yet the LNDLR's executive committee saw that it had no option but to obey the ecclesiastical hierarchy and accept the church's agreement with the government.

59. "Letter from Miguel Palomar y Vizcarra to Archbishop González Valencia of Durango," September 1, 1928, Section: *Organizaciones Católicas*, Series: *L.N.D.L.R.*, File #369, Box #50, *Archivo Histórico de la Universidad Nacional Autónoma de México*; and "Letter from Miguel Palomar y Vizcarra to Archbishop Francisco Orozco y Jiménez of Guadalajara," November 23, 1928, Miguel Palomar y Vizcarra Collection, Section: Organizaciones Católicas, Series: *L.N.D.L.R.*, File #371, Box #50, *Archivo Histórico de la Universidad Nacional Autónoma de México*.

60. "Report from Alberto María Carreño to the Directors of the 'Liga Nacional Defensora de la Libertad Religiosa,'" July 15, 1928, Miguel Palomar y

Vizcarra Collection, Series: *L.N.D.L.R.*, File #367, Box #50, *Archivo Histórico de la Universidad Nacional Autónoma de México*. Alberto María Carreño also questioned the morality of continuing a war that could not be won. The Cristeros's inability to capitalize on the ongoing bloodletting in the ranks of the governing "revolutionary family" (e.g., the Serrano and Gómez assassinations of 1927 and the Escobardista Revolt of 1929) is indicative of their military weakness.

61. Gianfranco Poggi, *Catholic Action in Italy: The Sociology of a Sponsored Organization* (Stanford: Stanford University Press, 1967), 12. Catholic Action originated in Italy.

62. "La Apoteosis de la Infamia . . . ," May 5, 1929, *Boletín de la Liga Nacional Defensora de la Libertad Religiosa*, II Series, no. 9., Miguel Palomar y Vizcarra Collection, Section: *Organizaciones Católicas*, Series: *L.N.D.L.R.*, File #377, Box #51, *Archivo Histórico de la Universidad Nacional Autónoma de México*.

63. "Letter of Octavio Elizalde to Archbishop Pascual Díaz," November 26, 1929, Pascual Díaz Archive, Section: *A.C.M.*, File #197, Box #3, *Archivo Histórico del Arzobispado Primado de México*.

64. Ibid.

65. "Letter from the A.C.J.M.'s General Committee to the Diocese Committees and Local Groups of the A.C.J.M.," December 31, 1929, Miguel Palomar y Vizcarra Collection, Section: *Organizaciones Católicas*, Series: *A.C.J.M.*, File #330, Box #46, *Archivo Histórico de la Universidad Nacional Autónoma de México*.

66. Ibid.

67. "Letter from Archbishop Pascual Díaz to R .P. Ramón Martínez Silva, S.J.," January 14, 1930, Pascual Díaz Archive, Section: *A.C.M.*, File #197, Box #3, *Archivo Histórico del Arzobispado Primado de México*.

68. "Letter from the A.C.J.M.'s General Committee to Archbishop Pascual Díaz," January 18, 1930, Pascual Díaz Archive, File #197, Box #3, *Archivo Histórico del Arzobispado Primado de México*; and "Letter from Archbishop Pascual Díaz to O. Elizondo [sic] and the other signers," February 1, 1930, Pascual Díaz Archive, File #197, Box #3, *Archivo Histórico del Arzobispado Primado de México*.

69. "Acta de fundación del Grupo Juventud Cívica, el 12 de marzo de 1930," Miguel Palomar y Vizcarra Collection, Section: *Organizaciones Católicas*, Series: *A.C.J.M.*, File #330, Box #46, *Archivo Histórico de la Universidad Nacional Autónoma de México*. The dramatic nature of this act was lost on no one, given importance the CEC's historical importance within the ACJM, having been its founding local and later serving as the organization's national headquarters.

70. Rius Facius, *Méjico Cristero*, 487.

71. "Acta de fundación del Grupo Juventud Cívica, el 12 de marzo de

1930," Miguel Palomar y Vizcarra Collection, Section: *Organizaciones Católicas*, Series: *A.C.J.M.*, File #330, Box #46, *Archivo Histórico de la Universidad Nacional Autónoma de México*; and untitled document written by Archbishop Pascual Díaz, August 1, 1930, Archbishop Dario Miranda Archive, File #197, Box #3, *Archivo Histórico del Arzobispado Primado de México*.

72. "Letter from Bernardo Bergöend, S.J. to Archbishop Pascual Díaz," October 7, 1930, Pascual Díaz Archive, Section: *Acción Católica Mexicana*, File #197, Box #3, *Archivo Histórico del Arzobispado Primado de México*.

73. Ibid.

74. "Acta de fundación del Grupo Juventud Cívica, el 12 de marzo de 1930," Miguel Palomar y Vizcarra Collection, Section: *Organizaciones Católicas*, Series: *A.C.J.M.*, File #330, Box #46, *Archivo Histórico de la Universidad Nacional Autónoma de México*; and Barquín y Ruíz, *Bernardo Bergöend*, 164–65.

75. Barquín y Ruíz, *Bernardo Bergöend*, 214–16.

76. Ibid. Like the old ACJM, Nationalist Youth promoted the trinity of "piety, study, and action." However, Nationalist Youth's statutes did contain one novelty that reflected one of the ideological currents of the time: it called for the creation of a Catholic corporatist state in Mexico.

77. The subsequent adoption, by some ACJM elements, of terrorist tactics is indicative of their military weakness. José de León Toral's assassination of Álvaro Obregón failed to prevent the federal security forces from militarily defeating the Cristeros; ironically, what it did do was to clear the path for Plutarco Elías Calles to become Mexico's undisputed political strongman. Calles then went on to found the ruling political party that governed Mexico from 1929 to 2000 and which returned to power in the 2012 presidential elections.

78. Oswaldo Robles Ochoa was a member of the same Daniel O'Connell ACJM local that produced Obregón's assassin, José de León Toral, and his would-be assassin Luis Segura Vilchis (untitled document, n.d., Pascual Díaz Archive, Section: *A.C.M.*, File #197, Box #3, *Archivo Histórico del Arzobispado Primado de México*; and Rius Facius, *De Don Porfirio a Plutarco*, 240).

79. Partido Acción Nacional, *Así Nacio el PAN* (Mexico City: Comisión Editorial, 1990), 77.

80. Ibid., 23.

81. Laura Patricia Romero, "Los estudiantes entre el socialismo y el neoconservadurismo," in *Jalisco desde la Revolución: movimientos sociales 1929–1940*, ed. Laura Patricia Romero (Guadalajara: Universidad de Guadalajara, 1988), 281.

Chapter Three

1. Rivero del Val, *Entre las Patas*, 25.

2. Untitled document, n.d., Pascual Díaz Archive, Section: *Acción Católica Mexicana*, File #197, Box #3, *Archivo Histórico del Arzobispado Primado de México*.

3. Ibid.

4. Luis Calderón Vega, *Cuba 88: Memorias de la UNEC* (Mexico City: n.p., 1959), 12. These included the positions of president, a vice president (one of two), and two secretaries.

5. The figure of Father Pro, SJ, represents an additional link between the ACJM's Daniel O'Connell chapter and the new Catholic Student Confederation, as his brother Humberto Pro was also a Daniel O'Connell group member.

6. Estatutos de la Confederación Nacional de Estudiantes Católicos de México, 1928, File #360, Box #46, Miguel Palomar y Vizcarra Collection, Archivo Histórico de la Universidad Nacional Autónoma de México.

7. The Cristero Rebellion broke out in 1926 shortly after the Mexican bishops declared a strike to protest the government's religious policies. Catholic peasant guerrilla groups began to emerge in historically Catholic regions in central and western Mexico, motivated by both religious and economic considerations. The LNDLR, which on July 25, 1926, had initiated a nationwide economic boycott as a means of pressuring Calles's government, moved in the fall of 1926 toward a policy of embracing the Cristeros's armed struggle. The League's dramatic decision was taken only after consulting the Mexican bishops, who agreed not to block the *Liga*'s entry into the Cristero Rebellion (*Programa de Boycott*, July 7, 1926, Pascual Díaz Archive, File #192, Box #5, *Archivo Histórico del Arzobispado de México*; and untitled document, May 13, 1929, Miguel Palomar y Vizcarra Collection, Section: *Organizaciones Católicas*, Series: *L.N.D.L.R.*, File #348, Box #47, *Archivo Histórico de la Universidad Nacional Autónoma de México*).

8. Luis Rivero del Val detailed his adventures as a Cristero guerrilla fighter in his autobiography *Entre las Patas de los Caballos* (1953).

9. Juan Hernández Luna, "Un diálogo con el restaurador en Mascarrones de la filosofia perrenes," in *Homenaje a Oswaldo Robles en su 25 Aniversario en Docencia* (Mexico City: Editorial Jus, 1963), 100.

10. "Letter from Daniel Tello to Miguel Palomar y Vizcarra," June 27, 1929, Section: *Organizaciones Católicas*, Series: *L.N.D.L.R.*, File #378, Box #51, *Archivo Histórico de la Universidad Nacional Autónomo de México*. League members had become increasingly alarmed by the negotiations that Díaz and Ruiz y Flores were carrying out and frustrated by their lack of input in the process. Lay Catholic militants and their allies in the church hierarchy feared that Díaz and Ruiz y Flores were going to reach an agreement based solely on

"promises of men without honor" ("Letter from Miguel Palomar y Vizcarra to Archbishop González Valencia of Durango," September 1, 1928, Section: *Organizaciones Católicas*, Series: *L.N.D.L.R.*, File #369, Box 50, *Archivo Histórico de la Universidad Nacional Autónoma de México*).

11. Díaz's reforms to the ACJM stripped from it its fundamental task of creating Catholic social and political activists. In addition, the ACJM's top leadership would no longer be elected by its members but appointed by Archbishop Díaz as head of Mexican Catholic Action. Although Archbishop Díaz's reforms faced fierce resistance from the ACJM's national leadership and much of its rank and file, the cleric managed to impose his will on the organization. As a consequence, many of the ACJM's hard-line members deserted the association and created a short-lived rival organization, *Nationalist Youth*, which was ultimately doomed due to its lack of official recognition. Bergöend remained the ACJM's spiritual director despite his strenuous opposition to Díaz's reforms, which he directly made known to the archbishop ("Letter from Bernardo Bergöend, S.J. to Archbishop Pascual Diaz," October 7, 1930, Pascual Díaz Archive, Section: *Acción Católica* Mexicana, File #197, Box #3, *Archivo Histórico del Arzobispado Primado de México*). Bergöend maintained secret ties to Nationalist Youth and hoped that it would carry on his goal of creating Catholic political activists (Barquín y Ruíz, *Bernardo Bergöend*, 214–16).

12. "Circular sent by the ACM to *Junta Diocesenas* discussing the C.N.E.C.M.," ACM, 1064 C.N.E.C. 1930–1944, *Unidad de Acervos Históricos de la Universidad Iberoamericana*.

13. Ibid.

14. Pascual Díaz Archive, Section: C.N.E.C. (1929), File #192, Box #5, *Archivo Histórico Primado de México*.

15. "Circular sent by the ACM to *Junta Diocesenas* discussing the C.N.E.C.M.," ACM, 1064 C.N.E.C. 1930–1944, *Unidad de Acervos Históricos de la Universidad Iberoamericana*. However, it is unclear whether any funds were obtained from this source.

16. Manuel Ulloa Ortíz, "Homenaje al R. R. Don Ramón Martínez Silva, S.J. en el Décimo Aniversario de su Fallecimiento," in *Semblanzas de un Maestro* (Mexico City: Editorial Jus, 1974), 8.

17. "Informe del Sr. Bustos al Comité Directivo de la Liga," August 12, 1927, Miguel Palomar y Vizcarra Collection, Section: *L.N.D.L.R.*, Series: *Organizaciones Católicas*, File #356, Box #48, *Archivo Histórico de la Universidad Nacional Autónoma de México*; and "Memorandum from Miguel Palomar y Vizcarra to Luis Bustos," October 8, 1927, Section: *L.N.D.L.R.* Series: *Organizaciones Católicas*, File #356, Box #48, *Archivo Histórico de la Universidad Nacional Autónoma de México*.

18. Calderón Vega, *Cuba 88*, 21.

19. Archbishop Díaz no doubt viewed the Catholic Student Union as a potential counterweight to Bergöend's troublesome ACJM. The Catholic Student Union's focus on issues surrounding higher education dovetailed with the church's overall concern with matters relating to education and its continued apprehension of the government's educational policies. Indeed, in the 1930s education became a major source of conflict in the relationship between Mexico's revolutionary leaders and the Roman Catholic Church.

20. Fernando Beluánde Terry, a future president of Peru, was one of the delegates at this congress.

21. "Convocatoría y Conclusiones de la Convención Iberoamericana de Estudiantes Católicos, 12 al 22 de diciembre 1931," in Calderón Vega, *Cuba 88*, appendix 2, 26.

22. Ibid., 31.

23. Calderón Vega, *Cuba 88*, appendix 2, 19.

24. Ibid., 42.

25. Ibid.

26. Bantjes, "Regional Dynamics," 118; and Sherman, *Mexican Right*, 38.

27. Mary Kay Vaughan, *Cultural Politics in Revolution: Teachers, Peasants, and Schools in Mexico, 1930–1940* (Tucson: The University of Arizona Press, 1997), 31–32.

28. Secretaría de Educación Pública, *Algunos Datos y Opiniones sobre la Educación Sexual en México* (Mexico City: Talleres Gráficos de la Nación, 1933), 5–6; and Ernesto Meneses Morales et al., *Tendencias Educativas Oficiales en México: 1911–1934* (Mexico City: Centro de Estudios Educativos, 1986), 630. The Mexican Eugenics Society proposal was inspired in a resolution in favor of sex education in public schools that had been passed in 1930 by the Sixth Pan-American Congress of the Child held in Lima, Peru (Vaughn, *Cultural Politics in Revolution*, 33).

29. Secretaría de Educación Pública, *Algunos Datos*, 34.

30. *La Palabra* (Mexico City), June 5, 1933.

31. Vaughn, *Cultural Politics in Revolution*, 34.

32. Ibid., 5.

33. Archbishop Leopoldo Ruiz y Flores, "Instrucción a los Católicos Mexicanos," December 20, 1934, Miguel Palomar y Vizcarra Collection, File #342, Box #43, *Archivo Histórico de la Universidad Nacional Autónoma de México*.

34. Cardinal Pacelli, "Instrucciones Sobre la Conducta Que el Episcopado y los Fieles les han de Observar acerca de la Enseñanza Socialista Impuesta por el Gobierno Mexicano," December 20, 1936, Miguel Palomar y Vizcarra Collection, File #342, Box #43, *Archivo Histórico de la Universidad Nacional*

Autónoma de México. This included the establishment of clandestine Catholic schools and the reclassifying of Catholic secondary schools as "commercial academies" free of government regulations. The latter often enjoyed the support of Mexico's conservative business community and efforts to close them down provoked conflict between this element of the Mexican Right and the government. This situation is illustrated by the example of the Commercial Academy of Morelia, a school founded in 1936 and supported financially by Morelia's chapter of the National Chamber of Commerce and Industry. President Lázaro Cárdenas's decision to close this school led to a flood of telegrams to the president's office from angry regional chapters of the National Chamber of Commerce and Industry ("Memorandum Relativo a la Clausura de la Academia de Enseñanza Mercantil de la Cámara Nacional de Comercio e Industria de Morelia, Michoacán, que presenta a la Considerción y Resolución del Señor Presidente de la República. La Confederación de Camaras Nacionales de Comercio e Industria y la Cámara Citada," January 26, 1938, File #XIII/162.1[723.4]/-1, Box #259, *Departamento Jurídico y Revalidación de Estudios* Collection, *Archivo Histórico de la Secretaría de la Educación Pública*).

35. Vaughn, *Cultural Politics in Revolution*, 35.

36. Bantjes, "Regional Dynamics," 118; and David Raby, "Los Maestros Rurales y los Conflictos Sociales en México (1931–1940)," *Historia Mexicana* 18.2 (Oct.–Dec. 1968): 190–226.

37. Sherman, *Mexican Right*, 45; and Bantjes, "Regional Dynamics," 119.

38. Vaughn, *Cultural Politics in Revolution*, 13.

39. Ibid., 35.

40. Mabry, *Mexican University*, 109–10; and Sherman, *Mexican Right*, 38.

41. Alberto Bremauntz, *La Educación Socialista en México* (Mexico City: Imprenta Rivadeneyra, 1943), 165–66.

42. Ibid., 411.

43. Vicente Lombardo Toledano, *Obra Educativa*, vol. 2 (Mexico City: Instituto Politécnico Nacional, 1987), 387.

44. Lombardo Toledano engaged in celebrated debate with former mentor, philosopher, and UNAM faculty member Antonio Caso on the merits of the curriculum reform program and the issue of academic freedom.

45. Rodolfo Brito Foucher's role in the creation of the Universidad Iberoamericana is analyzed in chapter 4. In 1935 the combative Brito Foucher went on to "invade" with a cohort of UNAM students the Tabascan fiefdom of the Calles stalwart Tomás Garrido Canabal, who was the most extreme of the nation's anticlerical governors. The gambit proved successful (Sherman, *Mexican Right*, 59).

46. Mabry, *Mexican University*, 119.

47. Fellow UNEC members Daniel Kuri Breña and Manuel Pacheco Moreno succeeded Chávez Camacho as presidents of the CNE.

48. "Memorandum que presenta la Unión Nacional de Estudiantes Católicos de México a la consideración del Venerable Episcopado," 1945, *Archivo del Arzobispo Luis Ma. Martínez*, File #83, Section: *Gobierno Civil, Memorandums Letra "M," Archivo Histórico del Arzobispado Primado de México*. It is impossible to corroborate these estimates that, on the face of it, appear to be significantly exaggerated.

49. The UNEC, as part of its crusade against its ideological adversaries, also supported anti-socialist curriculum reform efforts at the University of Guadalajara. In October 1934 a strike broke out at that institution led by secular and Catholic conservative faculty and students against a socialist curriculum reform effort endorsed by the school's rector and the state government. This time, however, the opponents of socialist education were unsuccessful. To break the strike, the government sent in the federal army to seize the university's buildings and then closed the institution for an indefinite amount of time (Romero, "Los estudiantes," 287).

50. The case of the elite Mexico City Jesuit preparatory school *Instituto Patria* serves to illustrate this point. The Jesuits selected a Catholic layman, Francisco Pérez Salazar, to present the school's application for incorporation into the UNAM. The school's name was changed to *Bachilleratos* and no mention was made of its previous incarnation as a Jesuit school, although it is hard to believe that university officials would not be aware of this fact, as the *Instituto Patria* was the most prestigious Catholic preparatory school in country and was located in Mexico City. However, both sides kept up with the charade and the *Bachilleratos* was granted incorporation in August 1934 ("Letter from Francisco Pérez Salazar to Rector Manuel Gómez Morín [UNAM]," April 13, 1934, Binder: 270, *Dirección General de Incorporación y de Revalidación* Collection, *Archivo Histórico de la Universidad Nacional Autónoma de México*; and "Letter from the *Oficial Mayor* of the UNAM Antonio Armendáriz to Director Francisco Pérez Salazar of *Bachilleratos*," August 15, 1934, Document: 150.4167.150/202.2/, Binder: 270, *Dirección General de Incorporación y de Revalidación* Collection, *Archivo Histórico de la Universidad Nacional Autónoma de México*).

51. José Luis Curiel, interview by author, Mexico City, October 27, 1993.

52. Its associate status meant that it had no voting rights within Catholic Action. More importantly, it meant that its future existence was always going to be uncertain.

53. Luis G. Bustos, "Fundamentalidad de la Unión National de Estudiantes Católicos," December 1935, 10.65 UNEC 1935–1936, *Unidad de Acervos Históricos de la Universidad Iberoamericana*.

54. In 1940 Mexico's population was still 78 percent rural with most living

in dire poverty despite President Cárdenas' massive land-reform program (Sherman, *Mexican Right*, 40).

55. Luis G. Bustos, "Fundamentalidad de la Unión National de Estudiantes Católicos," December 1935, 10.65 UNEC 1935–1936, *Unidad de Acervos Históricos de la Universidad Iberoamericana*.

56. "Letter from Archbishop Leopoldo Ruiz y Flores to Archbishop Pascual Díaz," July 22, 1935, 10.65 UNEC 1935–1936, *Unidad de Acervos Históricos de la Universidad Iberoamericana*.

57. "Letter from the *Vicario General* of the Archdiocese of Guadalajara to Luis G. Bustos, President of *Acción Católica Mexicana*," December 21, 1935, 10.65 UNEC 1935–1936, *Unidad de Acervos Históricos de la Universidad Iberoamericana*.

58. "Comunicación oficial que en su caracter de Director Pontíficio de la Acción Católica Mexicana, dirige el Exco. Sr. Arzobispo de México a la Junta Central y démas organos dirigentes de la ACM," N.D., 10.65 UNEC 1935–1936, *Unidad de Acervos Históricos de la Universidad Iberoamericana*.

59. "Letter from the Archbishop of Monterrey to Luis G. Bustos," December 26, 1935, 10.65 UNEC 1935–1936, *Unidad de Acervos Históricos de la Universidad Iberoamericana*.

60. "Comunicación oficial que en su caracter de Director Pontíficio de la Acción Católica Mexicana, dirige el Exco. Sr. Arzobispo de México a la Junta Central y démas organos dirigentes de la Acción Católica Mexicana," N.D., 10.65 UNEC 1935–1936, *Unidad de Acervos Históricos de la Universidad Iberoamericana*.

61. "Memorandum que presenta la Unión National de Estudiantes Católicos de México a la Consideración del Venerable Episcopado," 1945, *Archivo de Luis Ma. Martínez*, File #83, Section: *Gobierno Civil, Memorandums Letra "M," Archivo Histórico del Arzobispado Primado de México*.

62. Mabry, *Mexican University*, 158. Jesús Guísa y Acevedo, a Catholic activist and philosophy professor, was also removed from the UNAM because of his political activism.

63. Julio Jiménez Rueda, *Historia Jurídica de la Universidad de México* (Mexico City: Imprenta Universita, 1955), 225.

64. Mabry, *Mexican University*, 169.

65. Bantjes, "Regional Dynamics," 125; and Sherman, *Mexican Right*, 40. Mexican Catholics were grateful to Cárdenas who in 1936, for his own political reasons, had expelled Calles from Mexico.

66. Sherman, *Mexican Right*, 128. Sherman emphasizes the influence of the strength of right-wing opposition to Cárdenas' polices as evidenced by the vigor of General Juan Andreu Almazán's opposition candidacy in the 1940 presidential campaign.

67. Camp, *Crossing Swords*, 28.

68. José Gutiérrez Casillas, *Jesuitas en México durante el Siglo* XX (Mexico City: Editorial Porrúa, 1981), 555. See chapter 7 of Roderic Ai Camp's *Crossing Swords* (1997) for an excellent analysis of the critical role that the Seminario Montezuma had in training new generations of Mexican clerics during this era of intense anticlericalism.

69. Louis J. A. Mercier, preface to *A Humane Psychology of Education* by Jaime Castiello, SJ. (Chicago: Loyola University Press, 1962), xi–xii.

70. However, the UNEC did not retreat from the world of student politics during Castiello's tenure as its ecclesiastical representative. In an undated memorandum to Archbishop Luis Martínez, Jamie Castiello, SJ, proudly reported that the UNEC's candidate to the Mexico City–based FEU's Governing Board, José Campillo, had defeated a pro-government candidate by a vote margin of 550 (Jaime Castiello, "Informes," 1938 (?), *Archivo de Luis Ma. Martínez*, File #82, Section: *Diplomaticos, dictamenes, iniciatives y ministros. Letra "D", Archivo Histórico del Arzobispado Primado de México*).

71. José Campiello, "Presencia de Jaime Castiello: Semblanza," *Corporación* 66 (Jan.–Feb. 1963): 4.

72. For decades, its detractors have associated the UAG with extreme right-wing elements in Mexico's second largest city.

73. Calderón Vega, *Cuba 88*, 144. Cuesta Gallardo's activities were detailed in a report written in 1940 to Archbishop Martínez by the UNEC's president, Jesús Hernández Díaz.

74. "Memorandum presentado al Exmo. y Rvmo. Sr. Dr. D.N. Luis María Martínez, Dignísimo Arzobispo de México por el Asistente General de la Unión National de Estudiantes Católicos sobre el gravisimo problema que se plantea entre los universitarios católicos," 1945, *Archivo de Luis Ma. Martínez*, File #83, Section: *Gobierno Civil, Memorandums Letra "M," Archivo Histórico del Arzobispado Primado de México*.

75. "Memorandum que presenta la Unión National de Estudiantes Católicos de México a la Consideración del Venerable Episcopado," 1945, *Archivo de Luis Ma. Martínez*, File #83, Section: *Gobierno Civil, Memorandums Letra "M," Archivo Histórico del Arzobispado Primado de México*.

76. Calderón Vega, *Cuba 88*, 171–73.

77. "Memorandum que presenta la Unión National de Estudiantes Católicos de México a la Consideración del Venerable Episcopado," 1945, *Archivo de Luis Ma. Martínez*, File #83, Section: *Gobierno Civil, Memorandums Letra "M," Archivo Histórico del Arzobispado Primado de México*.

78. Sherman notes that during the Maximato, government policy, while anticlerical, had been conservative on economic matters and had alienated Mexico's business community as Cárdenas' administration managed to accomplish.

79. Donald J. Mabry, *Mexico's Acción Nacional: A Catholic Alternative to Revolution* (Syracuse, NY: Syracuse University Press, 1973), 21.

80. Partido Acción Nacional, *Así Nacio el PAN*, 23; and Mabry, *Mexico's Acción Nacional*, 34.

81. Partido Acción Nacional, *Así Nacio el PAN*, 23. This document was prepared by the PAN to celebrate the party's fiftieth anniversary in 1989. It is a reproduction of the programs and resolutions adopted by the PAN at its founding congress in 1939.

82. Ibid., 77.

83. José de Jesús Marinquez y Zarate, "Nueva Exposición y Protesta del Obispo de Huejutla," October 28, 1934, File #527, Box #64, Miguel Palomar y Vizcarra Collection, *Archivo Histórico de la Universidad Nacional Autónoma de México*.

84. Ibid.

Chapter Four

1. Roderic Ai Camp, *Mexico's Mandarins: Crafting a Power Elite for the Twenty-First Century* (Berkeley: University of California Press, 2002), 85.

2. Vicente Fox was a business administration major at the Universidad Iberoamericana (Camp, *Mexico's Mandarins*, 66).

3. Corporación de Estudiantes Católicos, *Memorias: Primer Congreso Nacional de Cultúra Católica del 18 al 23 de enero, 1953 Guadalajara, Jalisco* (Mexico City: Ediciones Corporación, 1953), 64.

4. Ibid.

5. Calderón Vega, *Cuba 88*, 186.

6. Universidad Iberoamericana, "Entrevista al Dr. Rodolfo Brito Foucher" (December 19, 1967), in "Historia de la UIA 1943–1956 [1968]," 20.

7. Ibid.

8. José Luis Curiel, interview by author, tape recording, Mexico City, October 27, 1993; and *Tiempo*, August 4, 1944, 10.

9. Hernández Luna, "Un diálogo con el restaurador," 100. The strongest assertion that Brito Foucher was pro-Sinarquista is made by none other than Salvador Abascal, the one-time Sinarquista leader, in his history of the National Sinarquista Union (Salvador Abascal, *Mis Recuerdos: Sinarquismo y Colonia María Auxiliadora* [Mexico City: Tradición, 1980]).

10. The *Colegio Motolinía* had been brought into the UNAM system of recognized schools as early as 1931, as certified by the documents preserved in the Dirección General de Incorporación y Revalidación de Estudios Collection of the UNAM's historical archive.

11. "Letter from Dr. Oswaldo Robles to the Señorita Directora of the Instituto Motolinía," February 18, 1943, Dirección General de Incorporación y Revalidación de Estudios Collection, *Archivo Histórico de la Universidad Nacional Autónoma de México*. An example of women's political marginality is seen by the fact that women were denied the right to vote in Mexico until 1952.

12. Universidad Iberoamericana, "Entrevista al Dr. Rodolfo Brito Foucher," 22.

13. The head of the Mexican province of the Jesuit order Francisco Robinson Bours, SJ.

14. José Luis Curiel, interview by author, tape recording, Mexico City, October 27, 1993. He was a Catholic student activist.

15. Ibid. The informant's observation is borne out by the fact that instead of pooling their resources with the Jesuit Universidad Iberoamericana, the Salesian order in Mexico utilized their own UNAM-affiliated preparatory school, the *Colegio Colón*, as the basis of their subsequent La Salle University.

16. Beatrice Estér Murguía, interview by author, tape recording, Mexico City, October 19, 1993; and "Letter from Alfonso Castiello, S.J. to Francisco Migoya, S.J., General Secretary of the Iberoamerican University," (no date) in "Historia de la UIA 1943–1956 [1968]," 49.

17. José de Jesús Hernández Chávez, S.J., interview by author, tape recording, Mexico City, October 13, 1993; and *Tiempo*, August 4, 1944, 10. A law professor at the UNAM, García Rojas was a former member of Bergöend's ACJM.

18. "Letter from Alfonso Castiello, S.J. to Francisco Migoya, S.J., General Secretary of the Iberoamerican University," (no date) in "Historia de la Universidad Iberoamericana 1943–1956 [1968]" (unpublished manuscript), 49. This unpublished manuscript also includes raw notes and documents. Torroella combined this responsibility with the directorship of the Instituto Patria.

19. "Letter from Dr. Everando Luna to Ramón Martínez Silva," April 11, 1945, Dirección General de Incorporación y Revalidación de Estudios Collection, *Archivo Histórico de la Universidad Nacional Autónoma de México*.

20. Centro Cultural Universitario, *Anuario del Centro Cultural Universitario* (Mexico City: n.p., 1950), no page numbers. This was the CCU's first and only yearbook.

21. José Ignacio Palencia, SJ, "Actividad Educativa y Cultural de los Jesuitas en la Ciudad de México y Alrededores (1572–1972)," in *La Compañía de Jesús en México: Cuatro Siglos de Labor Cultural 1572–1972* (Mexico City: Editorial Jus, 1972), 421.

22. Beatrice Estér Murguía, interview by author, tape recording, Mexico City, October 19, 1993.

23. J. Bronowski and Bruce Mazlish, *The Western Intellectual Tradition: From Leonardo to Hegel* (New York: Dorset Press, 1960), 478. This belief that morality was inborn in humans is presented formally in Kant's *Critique of Practical Reason* (1781).

24. At the CCU's philosophy school, both Jesuit and lay Catholics were faculty members. Among these lay neo-scholastic philosophers were men who had played an active role in the CCU's foundation: Oswaldo Robles and José Luis Curiel (CCU, *Anuario del Centro Cultural Universitario*).

25. Catholic social doctrine, as elaborated by the great papal encyclicals *Rerum Novarum* (1891) and *Quadragesimo Anno* (1931), formed the basis of the sociology taught in the Jesuit student organizations.

26. "Letter from Manuel Alcalá Anaya to Dr. Neftalí Rodríguez," March 7, 1944, Dirección General de Incorporación y Revalidación de Estudios Collection, *Archivo Histórico de la Universidad Nacional Autónoma de México*. The materials covered were Mexico's prehistory, the Pre-Cortesan era, and the "Spiritual Conquest" of Mexico by the Roman Catholic Church.

27. Ibid.

28. Cuevas, *História de la Iglesia*, 60–61.

29. Ibid., appendix 1, 423.

30. "Memorandum: Acuerdo #165," April 15, 1944, Dirección General de Incorporación y Revalidación de Estudios Collection, *Archivo Histórico de la Universidad Nacional Autónoma de México*.

31. José de Jesús Hernández Chávez, SJ, interview by author, tape recording, Mexico City, October 13, 1993.

32. "Letter from Dr. Everando Luna to Ramón Martínez Silva," April 11, 1945, Dirección General de Incorporación y Revalidación de Estudios Collection, *Archivo Histórico de la Universidad Nacional Autónoma de México*; and CCU, *Anuario del Centro Cultural Universitario*. The faculty at the CCU, like that of the UNAM itself, was heavily male at this time.

33. *El Popular* (July 11, 1944). *El Popular* was a newspaper controlled by Vicente Lombardo Toledano.

34. *El Popular* (July 4, 1944), 5; and *El Popular* (July 11, 1944).

35. *Tiempo* (July 21, 1944), 11.

36. *Tiempo* (August 4, 1944), 7.

37. Ibid.

38. Ibid., 8.

39. Mabry, *Mexican University*, 190.

40. "Acuerdo #165," April 15, 1944, Dirección General de Incorporación y Revalidación de Estudios Collection, *Archivo Histórico de la Universidad Nacional Autónoma de México*. The CCU also requested for the reincorporation

of its master's degree program in philosophy. UNAM regulations stipulated that the incorporated schools had to apply every year to the UNAM for the reincorporation for every course of study that they offered.

41. "Declaraciones del Rector," *Universidad de México* 1.9 (June 7, 1947).

42. "Acuerdo #53," July 25, 1945, Dirección General de Incorporación y Revalidación de Estudios Collection, *Archivo Histórico de la Universidad Nacional Autónoma de México*.

43. "Letter from Dr. Samuel Ramos to Lic. Juan Manuel Terán," August 13, 1945, File #12/218-203-/-1, Dirección General de Incorporación y Revalidación de Estudios Collection, *Archivo Histórico de la Universidad Nacional Autónoma de México*.

44. Ibid.

45. Ibid.

46. "Letter from Gilberto Loyo to Juan Manuel Terán," August 14, 1945, File #12/218-203-/1 /712-794, Dirección General de Incorporación y Revalidación de Estudios Collection, *Archivo Histórico de la Universidad Nacional Autónoma de México*. Loyo informed Terán that the Technical Commission of the UNAM's Economics School voted unanimously against the CCU's petition. In addition to being a distinguished economist and statistician, Loyo was concerned with educational matters. In his 1930 work *Sobre la enseñanza de la historia*, he called for a dogmatic teaching of Mexican history in order to form a national consciousness (Josefina Zoriada Vázquez, *Nacionalismo y Educación en México* [Mexico City: El Colegio de México, 1970], 186).

47. "H. Comisión de Grados y Revalidación Acuerdo #184," October 24, 1945, Dirección General de Incorporación y Revalidación de Estudios Collection, *Archivo Histórico de la Universidad Nacional Autónoma de México*.

48. "H. Comisión de Grados y Revalidación Acuerdo #224," November 30, 1945, Dirección General de Incorporación y Revalidación de Estudios Collection, *Archivo Histórico de la Universidad Nacional Autónoma de México*.

49. Universidad Iberoamericana, "Historia de la Universidad Iberoamericana 1943–1956 [1968]," 4. No documentation detailing the precise chain of events which led to the demise of the politically sensitive history course exits. It is not clear whether internal or external factors led to its end, and the Jesuits themselves claimed ignorance regarding this point.

50. Cuevas continued offering conferences at the CCU after the disappearance of its history program (CCU, *Anuario del Centro Cultural Universitario*).

51. Bravo Ugarte's *Historia de México* was published between 1941 and 1946.

52. Zoriada Vázquez, *Nacionalismo y Educación*, 260–61.

53. "Expediente del Ing. Rafael Illescas Frisbie," Document #XVI/131/-6, Box #4361, Consejo Nacional de la Educación Superior y la Investigación Científica Collection, *Archivo Histórico de la Secretaría de la Educación Pública*. Illescas Friesbie was appointed to this body on January 1, 1936, shortly after the founding of the council, and he remained in his position until March 1938, when his position was terminated by official decree.

54. Universidad Iberoamericana, "Historia de la Universidad Iberoamericana 1943–1956 [1968]," 4.

55. Identified as such in the CCU's 1950 *Anuario del Centro Cultural Universitario*.

56. "Letter from Alfonso Castiello S.J. to Francisco Migoya S.J., General Secretary of the Iberoamerican University," (no date) in "Historia de la Universidad Iberoamericana 1943–1956 [1968]," 49.

57. Ernesto Meneses Morales, *La Universidad Iberoamericana en el Contexto de la Educación Superior Contemporanea* (Mexico City: UIA, 1979), 70–71.

58. Rodrigo Mendirichaga, *El Tecnológico de Monterrey: sucesos, anécdotas, personajes* (Monterrey, Mexico: Editorial Castillo, 1982), 30–31.

59. Ibid., 180–81.

60. Universidad Iberoamericana, "Historia de la Universidad Iberoamericana: 1943–1956 [1968]," 5.

Chapter Five

1. Universidad Iberoamericana, "História de la Universidad Iberoamericana 1943–1956 [1968]," appendix 1, 1–2. The Universidad Iberoamericana's first rector was the Colombian Jesuit Félix Restrepo, and his successor was Ignacio Pérez Becerra.

2. "Estatuto Orgánico de la Universidad Iberoamericana," 13 de Abril de 1958, Actas del Consejo Universitario de la Universidad Iberoamericana Collection Centro de Información Académico, Unidad de Acervos Históricos de la Universidad Iberoamericana.

3. Fomento de Investigación y Cultura Superior A.C., "Mensaje del doctor Manuel Ignacio Pérez Alonso," in "30 Aniversario FICSAC," 1986, 6.

4. Acta #14 del Consejo Universitario 5 de Febrero de 1958," February 5, 1958, Actas del Consejo Universitario de la Universidad Iberoamericana Collection Centro de Información Académico, *Unidad de Acervos Históricos de la Universidad Iberoamericana*.

5. "Acta #1 del Consejo Universitario 1 de Mayo de 1956," Actas del Consejo Universitario de la Universidad Iberoamericana Collection Centro de Información Académico, *Unidad de Acervos Históricos de la Universidad Iberoamericana*.

6. José de Jesús Ledesma, *Trayectoria Histórico-Ideológico de la Universidad Iberoamericana* (Mexico City: Universidad Iberoamericana, 1987), 169.

7. Fomento de Investigación y Cultura Superior A.C., "Mensaje del doctor Manuel Ignacio Pérez Alonso," 7.

8. Ibid.

9. Fomento de Investigación y Cultura Superior A.C., "Presentación," in "30 Aniversario FICSAC," 3; and Franz A. von Sauer, *The Alienated "Loyal" Opposition: Mexico's Partido Acción Nacional* (Albuquerque: University of New Mexico Press, 1974), 3, 124.

10. Fomento de Investigación y Cultura Superior A.C., "Mensaje del ingeniero Cresencio Ballesteros," in "30 Aniversario FICSAC," 16.

11. Fomento de Investigación y Cultura Superior, A.C., "UIA-FICSAC 1962–1966" (1966), no page numbers; and Ernesto Meneses, *La Universidad Iberoamericana en el Contexto de la Educación Superior Contemporanea*, 149.

12. Fomento de Investigación y Cultura Superior, A.C., "UIA-FICSAC 1962–1966" (1966).

13. Universidad Iberoamericana, "Cronológia de la Universidad Iberoamericana," in "Historía de la Universidad Iberoamericana: 1943–1956 [1968]," appendix 1, 1–2. The first Jesuit rector was Félix Restrepo in 1952. The first Jesuit rector who was officially recognized by the UNAM was Manuel Ignacio Pérez Alonso, SJ, in 1956. The Iberoamericana's University Council was dominated by the Jesuit Order during this period.

14. Ernesto Meneses Morales, SJ, interview by author, tape recording, Mexico City, November 4, 1993.

15. "Acta #16 del Consejo Universitario 19 de Marzo de 1958," March 19, 1958, Actas del Consejo Universitario de la Universidad Iberoamericana Collection Centro de Información Académico, *Unidad de Acervos Históricos de la Universidad Iberoamericana*.

16. "Acta #20 del Consejo Universitario 14 de Abril de 1958," April 14, 1958, Actas del Consejo Universitario de la Universidad Iberoamericana Collection Centro de Información Académico, *Unidad de Acervos Históricos de la Universidad Iberoamericana*.

17. "Acta #7 del Consejo Universitario 25 de Julio de 1957," July 25, 1957, Actas del Consejo Universitario de la Universidad Iberoamericana Collection Centro de Información Académico, *Unidad de Acervos Históricos de la Universidad Iberoamericana*. Bouvier appeared as the director of the Iberoamericana's Industrial Relations School in the directory, which the University Council approved for publication.

18. Emile Bouvier, SJ, *Neither Right nor Left in Labor Relations* (Montreal: University of Montreal Press, 1951).

19. Ibid., 37. Marxism itself was presented as merely "the tools of war in the well-practiced hands of Free Masonry."

20. Ibid., 26.

21. Laborers had the right to work, to a fair wage, to good working conditions, to social security, and to organize. The working class in turn owed their employers a series of duties. They should "develop a passion for work well done" and demonstrate "proper respect" to their employer (Bouvier, *Neither Right nor Left*, 58, 62–63).

22. Universidad Iberoamericana, *Catálogo General: 1962* (Mexico City, Universidad Iberoamericana, 1962), 196.

23. Ibid., 202.

24. Ibid., 19, 194. The executives on the Iberoamericana Industrial Relations advisory board represented companies like the major electrical consumer goods manufacturer *IEM*, the luxury department store chain *Palacio de Hierro*, and the airline company *Aeronaves de México*.

25. Universidad Iberoamericana, "Historia de la Universidad Iberoamericana 1943–1956 [1968]," 42.

26. Ibid.

27. "Actas del Consejo Universitario," June 28, 1960, Actas del Consejo Universitario de la Universidad Iberoamericana Collection Centro de Información Académico, *Unidad de Acervos Históricos de la Universidad Iberoamericana*. Industrial Relations attracted 250 students in 1960, while its business administration program had 320 enrolled members.

28. Universidad Iberoamericana, *Catálogo General*, 59–61; and Universidad Iberoamericana, "Historia de la Universidad Iberoamericana 1943–1956 [1968]", 60. José Sánchez Villaseñor was credited with its establishment. Azcárraga, who at time of his death in 1997 was the head of the largest Spanish-language producer of television programming in the world, *Televisa*, was the head of production and sales of the *Telesistema Mexicano* in 1960. Other members of the advisory board were executives from other major television and radio stations. Emilio Azcárraga Milmo's son and current head of Televisa, Emilio Azcárraga Jean, is a graduate of the Universidad Iberoamericana.

29. Universidad Iberoamericana, *Catálogo General*, 61.

30. "Actas del Consejo Universitario," June 28, 1960, Actas del Consejo Universitario de la Universidad Iberoamericana Collection Centro de Información Académico, *Unidad de Acervos Históricos de la Universidad Iberoamericana*.

31. Universidad Iberoamericana, *Catálogo General*, 105.

32. Universidad Iberoamericana, "Historia de la Universidad Iberoamericana 1943–1956 [1968]," 57–58.

33. "Actas del Consejo Universitario," June 28, 1960, Actas del Consejo Universitario de la Universidad Iberoamericana Collection Centro de Información Académico, *Unidad de Acervos Históricos de la Universidad Iberoamericana*.

34. Ibid.

35. "Letter from Manuel Cavalla to Alonso Mariscal," June 19, 1956, Dirección General de Incorporación y Revalidación de Estudios Collection, *Archivo Histórico de la Universidad Nacional Autónoma de México*. Alonso Mariscal was the director of the UNAM's School of Architecture.

36. Fomento de Investigación y Cultura Superior A.C., "Mensaje del ingeniero Crescencio Ballesteros," in "30 Aniversario FICSAC," 17.

37. "Actas del Consejo Universitario," June 28, 1960, Actas del Consejo Universitario de la Universidad Iberoamericana Collection Centro de Información Académico, *Unidad de Acervos Históricos de la Universidad Iberoamericana*.

38. Meneses, *La Universidad*, 145–46.

39. Fomento de Investigación y Cultura Superior A.C., "Mensaje del ingeniero Crescencio Ballesteros," 16.

40. Ibid.

41. Ibid.

42. For an excellent analysis of Ballesteros's financial links to the Mexican economy, see Camp, *Mexico's Mandarins*, 74. In addition to his construction business, Ballesteros was also for a time the owner of Mexicana Airlines and president of the board of directors of John Deere of Mexico and Union Carbide of Mexico.

43. "Acta #7," July 25, 1957, Actas del Consejo Universitario de la Universidad Iberoamericana Collection Centro de Información Académico, *Unidad de Acervos Históricos de la Universidad Iberoamericana*.

44. Ibid.

45. Ibid.

46. Corporación de Estudiantes Mexicanos, *Memorias*, viii.

47. Ibid.

48. Sánchez Villaseñor's paper was titled "Christian Philosophy and Crisis of Values."

49. Corporación de Estudiantes Mexicanos, *Memorias*, 70.

50. Ibid., 73.

51. Ibid., 73–74, 76. Sartre's philosophy had been the target of Sánchez Villaseñor's scholarly writings before this congress on Catholic culture. In an article published in the Jesuit student journal, Corporación had stated that this

"pessimistic and destructive philosophy," symptomatic of the crisis of values in Western Culture, was due to mankind's rejection of the authority of God.

52. Corporación de Estudiantes Mexicanos, *Memorias*, 74.

53. Immanuel Kant.

54. Sartrian existentialism.

55. Corporación de Estudiantes Mexicanos, *Memorias*, 77–78.

56. Ibid., 56.

57. Ibid., 64.

58. Penny Lernoux, *Cry of the People* (New York: Penguin Books, 1982), 31.

59. Schwaller, *History of the Catholic Church*, 229.

60. Lernoux, *Cry of the People*, 31; and Schwaller, *History of the Catholic Church*, 228.

61. "Popularum Progressio," *Corporación* no. 90 (March–April 1967): 14.

62. Ibid., 15.

63. Ibid.

64. Ibid., 16.

65. Ibid.

66. Lernoux, *Cry of the People*, 31.

67. Camp, *Crossing Swords*, 86.

68. Scott Mainwaring and Alexander Wilde, eds., *The Progressive Church in Latin America* (Notre Dame, IN: University of Notre Dame Press, 1989), 11; and "Popularum Progressio," 18. Pope Paul VI's encyclical *Popularum Progressio* had decried the "oppressive structure derived from the abuse of plenty or from the abuse of power, from the exploitation of workers" ("Popularum Progressio," 18).

69. "Segunda Conferencia General del Episcopado Latinoamericano. Documento Final de la Comisión No. 1 Sub-Comisión A: Justicia. Hechos," *Christus* 33.2 (1968): 1027.

70. "Segunda Conferencia General del Episcopado Latinoamericano: Educación, Documento Final de la Comisión No. 3," *Christus* 33.2 (1968): 1054.

71. Ibid., 1055.

72. "Segunda Conferencia General del Episcopado Latinoamericano: Educación Documento Final de la Comisión No. 3: Educación" *Christus* 33.2 (1968): 1055; Thomas C. Bruneau, *The Political Transformation of the Brazilian Catholic Church* (Cambridge: Cambridge University Press, 1974), 79; and Lernoux, *Cry of the People*, 40.

73. "Segunda Conferencia General del Episcopado Latinoamericano: Educación Documento Final de la Comisión No. 1 Sub-Comisión B: Paz. Conclusiones Finales," *Christus* 33.2 (1968): 1044.

74. "Documento Básico preliminar para la II Conferencia General del Episcopado Latino Americano (CELAM): Secularización Cultural," *Christus* 33.2 (1968): 750.

75. Ibid., 754.

76. Arrupe assumed this post in 1965 in the middle of a rising wave of change within the Roman Catholic Church. This radical shift is consistent with the Order's traditional relationship with the papacy and with its historic political acumen.

77. Joaquín Saénz y Arriaga, *The New Post-Conciliar or Montinian Church*, trans. Edgar A. Lucidi (San Diego: n.p., 1985), 227.

78. Ibid., 229.

79. Lernoux, *Cry of the People*, 361.

80. Ibid.

81. Camp, *Crossing Swords*, 80.

82. Ernesto Meneses Morales, SJ, interview by author, tape recording, Mexico City, November 4, 1993. Palencia notes that many of the Jesuit faculty at the Iberoamericana also taught at the Instituto Patria (Palencia, "Actividad educativa," 419).

83. Palencia, "Actividad educativa," 419. The decision for closing the school was taken by the superior of the Jesuit's Mexican Province, Enrique Martín del Campo, SJ. My informants Antonio Penella and his wife Ester, both of whom had attended the Iberoamericana during the 1940s, were among those parents who protested the decision to close down the Instituto Patria.

84. Gutiérrez Casillas, *Jesuitas en México durante el Siglo XX*, 437–38.

85. Universidad Iberoamericana, "Filosofía Educativa: Inspiración," in "La Universidad de Inspiración Cristiana (1969)" (Mexico City: Universidad Iberoamericana, 1969), no page numbers.

86. Ibid.

87. Ibid.

88. Ibid.

89. Ernesto Meneses Morales, SJ, interview by author, tape recording, Mexico City, November 4, 1993.

90. Universidad Iberoamericana, "Conciencia Social," in "La Universidad de Inspiración Cristiana."

91. "Reglamento Para las Actividades Políticas de los Estudiantes de la Escuela de Ciencias Políticas y Sociales de la U.I.A.," 1965, Actas del Consejo Universitario Collection, *Unidad de Acervos Históricos de la Universidad Iberoamericana*.

92. "Resumen del Acta y Acuerdos tomados en la Junta del Consejo Universitario del día 24 de junio de 1965," June 24, 1965, Actas del Consejo Universitario Collection, *Unidad de Acervos Históricos de la Universidad Iberoamericana*; and "Reglamento Para las Actividades Políticas de los Estudiantes de la Escuela de Ciencias Políticas y Sociales de la U.I.A.," Actas del Consejo Universitario Collection, *Unidad de Acervos Históricos de la Universidad Iberoamericana*.

93. Felipe Pardinas, SJ, "Carta del Editor," *Comunidad* 1.1 (March 1966): 3–8.

94. Ibid.

95. Ibid., 7.

96. Ibid.

97. Ibid., 8.

98. Raúl Olmedo, "El Estructuralismo y las Teórias de Althusser, Debray y Gunder Frank Sobre el Funcionamiento del Capitalismo Actual," *Comunidad* 3.11 (February, 1968): 17.

99. Raúl V. Duarte, "Hacia un Dialógo con los Marxistas," *Comunidad* 2.8 (August, 1967): 343.

100. Raymundo Oznam de Andrade, "Popularum Progressio: neo-capitalismo o revolución," *Comunidad* 2.9 (October 1967): 474.

101. At that time, he was the PRI's president.

102. Saénz y Arriaga, *New Post-Conciliar*, 387.

103. Joaquín Saénz y Arriaga, *Cuernavaca y El Progresismo Religioso en México* (Mexico City: Author, 1967), 11.

104. Ibid., 14. The Holy Office also exiled Lemercier from Mexico to his native Belgium.

105. Ibid., 26–27.

106. Ibid., 28.

107. Ibid., 45.

108. Ibid., 46.

109. Ibid., 44.

110. Saénz y Arriaga, *New Post-Conciliar*, 16. Saénz y Arriaga saw the House of Emaus as a component of a greater program by the Bishop of Cuernavaca, Sergio Méndez y Arceo, to introduce far-reaching reforms which Saénz y Arriaga felt would destroy Mexico's Catholic community.

111. René Capistran Garza, prologue to *New Post-Conciliar*, by Saénz y Arriaga, xviii.

Chapter Six

1. Donald C. Hodges, *Mexican Anarchism after the Revolution* (Austin: University of Texas Press, 1995), 87–88, 92.

2. Ibid. A separate guerrilla band developed in Guerrero under the leadership of Genaro Vázquez, who like Lucio Cabañas was a rural school teacher.

3. Barry Carr, *Marxism and Communism in Twentieth-century Mexico* (Lincoln: University of Nebraska Press, 1992), 229.

4. The extreme inequality in the allocation of federal resources within the public university system that overwhelmingly favored the Mexico City–based UNAM and the IPN was a major issue in the student unrest in the provincial universities. This issue is addressed in detail in Jaime Castrejón Diez's *La Educación Superior en México* (Mexico City: Editorial Edicol, 1979).

5. The PRI was the latest name given to the ruling party that was founded in 1929 by Plutarco Elías Calles in the wake of the assassination of Álvaro Obregón.

6. Roger D. Hansen, *The Politics of Mexican Development* (Baltimore: Johns Hopkins University Press, 1971), 123.

7. Michoacán has been governed by Lázaro Cárdenas's brother, son, and, most recently, his grandson Lázaro Cárdenas Batal. Tabasco has been governed by Carlos Madrazo's son Roberto Madrazo and is the political base of his disciple Andrés Manuel López Obrador, a former mayor of Mexico City. López Obrador ran against Roberto Madrazo and the PAN's candidate Felipe Calderón in a highly disputed election in which Calderón won by a razor-thin margin over López Obrador. He was also the PRD's candidate in the 2012 presidential elections. President Felipe Calderón's father was a president of the UNEC during the late 1930s and a nemesis of Carlos Madrazo and the labor leader Vicente Lombardo Toledano.

8. Ramón Ramirez, *El Movimiento Estudiantil de México: Julio/diciembre de 1968*, vol. 1 (Mexico City: Ediciones Era, 1969), 145–47.

9. Ibid., 149–52.

10. The example of anti-Gaullist student protests in France were also on the minds of these Mexican student activists, encouraging them to believe that their growing movement could actually achieve significant change to Mexico's political culture.

11. Mabry, *Mexican University*, 244.

12. The event was named after the US-made anti-tank weapon used in the assault, the World War II vintage "Bazooka."

13. Mabry, *Mexican University*, 265.

14. Meneses, *La Universidad Iberoamericana*, 98; and José de Jesús

Ledesma, *Trayectoria Histórico-Ideológica de la Universidad Iberoamericana* (Mexico City: UIA, 1987), 431.

15. Meneses, *La Universidad Iberoamericana*, 99; and Ledesma, *Trayectoria Histórico-Ideológica*, 432.

16. Ledesma, *Trayectoria Histórico-Ideológica*, 432.

17. Meneses, *La Universidad Iberoamericana*, 98; and Ledesma, *Trayectoria Histórico-Ideológica*, 432.

18. José Ignacio Palencia, SJ, "El Movimiento Estudiantil y Nosotros: Hechos y Participación," *Pulgas* no. 16 (October 1968): 17.

19. Ángel Palerm (Prof. A. [pseudo.]), "El movimiento estudiantil: notas sobre un caso (3)," *Comunidad* 6.19 (June 1969): 381.

20. Ibid.

21. Rector Barrios had resigned his post to protest the government's violation of the UNAM's autonomy.

22. "Acta del Consejo Universitario celebrado el día 27 de septiembre de 1968," September 27, 1968, Actas del Consejo Universitario Collection AHUIA.

23. Ibid.

24. "Acta del Consejo Universitario celebrado el día 21 de noviembre de 1968," November 21, 1968, Actas del Consejo Universitario Collection AHUIA.

25. Ibid.

26. The origins of MURO are discussed in Roberto Blancarte's *Historia de la Iglesia Católica en México* (Mexico City: Fondo de la Cultura Económica/El Colegio Mexiquense, 1992), 205–6. MURO was blamed for numerous attacks on left-wing student activists in 1968.

27. "Acta del Consejo Universitario celebrado el día 21 de noviembre de 1968," November 21, 1968, Actas del Consejo Universitario Collection AHUIA.

28. Juan Antonio Ortega y Medina, "Antropología: Angel Palerm Vich," in *El Exilio Español en México: 1939–1982* (Mexico City: Fondo de la Cultura Económica/Salvat, 1982), 345; and *Diccionario Porrúa de Historia, Biografía, y Geografía de México* (Mexico City: Editorial Porrúa, 1986), 2185. Spanish anarchism was noted for its particularly fierce anti-clericalism which had been amply demonstrated during the course of the Spanish Civil War. Palerm's background was ironic for a faculty member of a Mexican Jesuit university.

29. Ángel Palerm (Prof. A. [pseudo.]), "El movimiento estudiantil: notas sobre un caso (4)," *Comunidad* 6.20 (August 1969): 522.

30. The writer José Revueltas and the IPN chemistry professor Heberto

Castillo were among the political prisoners imprisoned at Lecumberri, along with National Strike Committee survivors like Eduardo del Valle.

31. Mabry, *Mexican University*, 267.

32. "Acta del Consejo Universitario celebrado el día 15 de enero de 1970," January 15, 1970, Actas del Consejo Universitario Collection AHUIA.

33. Ibid.

34. Ibid.

35. Palencia, "El Movimiento Estudiantil," 17.

36. Ibid.

37. Ibid., 18–19.

38. The Mexican Province was headed at the time by Enrique Gutiérrez Martín del Campo, SJ.

39. Palencia, "El Movimiento Estudiantil," 6.

40. Blancarte, *Historia de la Iglesia Católica*, 243; and Palencia, "El Movimiento Estudiantil," 10–11.

41. Ibid.

42. Palomar entered the Jesuit Order in 1942 and left it in 1971 (Gutiérrez Casillas, SJ, *Jesuitas en México Durante el Siglo XX*, appendix 7).

43. Carlos Palomar, SJ, "Solicito ser detenido por el delito de disolución social," *Pulgas* no. 16 (October 1968): 30.

44. Ibid.

45. Ibid., 31.

46. Enrique Maza was the same Jesuit who had been identified by Saénz y Arriaga as being, along with Felipe Pardinas of the Universidad Iberoamericana, prime exponents of church reform in Mexico.

47. Enrique Maza, SJ, "El movimiento estudiantil y sus repercusiones para la Iglesia," *Christus* 33.2 (1968): 1247.

48. Ibid., 1248. Many of these observations still hold true in contemporary Mexico.

49. Ibid., 1250.

50. Ibid., 1261.

51. Ibid., 1262.

52. Ibid., 1263.

53. Ibid., 1262. As noted previously, among those slandering Bishop Méndez Arceo was Saénz y Arriaga and the veteran lay Catholic activist Antonio Ríus Facius.

54. Camp, *Crossing Swords*, 30.

55. Ernesto Corrupio Ahumada, Arz. de Oaxaca, "Mensaje Pastoral Sobre el Movimiento Estudiantil (October 9, 1968)," *Christus* 34.1 (1969): 13.

56. Hodges, *Mexican Anarchism*, 121.

57. Víctor Bravo Ahuja had excellent connections in Monterrey among academic, political, and business circles. He had been the long-serving rector of the Technological Institute of Monterrey, a privately operated university founded by the leading businessmen of Monterrey in 1943, before entering governmental service.

58. Hodges, *Mexican Anarchism*, 122. The umbrella student organization represented the university community of Mexico City. The leaders of CoCo were for the most part survivors of the CNH who had been released from prison or had returned from exile.

59. "Testimonio Número 1.: Anexo único al Informe de la Comisión de Testimonios Sobre los Sucesos del Diez de Junio de 1971 y los Estudiantes de la Universidad Iberoamericana de México," in "Junio Diez, 1971," *Comunidad* 6.32 (August 1971): no page numbers. The Monterrey students' apparent victory discouraged large-scale participation by Iberoamerican students at the march, however. The Iberoamericana's School of Anthropology was the only school that voted to heed the National Council of Struggle's call. Individual students from the Iberoamericana's sociology, law, psychology, sociology, and political science majors joined the anthropology students, although their respective schools had voted not to participate in the marches.

60. Orlando Ortíz, ed., *Jueves de Corpus* (Mexico City: Editorial Diogenes, 1971), 37–38.

61. Hodges, *Mexican Anarchism*, 122.

62. Ortiz, ed., *Jueves de Corpus*, 25.

63. Hodges, *Mexican Anarchism*, 126.

64. Ortiz, ed., *Jueves de Corpus*, 36.

65. Hodges, *Mexican Anarchism*, 120–23.

66. The government's position, as expressed in an official communiqué from the Attorney General's office based on purported declarations of students, was that it had been the marchers who had carried the firearms and had killed each other ("Texto del informe de la Procuraduría General de la República . . . ," June 15, 1971, *El Nacional*).

67. Hence the Universidad Iberoamericana could hardly have been an arsenal if the demonstrators did not have any weapons.

68. Ledesma, *Trayectoria Histórico-Ideológica*, 302.

69. Ernesto Meneses Morales, SJ, interview by author, tape recording, Mexico City, November 4, 1993.

70. Ledesma, "Relación de la Crisis de la U.I.A. en 1968, por el Dr. Ernesto Meneses," in José de Jesús Ledesma, *Trayectoria Histórico-Ideológico*

de la Universidad Iberoamericana, Vol. III, appendix 2 (Mexico City: Universidad Iberoamericana Press, 1987), 497. Xavier Mesa had been serving as the university's secretary general in 1964 and as such was in the line of succession.

71. Ibid., 501.

72. "Acta del Consejo Universitario celebrado el día 27 de febrero de 1969," February 27, 1969, Actas del Consejo Universitario Collection AHUIA.

73. Ibid.

74. Ibid.

75. Ibid.

76. Meneses, *La Universidad Iberoamericana*, 111.

77. Ibid., 109.

78. Ibid.

79. Ibid., 110.

80. "Marco Histórico," August 1970, Actas del Consejo Universitario Collection AHUIA.

81. Ibid.

82. Ibid.

83. "Consideraciones básicas para constituir un Senado o Junta Universitario como Autoridad principal de la UIA," Actas del Consejo Universitario Collection.

84. "Reglamento del Senado Universitario que sustituye a la Junta de Gobierno: Capítulo V, De las Facultades del Senado," Actas del Consejo Universitario Collection AHUIA.

85. "Reglamento del Senado Universitario que sustituye a la Junta de Gobierno: Capítulo I, De su Naturaleza y Finalidades," Actas del Consejo Universitario Collection AHUIA.

86. Ibid. The Senate also had a representative from the non-academic personal, as well as one from the Universidad Iberoamericana's alumni.

87. Universidad Iberoamericana, *Informe del Rector 1977–1979* (1980), 39.

88. Ibid., 40.

89. Universidad Iberoamericana, "Mensaje del ingeniero Crescencio Ballesteros," in "30 Aniversario FICSAC," 16–17.

90. *Excélsior*, Mexico City, March 15, 1979.

91. Raul Sobrino V., *del derrumbe* . . . , in *Boletín UIA*, March 1979, no. 110.

92. "Acuerdo número 8818 por el que la Secretaría de Educación Pública, otorga reconocimiento de valídez oficial a los estudios de tipo superior que imparte la Universidad Iberoamericana," *Diario Oficial* (June 17, 1974).

BIBLIOGRAPHY

Archival Collections

    MEXICO CITY, ARCHIVO HISTÓRICO DEL
    ARZOBISPADO PRIMADO DE MÉXICO

Archbishop Pascual Díaz Archive
Archbishop Luis María Martínez Archive
Archbishop Dario Miranda Archive

    MEXICO CITY, ARCHIVO HISTÓRICO DE LA
    SECRETARÍA DE LA EDUCACIÓN PÚBLICA

Departamento Jurídico y Revalidación de Estudios Collection
Consejo Nacional de la Educación Superior y la Investigación Científica
    Collection

    MEXICO CITY, ARCHIVO HISTÓRICO DE LA
    UNIVERSIDAD NACIONAL AUTÓNOMA DE MÉXICO

Miguel Palomar y Vizcarra Collection
Dirección General de Incorporación y de Revalidación Collection

    MEXICO CITY, UNIDAD DE ACERVOS HISTÓRICOS
    DE LA UNIVERSIDAD IBEROAMERICANA

Acción Católica Mexicana Collection
Unión National de Estudiantes Católicos Collection
Actas del Consejo Universitario Collection

NEWSPAPERS AND PERIODICALS

Christus
Comunidad
Corporación
Diario Oficial
El Nacional
El Sinarquista
Excélsior
La Nación
PROA
PROCESO
Tiempo

Published Primary Sources

Abascal, Salvador. *Mis Recuerdos: Sinarquismo y Colonia María Auxiliadora 1935-1944*. Mexico City: Editorial Tradición, 1980.
"Acuerdo número 8818 por el que la Secretaría de Educación Pública, otorga reconocimiento de valídez oficial a los estudios de tipo superior que imparte la Universidad Iberoamericana." *Diario Oficial* (June 17, 1974).
Alvear Acevedo, Carlos. *La Educación y la Ley: La Legislación en Materia Educativa en el México Independiente*. Mexico City: Editorial Jus, 1963.
Bassols, Narciso. *Obras*. Mexico City: Fondo de la Cultura Económica, 1964.
Bremauntz, Alberto. *La Educación Socialista en México*. Mexico City: Imprenta Rivadeneyra, 1943.
Calderón Vega, Luis. *Cuba 88: Memorias de la UNEC*. Mexico City: n.p., 1959.
Carreño, Alberto María, ed. Pastorales, Edictos y otros Documentos del Execmo. y Rvmo. Sr. Dr. D. Pascual Díaz, Arzobispo de México. Mexico City: Ediciones Victoria, 1938.
Castiello, Jaime, SJ. *A Human Psychology of Education*. Chicago: Loyola University Press, 1962.
Centro Cultural Universitario. *Anuario del Centro Cultural Universitario*. Mexico City: n.p., 1950.
Corporación de Estudiantes Mexicanos. *Memorias: Primer Congreso Nacional de Cultúra Católica del 18 al 23 de enero, 1953*. Mexico City: Ediciones Corporación, 1953.
"Declaraciones del Rector." *Universidad de México* 1.9 (June 7, 1947).
"Estatutos Generales de la Unión Nacional de Damas Católicas Medicines." In *Primer Congreso Nacional Unión de Damas Católicas, noviembre de 1922*. Tlalpam, Mexico: Imprenta Patricio Saenz, 1922.
Fomento de Investigación y Cultura Superior, A.C. "30 Aniversario FICSAC." 1986.

Lara y Torres, Leopoldo. *Documentos para la Historia de la Persecución Religiosa en México de Mons. Leopoldo y Torres Primer Obispo de Tacámbaro*. Mexico City: Editorial Jus, 1972.
Ledesma, José de Jesús. "Relación de la Crisis de la U.I.A. en 1968, por el Dr. Ernesto Meneses." In José de Jesús Ledesma, *Trayectoria Histórico-Ideológico de la Universidad Iberoamericana*. Vol. III, 495–503. (Mexico City: Universidad Iberoamericana Press, 1987).
Lombardo Toledano, Vicente. *Obra Educativa*. Vol. 2. Mexico City: Instituto Politécnico Nacional, 1987.
Partido Acción Nacional. *Así Nacio el PAN*. Mexico City: Comisión Editorial, 1990.
Partido Socialista del Sureste de México. *Congreso Obrero de Izamal: Segunda Gran Convención de Trabajadores convocada por el Partido Socialista del Sureste de México*. Mérida, Mexico: Compañía del Sureste, 1922.
Rius Facius, Antonio. *De Don Porfirio a Plutarco: Historia de la A.C.J.M.* Mexico City: Editorial Jus, 1958.
Secretaría de Educación Pública. *Algunos Datos y Opiniones Sobre la Educación Sexual en México*. Mexico City: Talleres Gráficos de la Nación, 1933.
———. *Boletín de la Secretaría de Educación Publica* (January, 1923).
Secretaría de Educación Pública. *El Esfuerzo Educativo en México: La Obra del Gobierno Federal en el Ramo de Educación Pública durante la Administración del Presidente Plutarco Elías Calles 1924–1928*. Mexico City: Publicaciones de Secretaría de Educación Pública, 1928.
"Segunda Conferencia General del Episcopado Latinoamericano. Documento Final de la Comisión No. 1 Sub-Comisión A: Justicia. Hechos." *Christus* 33.2 (1968): 1026–35.
Sobrino V., Raul. *del derrumbe . . .* In *Boletín UIA*, March 1979, no. 110: 6–7.
Tena Ramírez, Felipe. *Leyes Fundamentales de México*. Mexico City: Editorial Porrúa, 1957.
"Texto del informe de la Procuraduría General de la República . . ." June 15, 1971, *El Nacional*.
Tovar, Pbro. Librado. *Crónica y Trabajos Principales de Primer Congreso Católico-Regional-Obrero Celebrado en Guadalajara, Jalisco, en Abril de 1919*. Guadalajara: Tip. C. M. Sainz, 1920.
Unión Nacional Sinarquista. *El Sinarquismo: su ruta histórica, ideario y postulados, documentos*. Mexico City: Ediciones UNS, 1953.
Universidad Iberoamericana. *Catálogo General: 1962*. Mexico City: Universidad Iberoamericana, 1962.
———. "La Universidad de Inspiración Cristiana." Mexico City: Universidad Iberoamericana, 1969.
Wilkie, James W., and Edna Monzón de Wilkie. *México visto en el Siglo XX: Entrevistas de Historia Oral*. Mexico City: Instituto Mexicano de Investigaciones, 1969.

Secondary Sources

Anderson, Robin. *Between Two Wars: The Story of Pope Pius XI (Achille Ratti) 1922–1939*. Chicago: Francisco Herald Press, 1977.
Banegas Galván, Francisco. *El Porque del Partido Católico Nacional*. Mexico City: Editorial Jus, 1960.
Bantjes, Adrian A. "The Regional Dynamics of Anticlericalism and Defanaticization in Revolutionary Mexico." In *Faith and Impiety in Revolutionary Mexico*, edited by Matthew Butler, 111–30. New York: Palgrave MacMillan, 2007.
Barquín y Ruíz, Andrés. *Bernardo Bergöend, S.J.* Mexico City: Editorial Jus, 1968.
———. *José María González Valencia: Arzobispo de Durango*. Mexico City: Editorial Jus, 1967.
———. *Luis Segura Vilchis*. Mexico City: Editoral Jus, 1967.
Bastian, Jean-Pierre. *Los Disidentes: sociedades Protestantes y Revolución en México, 1872–1911*. Mexico City: Fondo de la Cultura Económica/El Colegio de México, 1989.
Blancarte, Roberto. *Historia de la Iglesia Católica en México*. Mexico City: Fondo de la Cultura Económica/ El Colegio Mexiquense, 1992.
Bock, Edward C. *Wilhelm von Kettler, Bishop of Mainz: His Life, Times and Ideas*. Lanham, MD: University Press of America, 1977.
Bouvier, Emile, SJ. *Neither Right nor Left in Labor Relations*. Montreal: University of Montreal, 1951.
Bravo Ugarte, José, SJ. *La Educación en México: (. . . –1965)*. Mexico City: Editorial Jus, 1966.
———. *Historia de México: Independencia, Caracterización Política e Integración Social*. Vol. 3. Mexico City: Editorial Jus, 1962.
Bronowski, J., and Bruce Mazlish. *The Western Intellectual Tradition: from Leonardo to Hegel*. New York: Dorset Press, 1960.
Bruneau, Thomas C. *The Political Transformation of the Brazilian Catholic Church*. Cambridge: Cambridge University Press, 1974.
Butler, Matthew, ed. *Faith and Impiety in Revolutionary Mexico*. New York: Palgrave Macmillan, 2007.
Camp, Roderic Ai. *Crossing Swords: Politics and Religion in Mexico*. New York: Oxford University Press, 1997.
———. *Mexico's Mandarins: Crafting a Power Elite for the Twenty-First Century*. Berkeley: University of California Press, 2002.
Campillo, José. "Presencia de Jaime Castiello: Semblanza." *Corporación* no. 66 (January–February 1963).
Campbell, Hugh G. *La Derecha Radical en México, 1929–1949*. Translated by Pilar Martínez Negrete. Mexico City: Secretaría de Educación Pública, 1976.
Capistran Garza, René. Prologue to *The New Post-Conciliar or Montinian Church*, by Joaquín Saénz y Arriaga. San Diego: n.p., 1985.

Carr, Barry. *Marxism and Communism in Twentieth-Century Mexico.* Lincoln: University of Nebraska Press, 1992.
Castrejón Diez, Jaime. *La Educación Superior en México.* Mexico City: Editorial Edicol, 1979.
Ceballos Ramírez, Manuel. *El Catolicismo Social: Un Tercero en discordia (Rerum Novarum, la "cuestión social" y la movilización de los católicos mexicanos [1891–1911]).* Mexico City: El Colegio de México, 1991.
———. "Rerum Novarum en México: cuarenta años entre la conciliación y la intrasigencia (1891–1931)." *Revista Mexicana de Sociología* 49.3 (July–September 1987): 151–70.
Chávez, Julio. "Enfermedades Mexicanas." *PROA* no. 5 (June–August 1939): 5–7.
Corrupio Ahumada, Ernesto, Archbishop of Oaxaca. "Mensaje Pastoral sobre el Movimiento Estudiantil (October 9, 1968)." *Christus* 34.1 (1969): 12–15.
Cosio Villegas, Daniel. *Historia Moderna de México: El Porfiriato, La Vida Política Interior.* Part 2. Mexico City: Editorial Hermes, 1972.
Cuevas, Mariano, SJ. *Historía de la Iglesia en México.* Vol. 5. El Paso, TX: Editorial *Revista Católica*, 1928.
Decorme, Gerardo, SJ. *Historia de la Compañía de Jesús en la República Mexicana durante el Siglo XIX: Restauración y Vida Secularizada 1848–1880.* Vol 2. Guadalajara: J. M. Yguiniz, 1921.
De la Mora, Francisco T. "El Ideal Sinarquista." *El Sinarquista* (January 7, 1943).
Diccionario Porrúa de Historia, Biografía, y Geografía de México. Mexico City: Editorial Porrúa, 1986.
Duarte, Raúl V. "Hacia un Diálogo con los Marxistas." *Comunidad* 2.8 (August 1967): 343–51.
Dulles, John W. F. *Yesterday in Mexico: A Chronicle of the Mexican Revolution, 1919–1936.* Austin: University of Texas Press, 1961.
"El pueblo mexicano se organiza para defender sus libertades." *El País*, March 22, 1925.
Espinosa, David. "'Restoring Christian Social Order': The Mexican Catholic Youth Association (1913–1932)." *The Americas* 59.4 (April 2003): 451–74.
———. "Student Politics, National Politics: Mexico's National Student Union, 1926–1943." *The Americas* 62.4 (April 2006): 533–62.
Fomento de Investigación y Cultura Superior, A.C. "UIA-FICSAC 1962–1966." 1966.
Franco, José Miguel . "La Rojería está Agazapada." *El Sinarquista* (August 2, 1942).
Garay, Luis de. "Acción Nacional." *PROA* 9.1 (November 1939): 22–23.
Gómez Morín, Manuel. "La Verdad sobre México." *PROA* 9.6 (April 1940): 18–32.
Gómez Navas, Leonardo. "La Revolución Mexicana y la Educación Popular."

In *História de la Educación Pública en México*, edited by Fernando Solana, Raúl Reyes, and Raúl Bolanos, 116–56. Mexico City: Fondo de la Cultura Económica, 1981.

González, Joaquín. "Don Bernardo Bergöend." *Excélsior*, October 20, 1943.

González Luna, Efraín. "El Hombre." *PROA* 9.6 (April 1940): 12–15.

Gonzálo Aizpuru, Pilar. "Paideia Cristiana o Educación Elista: un dilema en la Nueva España del Siglo XVI." *Historia Mexicana* 33.3 (January–March 1984): 185–213.

Guisa y Acevedo, Jesús. *Doctrina Política de la Reacción*. Mexico City: Editorial Polis, 1941.

———. *Lovaina, de donde vengo. . . .* Mexico City: Excelsior, 1934.

Gutiérrez Casillas, José, SJ. *Jesuitas en México durante el Siglo XIX*. Mexico City: Editorial Porrúa, 1972.

———. *Jesuitas en México durante el Siglo XX*. Mexico City: Editorial Porrúa, 1981.

Haber, Stephen H. *Industry and Underdevelopment: The Industrialization of Mexico, 1890–1940*. Stanford, CA: Stanford University Press, 1989.

Hansen, Roger D. *The Politics of Mexican Development*. Baltimore MD: Johns Hopkins University Press, 1971.

Hernández Chávez, José de Jesús, SJ. Interview by author. Tape Recording. Mexico City, October 13, 1993.

Hernández Díaz, Jesús. "Ignacio de Loyola, Jefe." *PROA* no. 5 (June–August 1939): 3–4.

Hernández Luna, Juan. "Un diálogo con el restaurador en Mascarrones de la filosofía perrenís." In *Homenaje a Oswaldo Robles en su 25 Aniversario de Docencia*, 95–112. Mexico City: Editorial Jus, 1963.

Hodges, Donald C. *Mexican Anarchism after the Revolution*. Austin: University of Texas Press, 1995.

Jarquín Gálvez, Uriel, and Jorge Javier Romero Valdillo. *Un Pan que no se Come: Biografía de Acción Nacional*. Mexico City: Ediciones de Cultura Popular, 1985.

Jiménez Rueda, Julio. *Historia Jurídica de la Universidad de México*. Mexico City: Imprenta Universitaria, 1955.

Kirchner, Alan M. *Tomás Garrido Canabal y el Movimiento de los Camisas Rojas*. Mexico City: SEPSETENTAS, 1976.

Knight, Alan. "The Mentality and Modus Operandi of Revolutionary Anticlericalism." In *Faith and Impiety in Revolutionary Mexico*, edited by Matthew Butler, 21–56. New York: Palgrave MacMillan, 2007.

Krauze, Enrique. *Caudillos Culturales en la Revolución Mexicana*. Mexico City: SEP Cultura, 1985.

Larroyo, Francisco. *Historia Comparada de la Educación en México*. Mexico City: Editorial Porrúa, 1956.

Ledesma, José de Jesús. *Trayectoria Histórico-Ideológico de la Universidad Iberoamericana*. Mexico City: UIA, 1987.

León López, Enrique G. *El Instituto Politécnico Nacional: Origen y Evolución Histórica*. Mexico City: Instituto Politécnico Nacional, 1986.
Leonardo R., Patricia de. *La Educación Superior Privada en México: Bosquejo Histórico*. Mexico City: Editorial Línea, 1983.
Lernoux, Penny. *Cry of the People*. New York: Penguin Books, 1982.
Loaeza, Soledad. *Clases Medias y Política en México*. Mexico City: El Colegio de México, 1988.
Mabry, Donald J. *The Mexican University and the State*. College Station: Texas A&M University Press, 1982.
———. *Mexico's Acción Nacional: A Catholic Alternative to Revolution*. Syracuse, NY: Syracuse University Press, 1973.
Mainwaring, Scott, and Alexander Wilde, eds. *The Progressive Church in Latin America*. Notre Dame, IN: University of Notre Dame Press, 1989.
Martin, Benjamin F. *Count Albert de Mun: Paladin of the Third Republic*. Chapel Hill: University of North Carolina Press, 1978.
Martínez Assad, Carlos. *El Laboratorio de la Revolución; el Tabasco Garridista*. Mexico City: Siglo Veintiuno, 1979.
Martínez Assad, Carlos, ed. *En el País de Autonomía: La Escuela Moderna*. Mexico City: El Caballito, 1985.
Mayo, Sebastián. *La Educación Socialista en México: El Asalto a la Universidad Nacional*. Rosario, Argentina: Editorial Bear, 1964.
Maza, Enrique, SJ. "El movimiento estudiantil y sus repercusiones para la Iglesia." *Christus* 33.2 (1968): 1234–67.
Medin, Tzvi. *El Minimato Presidencial: Historia Política del Maximato, 1928–1935*. Mexico City: Ediciones Era, 1982.
———. *El Sexenio Alemanista*. Mexico City: Ediciones Era, 1990.
Mendirichaga, Rodrigo. *El Tecnológico de Monterrey: sucesos, anécdotas, personajes*. Monterrey, Mexico: Editorial Castillo, 1982.
Meneses Morales, Ernesto, SJ. Interview by author. Tape recording. Mexico City, November 4, 1993.
Meneses Morales, Ernesto, Liliana Bedoy, Dorothy Huacuja, Frederika Moreno Stein, and Virginia Olaeta Elizalde. *Tendencias Educativas Oficiales en México 1821–1911*. Mexico City: Editorial Porrúa, 1983.
———. *Tendencias Educativas Oficiales en México 1911–1934*. Mexico City: Centro de Estudios Educativos, 1986.
———. *Tendencias Educativas Oficiales en México 1934–1964*. Mexico City: Centro de Estudios Educativos/UIA, 1988.
———. *La Universidad Iberoamericana en el Contexto de la Educación Superior Contemporanea*. Mexico City: UIA, 1979.
Meyer, Jean. *La Cristiada: 2-el conflicto entre la iglesia y el estado 1926–1929*. 3 vols. Mexico City: Siglo Veintiuno, 1973.
———. *El Sinarquismo ¿un fascismo mexicano?* Mexico City: Editorial Joaquín Mortiz, 1979.
Meyer, Michael. *Huerta: A Political Portrait*. Lincoln: University of Nebraska Press, 1972.

Monge, Luis [pseud.]. Interview by author. Mexico City, October 27, 1993.
Mora Forero, Jorge Rafael. *Historia de una Reforma Educativa Socialista*. Bogotá: Ediciones Cupenal, 1982.
Murguía, Beatrice Ester. Interview by author. Tape recording. Mexico City, October 19, 1993.
Navarrete, Félix, and Eduardo Pallares. *La Persecución Religiosa en México desde el punto de vista jurídico*. Mexico City: n.p., 1939.
Nolte, Ernest. *Three faces of Fascism: Action Française, Italian Fascism, National Socialism*. New York: Holt, Rinehart and Winston, 1966.
Olmedo, Raúl. "El Estructuralismo y las Teórias de Althusser, Debray y Gunder Frank sobre el Funcionamiento del Capitalismo Actual." *Comunidad* 3.11 (February 1968): 13–17.
Ortega y Medina, Juan Antonio. "Antropología: Angel Palerm Vich." In *El Exilio Español en México: 1939–1982*. Mexico City: Fondo de la Cultúra Económica/Salvat, 1982.
Ortiz, Orlando, ed. *Jueves de Corpus*. Mexico City: Editorial Diogenes, 1971.
Ortoll, Servando. "Acción Católica y Sinarquismo, ¿Dos Alternativas para Controlar a los Disidentes?" In *Religiosidad y Política en México*, edited by Carlos Martínez Assad, 133–59. Mexico City: Universidad Iberoamericana, 1992.
Oznam de Andrade, Raymundo. "Popularum Progressio: neo-capitalismo o revolución." *Comunidad* 2.9 (October 1967): 465–74.
Palencia, José Ignacio, SJ. "Actividad educativa y cultural de los Jesuitas en la Ciudad de México y Alrededores (1572–1972)." In *La Compañía de Jesús en México: Cuatro Siglos de Labor Cultural 1572–1972*, edited by Manuel Ignacio Pérez Alonso, 379–439. Mexico City: Editorial Jus, 1972.
———. "El Movimiento Estudiantil y Nosotros: Hechos y Participación." *Pulgas* no. 16 (October 1968): 6–19.
Palerm, Ángel (Prof A. [pseud.]). "El movimiento estudiantil: notas sobre un caso (3)." *Comunidad* 6.19 (June 1969): 371–83.
———. "El movimiento estudiantil: notas sobre un caso (4)." *Comunidad* 6.20 (August 1969): 521–29.
Palomar, Carlos, SJ. "Solicito ser detenido por el delito de disolución social." *Pulgas* no. 16 (October 1968): 28–31.
Pardinas, Felipe, SJ. "Carta del Editor." *Comunidad* 1.1 (March 1966): 3–8.
Poggi, Gianfranco. *Catholic Action in Italy: The Sociology of a Sponsored Organization*. Stanford, CA: Stanford University Press, 1967.
"Popularum Progressio," *Corporación* no. 90 (March–April 1967): 14.
Quirk, Robert E. *The Mexican Revolution and the Catholic Church: 1910–1929*. Bloomington: Indiana University Press, 1973.
Raby, David L. "Los Maestros Rurales y los Conflictos Sociales en México (1931–1940)." *Historia Mexicana* 18.2 (October–December 1968): 190–226.

Ramírez, Ramón. *El movimiento estudiantil de México: Julio/diciembre de 1968.* Vol. 1. Mexico City: Ediciones Era, 1969.
Rius Facius, Antonio. *La Juventud Católica y la Revolución Mejicana: 1910–1925.* Mexico City: Editorial Jus, 1963.
———. *Lanza en Ristre: Frente a los Ataques del Progresismo Marxista.* Mexico City: n.p., 1968.
———. *Méjico Cristero: Historia de la ACJM 1925 a 1931.* Mexico City: Editorial Patria, 1960.
Rivera del Val, Luis. *Entre las Patas de los Caballos: Diario de un Cristero.* Mexico City: Editorial Jus, 1953.
Robles, Martha. *Educación y Sociedad en la Historia de México.* Mexico City: Siglo XXI, 1977.
Romero, Laura Patricia. "Los Estudiantes entre el socialismo y el neoconservadurismo." In *Jalisco desde la Revolución: movimientos sociales 1929–1940,* edited by Laura Patricia Romero, 263–337. Guadalajara: Universidad de Guadalajara, 1987.
Saénz y Arriaga, Joaquín. *Cuernavaca y el Progresismo Religioso en México.* Mexico City: n.p., 1967.
———. *The New Post-Conciliar or Montinian Church.* Translated by Edgar A. Lucidi. San Diego: n.p., 1985.
Sherman, John W. *The Mexican Right: The End of Revolutionary Reform, 1929–1940.* Westport, CT: Praeger, 1997.
Schimberg, Albert Paul. *The Great Friend: Frederick Ozanam.* Milwaukee, WI: Bruce Publishing Company, 1946.
Schwaller, John Frederick. *The History of the Catholic Church in Latin America: From Conquest to Revolution and Beyond.* New York: New York University Press, 2011.
Sutton, Michael. *Nationalism, Positivism, and Catholicism: The Politics of Charles Maurras and French Catholics 1890–1914.* Cambridge: Cambridge University Press, 1982.
Tanck Estrada, Dorothy. *La Educación primaria en la Ciudad de México.* Mexico City: El Colegio de México, 1977.
Torres Bueno, Manuel. "El Problema Educativo." *El Sinarquista* (May 7, 1943).
Tuck, Jim. *The Holy War in Los Altos.* Tucson: University of Arizona, 1982.
Ulloa Ortíz, Manuel. "Homenaje al R. R. Don Ramón Martínez Silva, S.J. en el Décimo Aniversario de su Fallecimiento." In *Semblanzas de un Maestro,* 63–90. Mexico City: Editorial Jus, 1974.
Universidad Iberoamericana. "Entrevista al Dr. Rodolfo Brito Foucher." December 19, 1967, in "Historia de la UIA 1943–1956 [1968]."
———. "Historia de la UIA 1943–1956 [1968]." Unpublished manuscript.
———. *Informe del Rector 1977–1979.* 1980.
Vaughan, Mary Kay. *Cultural Politics in Revolution: Teachers, Peasants, and Schools in Mexico, 1930–1940.* Tucson: University of Arizona Press, 1997.

———. *The State, Education, and Social Class, 1880–1928*. De Kalb: Northern Illinois University, 1986.
Vera Estañol, Jorge. *La Revolución Mexicana: Orígenes y resultados*. Mexico City: Porrúa, 1957.
Von Sauer, Franz. A. *The Alienated "Loyal" Opposition: Mexico's Partido Acción Nacional*. Albuquerque: University of New Mexico Press, 1974.
Wallace, Lillian Parker. *Leo XIII and the Rise of Socialism*. Durham, NC: Duke University Press, 1966.
Wences Reza, Rosalío. *La Universidad en la historia de México*. Mexico City: Editorial Línea, 1984.
Williams, Margaret, RSCJ. *A Society of the Sacred Heart: History of a Spirit 1800–1975*. London: Darton, Longman and Todd, 1978.
Wright-Rios, Edward. *Revolutions in Mexican Catholicism: Reform and Revelation in Oaxaca, 1887–1934*. Durham, NC: Duke University Press, 2009.
Zea, Leopoldo. *Positivism in México*. Austin: University of Texas Press, 1974.
Zoraida Vázquez, Josefina, Dorothy Tank de Estrada, Ann Staples, and Francisco Arce Gurza. *Ensayos sobre la Historia de la Educación en México*. Mexico City: El Colegio de México, 1981.
Zoraida Vázquez, Josefina. *Nacionalismo y Educación en México*. Mexico City: El Colegio de México, 1971.
Zuloaga, Pedro. "Las Ideas Fuerzas y nuestro Destino Manifesto." *PROA* no. 1 (March 15, 1939): 2–5.

INDEX

23 of September Movement, 115

Acevedo y de la Llata, María Concepción (Madre Conchita), 45–46
Alemán, Miguel (president), 87–88
Arrupe, Pedro, SJ (superior general of the Society of Jesus), 104–5, 137
Asociación Católica de la Juventud Mexicana (ACJM), 1, 3, 5, 8–11, 13, 34–55, 58, 66–67, 77, 140–41, 143–44; ACJM and the Arreglos of 1929, 46–50; ACJM and the Cristero Rebellion, 39–46; origins, 16–39
Ávila Camacho, Manuel (president), 69, 105
Azcárraga Milmo, Emilio, 97

Ballesteros, Crescencio, 98, 135–36
Ballesteros, Jorge, 135
Barrios Sierra, Javier (rector of UNAM), 121
Basilica of Guadalupe (bombing), 40
Bassols, Narciso, 60–61, 63
bazukazo, 118

Bergöend, Bernardo, SJ, 2, 5, 6, 10, 34–35, 38–39, 41, 51–54, 68, 105, 143; background, 36; conflict with the UNEC, 58, 66–68; creation of the ACJM, 37; death, 50; opposition to the Arreglos of 1929, 48–50
Berzelius Institute, 86–87
Bouvier, Emile, SJ, 95–96
Bravo Ahuja, Víctor, 127
Bravo Ugarte, José, SJ, 86
Brito Foucher, Rodolfo (rector of UNAM), 75, 88–89, 132; creation of the Centro Cultural Universitario, 77–79; UNAM Strike of 1933, 64–65; UNAM Strike of 1944, 82–88
Burke, John, SJ, 46
Bustos, Luis, 67

Cabañas, Lucio, 115
Calderón, Felipe (president), 73, 139
Calderón Vega, Luis, 10, 73, 77; father of President Felipe Calderón (2006–2012), 36; founding member of the PAN, 72; UNEC president, 70
Calles, Plutarco Elías (president), 17,

191

59, 63; and the Cristero Rebellion, 40–46
Cananea copper mine strike, 20, 22
Capistrán Garza, René, 111; ACJM president, 42
Cárdenas, Lázaro (president), 6, 52, 72, 135, 143; and the CNE, 68–69; and the National Liberation Movement, 114; and Socialist Education, 61–63
Carranza, Venustiano (president), 30–32
Carreño, Alberto María, 47
Castiello, Jamie, SJ, 70
Catholic Action (Mexico), 2, 56; and the CNECM, 57; conflict with the UNEC, 66–68; and the LNDLR, 36; Pope Pius XI's mandate to Archbishop Pascual Díaz, 47
Catholic University of America, 78
Centro Cultural Universitario (CCU), 89; origins of, 77–82; Rector MacGregor, 83–88
Centro de Estudiantes Católicos (CEC): and the ACJM, 17; attacked by anarchists, 40
Chávez Camacho, Armando: CNE president, 65; FICSAC member, 93; PAN founding member, 72; Universidad Iberoamericana's communications major advisory board member, 97
Chico Goerne, Luis, 68
Christlieb Ibarra, Adolfo, 93
Christus (magazine), 125
Confederación General de los Trabajadores (CGT), 40
Confederación Nacional de Estudiantes (CNE), 63; creation of a rump CNE, 68–69; under UNEC control, 65
Confederación Regional Obrera Mexicana (CROM), 40

Conference of Latin American Bishops of Medellín, 4, 13, 106; Liberation Theology, 103–4
Constitution of 1857, 17–18
Constitution of 1917, 3, 5, 39, 40; anti-clerical provisions and Catholic opposition, 30–34, 37; and Socialist Education, 62
Corona del Rosal, Alfonso, 116–17
Corpus Christi Massacre of 1971, 127–31
Corripio Ahumada, Ernesto (archbishop), 126
Cristero Rebellion, 1–2, 5–6, 11–12, 33–34, 38, 51, 142; and the ACJM, 39, 42, 44, 46, and the Arreglos of 1929, 47; casualties, 35; and the CNCEM, 54, 56
Cuesta Gallardo, Carlos, 70–71
Cuevas, Mariano, SJ, 81
Curiel, José Luis, 77–79, 81

Dávalos Lozada, Manuel, 43
Díaz, Pascual (archbishop of Mexico), 35; Arreglos, 46–47; demobilization of the ACJM, 47–50; negotiating conflict between the UNEC and the ACJM, 66–68; support for the UNEC, 54, 56–58
Díaz, Porfirio (president), 2, 4–5, 15, 20–21, 23, 33–34, 36–37; friendship with Bishop Gillow, 24; Mexican Revolution, 24–27; religious policies, 17–18; repression of organized labor, 20
Díaz Ordaz, Gustavo (president), 113, 115, 121, 123, 127; Carlos Madrazo's sacking, 116; Demetrio Vallejo, 117; repression of the 1968 Student Movement, 118–19
Domínguez, Belisario (senator), 28
Duarte, Raúl V., 109

INDEX

Echeverría, Dolores, 78
Echeverría, Luis (president), 127–28, 142
Elizalde, Octavio, 48–49
Elizondo, Eduardo (governor), 127
El País (Mexico City newspaper), 29
Elquero, José, 23–24
Escuela Libre de Derecho, 87
Espinosa Iglesias, Manuel, 94

Fernández de Cevallos, Diego, 77
Fernández Smollera, Gabriel, 25, 29
First National Congress of Catholic Culture (1953), 99–101
Fomento de Investigación y Cultura Superior Asociación Civil (FIC-SAC), 94, 98; conflict between FIC-SAC and the UIA, 130–36; Junta de Gobierno, 94; origins, 92–93
Fox Quesada, Vicente (president), 76–77
Freire, Paolo, 104

Gamboa, Federico, 28
Gámiz, Arturo, 115
Garay, Luis de, 72, 78, 81
García Rojas, Gabriel, 79–80
Garza Sada, Eugenio, 87
Gómez Morín, Juan Manuel, 93
Gómez Morín, Manuel, 12; PAN founder, 72; UNAM rector, 65
González, José, 45
González Flores, Anacleto, 43
González Luna, Efraín, 52, 143; PAN founding member, 72
granaderos, 116
Guerra, Roberto, SJ, 98
Guisa y Acevedo, Jesús, 78
Gutiérrez, Gustavo, 103
Gutiérrez Lauscuraín, Juan, 52

Halcones, 128–29
Hernández Prieto, Carlos, SJ, 130

"House of Emmaus," 110
Huerta, Victoriano (president), 5, 16, 30, 34, 39, 81; coup against Madero, 27; relationship with the PCN, 28–29

Iberoamerican Conference (1931), 58–59
Ideario, 106–7, 114
Illescas Friesbie, Rafael, 86
Instituto Patria, 105–6
Instituto Politécnico Nacional, 8, 116, 118, 120, 128, 135
Instituto Tecnológico y de Estudios Superiores del Occidente (ITESO), 142–43
Instituto Tecnológico y de Estudios Superiores de Monterrey (Tecnológico), 76–77, 87

John XXIII (pope), 101–2, 111
Juárez, Benito, 17, 39

Ketteler, Wilhelm (bishop), 19
Knights of Columbus, 41
Kuri Breña, Daniel, 72, 97; CCU faculty member, 81, FICSAC member, 93

Lamberto Ruiz, Nahum, 45
La Nación (Mexico City newspaper), 29
Leaño, Nicolás, 22
Lecumberri Penitentiary, 123
Lemecier Affair, 110–11
León de la Barra, Francisco, 25–26
León Toral, José de, 45–46, 51, 143
Leo XIII (pope), 19–22, 80
Lerdo de Tejada, Sebastián, 18
Liga Nacional Defensora de las Libertades Religiosas (LNDLR), 5, 56–57, 143; ACJM and the LNDLR, 41–44; Arreglos, 47, 49

Loaeza, Soledad, 143
Lombardo Toledano, Vicente, 12, 69; National Liberation Movement, 114; role in 1944 UNAM strike, 82; Socialist Education controversy, 63–65; speech at UIA, 109
López Obrador, Andrés Manuel, 139–40
Loyo, Gilberto, 85

MacGregor, Fernando (rector of UNAM), 83–85
Madera assault, 115
Madero, Francisco (president), 5, 16, 24, 34, 37; assassination, 27; relations with the PCN, 25–27
Madrazo, Carlos, 109, 116
Manríquez y Zarate, José y Jesús (bishop), 44
Martínez, Luis María (archbishop of Mexico), 69; curbing the UNEC, 70–71; founding the CCU, 77
Martínez Silva, Ramón, SJ, 6, 10, 73, 105; conflict with ACJM, 67; private director of the CCU, 80; removal from UNEC, 70; revival of the Student Union, 57–58; Socialist Education, 63–64
Mary Street Jenkins Foundation, 94
Maximilian, (archduke and emperor), 15, 17
Maza, Enrique, SJ, 125–26
Medellín, Roberto (rector of UNAM), 64–65
Méndez Arceo, Sergio (bishop), 126
Meneses, Ernesto, SJ (rector of the UIA), 106; conflict with FICSAC, 132; Corpus Christi Massacre, 129; Student Movement of 1968, 120–21
Mexican Apostolic Catholic church, 41
Mexican Revolution, 4, 24–34, 37
Mexican Student Movement of 1968, 4, 8, 92, 113–14, 116–24, 131, 133, 141; Jesuits and the Mexican Student Movement, 125–27
Mora y del Río, José (archbishop of Mexico), 23, 25, 37, 40, 44, 55, 57; appointment of Miguel Agustín Pro, SJ, to the Student Union, 55; appointment of Ramón Martínez Silva, SJ, to the Student Union, 57; assassination attempt, 40; creation of the ACJM, 37; creation of PCN, 25
Morrow, Dwight (ambassador), 46
Movimiento Universitario de Renovadora Orientación (MURO), 121–22
Múgica, Francisco, 31
Mun, Albert de (count), 19

National Catholic Congresses, 21–24
Nationalist Youth, 50
National Sinarquista Union, 78
National Strike Committee, 118
Natividad Macías, José, 32

Obregón, Álvaro (president), 5; ACJM assassination plots, 44–46, 143; administration's relations with the Catholic church, 40; Constitution of 1917, 30–32
Ocaranza, Fernando, 65–66
Olmedo, Raúl, 108
Operarios Guadalupanos, 22–23
Orozco y Jiménez, Francisco (archbishop), 44

Pacto de la Ciudadela, 28
Palavicini, Félix, 31
Palencia, José Ignacio, SJ, 124
Palerm, Ángel, 9; articles on the 1968 Tlatelolco Massacre, 122–23; commission on Corpus Christi allegations, 129; FICSAC controversy, 131–33; Spanish Republican exile, 122
Palomar, Carlos, SJ, 124–25

Palomar y Vizcarra, Miguel, 15; First National Eucharist of 1924, 40–41; José Elguero letter, 23; LNDLR mission to The Vatican, 49–50; Rafael Contreras letter, 29

Pardinas, Felipe, SJ, 94, 107–8, 131; criticism directed against him by Joaquín Saénz y Arriaga, 109–10; editor of *Comunidad*, 107–9; industrial design major, 97

Partido Acción Nacional (PAN), 3, 6, 36, 52, 54, 139, 142; UNEC's contribution in the creation of the PAN, 71–73; 76–77

Partido Católico Nacional (PCN), 5, 11, 16, 24–29, 34, 37; Huerta, 27–29; Madero, 25–27; origins, 24–25

Partido Nacional Revolucionario (PNR), 61–62

Partido Revolucionario Institucional (PRI), 72, 91, 139–40, 144

Paul VI (pope), 103, 110; *Popularum Progressio*, 102

Peña Nieto, Enrique (president), 139; #YOSOY132, 140–41

Pérez Alonso, Manuel Ignacio, SJ, 92, 98–99

Pino Suárez, José María (vice-president), 25, 27

Pius XI (pope), 44, 47

Plan of Ayala (1911), 26

Plan of San Luis Potosí (1910), 24

porras, 83

Portes Gil, Emilio (president), 46

Portilla Osorio, Enrique, SJ (rector of UIA), 135

Pro, Humberto, 45

Pro, Miguel Agustín, SJ, 45, 55

Protocols of the Elders of Zion (forgery), 71

Pulgas (magazine), 124

Quadragesimo Anno (papal encyclical), 52, 58

Ramos, Samuel, 84–85

Real y Pontifícia Universidad de México (1551), 75

Rerum Novarum (papal encyclical), 2–5, 18–22, 26–27, 34, 52, 73

Restrepo, Félix, SJ, 87–88

Río Blanco Strike, 20

Rivas de la Chica, Evangelina, 93

Rivero del Val, Luis, 56

Robles, Oswaldo, 51–52; and the CCU, 77–81; and the Student Union, 55–56

Ruiz y Flores, Leopoldo (archbishop), 44; Arreglos, 47; denunciation of socialist education, 62; return from US exile, 69; support for UNEC, 67

Saénz y Arriaga, Joaquín, SJ, 109–11

Sánchez Villaseñor, José, SJ, 95; creation of UIA's business administration major, 96; First National Congress of Catholic Culture (1953); 99–100

San Salvador Atenco, 139

Secretaría de Educación Pública (SEP), 76; defanatization campaigns, 60; purge of Marxists, 69; Second Cristiada, 62

Segura Vilchis, Luis, 44–45, 51

Seminario Montezuma, 70

Séptien García, Carlos, 73

sex education (controversy), 60–61

"Silent March," 118

Socialist Education, 2, 6, 12–13, 62–66, 69

Summer Olympics (1968), 116, 118–19

Tamariz, Eduardo, 18

Televisa, 140

Televisión Azteca, 140

Tirado, Juan, 45

Torroella, Enrique, SJ, 79–80

Treaty of Ciudad Juárez, 26

Trouyet, Carlos, 131

Ulloa Ortíz, Manuel, 78, 93; CCU faculty, 81; PAN, 72
Unión Nacional de Damas Católicas (UNDC), 38, 41
Unión Nacional de Estudiantes Católicos (UNEC), 1, 2, 6–7, 9–10, 13, 36, 53–54, 72–73, 75, 77–79, 140–41, 143–44; origins of the UNEC, 55–56; UNEC and Catholic Action, 66–71; UNEC and Socialist Education, 63–66
Unión Nacional de Padres de Familia, 38, 41, 61
Universidad Autónoma de Guadalajara (UAG), 70, 143
Universidad Iberoamericana (UIA), 2–4, 6–9, 12–13, 51, 55, 75–76, 91–94, 137, 139–42; Church Reform Movement and the UIA, 104–11; Corpus Christi Massacre and the UIA, 127–34; curricular development, 95–99; destruction of the UIA campus, 134–36; University of Christian Inspiration, 106–11
Universidad Nacional Autónoma de México (UNAM), 6, 8–9, 12–13, 51, 53–54, 66, 69–72, 76, 91–92, 96–99, 111, 121, 124, 128, 130, 135–36; crackdown on UNEC activists, 68; military occupation of the UNAM, 120; socialist education and the 1933 UNAM strike, 63–65; UNAM and the CCU, 77–82, 83–89; UNAM and the Corpus Christi Massacre, 128; UNAM and the 1968 Student Movement, 116–18
University of Nuevo León, 127–28

Vallejo, Demetrio, 117
Vatican II Council, 3–4, 7–8, 13, 91, 100, 112, 114, 133, 141; Church Reform Movement and Vatican II, 101–4
Vázquez Mota, Josefina, 77
Verea, Luis, SJ, 86
Vértiz, Julio, SJ, 70–71, 93, 99–101
Villa, Francisco, 32
Vogelsang, Karl von (baron), 19

Walsh, Edmund, SJ, 46
Wilson, Henry Lane (ambassador), 28

Xavier Mesa, Francisco, SJ (rector of UIA), 130–31

#YOSOY132, 140–41

Zapata, Emiliano, 26, 30

www.ingramcontent.com/pod-product-compliance
Lightning Source LLC
Chambersburg PA
CBHW020917230426
43666CB00008B/1480